CHARLES   GLEED

CHARLES   GLEED

VISIONS
OF THE
WORLD

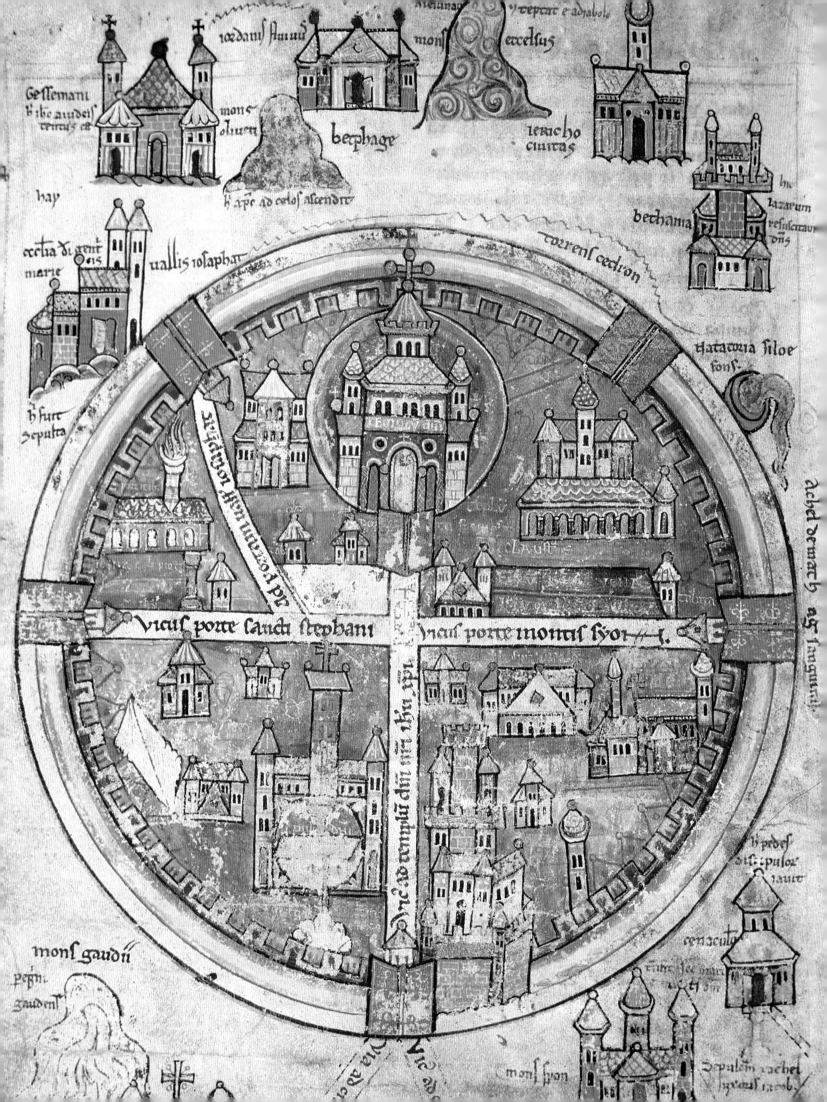

VISIONS
OF THE
WORLD

A HISTORY OF MAPS

JEREMY BLACK

MITCHELL BEAZLEY

For Jill and Peter

Visions of the World

by Jeremy Black

First published in Great Britain in 2003 by Mitchell Beazley,

an imprint of Octopus Publishing Group Ltd,

2–4 Heron Quays, London E14 4JP

Rprinted 2005

ISBN 1 84000 834 2

A CIP record for this book is available from the British Library

Set in Gill Sans and Versailles

Printed and bound in China

Commission Editors: Vivien Antwi and Kate John

Executive Art Editor: Christine Keilty

Project Editor: Naomi Waters

Design: Colin Goody

Picture Research: Jenny Faithfull

Production: Gary Hayes

Copy-editors: Adrian Morgan and Rona Johnson

Proofreader: Siobhan O'Connor

Indexer: Sandra Shotter

Page 1: *Two patrons and a sailor discussing the route to and geography of Asia with
the help of a globe, in a painting by Cornelis de Man (1621–1706). This painting has
been given various titles, including* The Geographers *and* Three Scholars with a
Globe. *Kees Zandvliet has suggested that the man wearing a fur cap may have
been Barents, an explorer of the Northern Passage to Asia, who crossed the Barents
Sea on expeditions in 1504, 1595, and 1596, exploring Novaya Zemlya and dying at
sea in 1597. His map of the Arctic region was published posthumously by Cornelis
Claesz in 1598. The painting dates from about 1670 and brings together men of
action and supporters, who may have been educated merchants or scholars. One of
the latter holds a pair of dividers.*

Page 2: *Map of Jerusalem, from* Chronicles of the Crusades *by Robert le Moine de
Reims, French abbot of St Remy, who was present at the conquest of Jerusalem in
909. Although plans of Jerusalem and the holy places had accompanied the account
of Arculf's pilgrimage in 670, a regular sequence of maps of the city followed its
capture in the First Crusade. Most of the maps are stylized, giving the works a
circular, diagrammatic wall within which the thoroughfares comprise a cross. Thus
symbolism took precedence over accuracy.*

Contents

The World through Ancient Eyes 14

Before the age of printing different civilizations and cultures had developed diverse mapmaking traditions, although varying degrees of cultural and technological exchange meant that only some flourished and spread.

In the Wake of Columbus 38

The mapping of the New World by Europeans gradually sublimated indigenous mapmaking traditions. Printing encouraged demand for maps and other technological advances led to greater accuracy in surveying. The Dutch rise to become the preeminent mapmakers of Europe in the 17th century.

The Age of Enlightenment 68

As exploration of the world continued and the tools of the mapmaker's craft improved, maps came to be used for military planning and territorial definition. Substantial errors remained in the maps of some territories, but this did not dampen public demand for more maps.

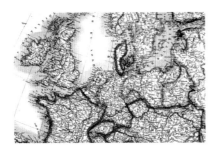

Commerce and Empire 98

European colonial powers use maps to impose boundaries on their native subjects, and to project their imperial goals, as well as to plan roads and railways. Standard scales and colour appear, which heightens the popular appeal of maps, which are sought by the public in order to follow the progress of wars.

The Modern Age 132

Revolutions in technology – the advent of aerial photography, computer software, space rockets, and satellites – have enabled us to map the unmappable, from the topography of the ocean floor to the surface of the Moon and the galaxies in the distant reaches of the universe.

Preface

Maps have given me great pleasure for years, and I was delighted to be asked to write this book. I hope I have communicated the fascination and importance of maps and mapmaking. In writing this book, I have benefited greatly from teaching a course on Historical Cartography at the University of Exeter and from the opportunity to deliver papers at Georgetown and Lamar universities, and at conferences held by the Newberry Library, the Foreign Policy Research Institute, and the Historical Service of the French army. I would like to thank Vivien Antwi and Kate John, the commissioning editors, Naomi Waters, the project editor, the design team of Christine Keilty and Colin Goody, and Jenny Faithfull, the picture researcher.

The book is dedicated to two wonderful people, Jill and Peter, who give me and many others great pleasure with their hospitality at my favourite pub, the Beer Engine at Newton St Cyres.

Jeremy Black
Exeter, May 2003

➢ Part of a sixth-century (between 542 and 565) mosaic map now preserved in a church in Madaba, Jordan. The map only survives in fragments, but it is thought to have shown the area from Byblos and Damascus to Mount Sinai and Thebes in Egypt. The full map would have used over two million mosaic squares. The section depicted is part of the Jordan valley, with the Dead Sea at the right. The map incorporates pictures, including fish in the River Jordan. The legends are in Greek.

Introduction

Y ou may be forgiven for thinking that a book containing sumptuous reproductions of maps means that the question "What is a map?" has an easy answer. To a boy growing up in the 1950s and 1960s in Edgware, a suburb of London, a map meant first a diagram of my surrounding streets, then a reproduction of the street plan of Edgware, and, lastly, the tube map which showed me the routes on the London Underground that would carry me from Edgware to Hendon and other exotic places southwards along the Northern Line.

A map is a map, isn't it?

Sounds reasonable, does it not? Most of us will share similar experiences, with maps providing detail and structure to our immediate environs, then guidance to how our home area fits into the wider world. So, we think we know what a map is and what it looks like: it has purpose and form, which are closely linked, each providing meaning for the other.

But there are other purposes, other forms, and other eras. The definitions that worked for the Western world in the late 20th century do not look so clear-cut today. First, within our world, there has been a move away from the dominance of paper products and, now, maps appear increasingly on screen: as weather and news maps on television and as road and air routes available on computers.

Thanks to the computer, the difference between a cartographer and a graphic designer has become relatively small. And, again thanks to the computer, mapping has become interactive, with individuals able to design and adapt maps using software packages. In the case of the interactive maps designed to prepare the American troops for war with Iraq, used in training exercises during the winter of 2002–3, mapping is not too different from aspects of computer games.

Secondly, we are ever more aware of other, non-Western cartographic traditions which use different systems of representation designed for other purposes. This awareness increasingly requires a careful scrutiny of surviving artefacts in order to establish the degree to which they can be considered as having maplike characteristics, if not as being maps. For example, the Pitt Rivers Museum in Oxford displays what is captioned as a "painting on sealskin representing men performing various activities", including harpooning whales and riding in sledges drawn by reindeers. It is also possible to see the sealskin as a map, marking where this trading took place by depicting Western sailing ships alongside native canoes in an anchorage, which is positioned both geographically and with reference to the range of Chukchi activities.

An awareness of other mapping traditions leads to a questioning of the notion that Western cartography was, and is, automatically better, and that it is valid to conduct the debate solely in terms of Western assumptions. Other cultures had different ways of conveying the information we also seek to convey, for example, distance, routes, and terrain such as mountains and rivers.

Other purposes can also be served by mapping, or the same purposes with a different emphasis. In many cultures, to know where you were and where you were going meant to depict, and thus map, the Earth as part of a cosmological world that included other planets, heaven and hell.

Thirdly, and in a way that is largely forgotten today, this was also true of the culture throughout the Christian world; here, too, what was shown took on meaning as part of a mapping in the mind. The "maps" that counted were those of the route to salvation, whether literally so, as in pre-Reformation pilgrimage journeys or maps of routes to Mecca

◅ This painting on a sealskin, produced by the Chukchi people on the Russian shore of the Bering Strait, challenges our ideas of what constitutes a map. It was obtained by the captain of an Arctic whaler in the late 19th century. Donated to the Ashmolean Museum in 1958 it was transferred to the Pitt-Rivers Museum in 1966.

for modern Muslims, or symbolically. Consider the more symbolic but still real journeys, such as the *Pilgrim's Progress* (1678) of John Bunyan's religious allegory. The understanding of direct providential intervention, of a daily interaction between the human world and wider spheres of good and evil, of heaven and hell, of sacred places and saintly lives, varied across the world. However, it ensured that space took on meaning in a fashion that was very different to that in a modern world, a world where mapping is part of a culture of secularism and science, and rests on the assumption that different people will produce similar maps that vary only in accordance with agreed conventions – in the scale chosen, for example. Thus, to understand mental mapping, cartographic culture, and the different maps and globes produced in many societies, it is necessary to appreciate that they should not be judged by how far they conform to our assumptions.

We also need to be aware that cartographic conventions play an important role in mapping in our society. In December 2002 I was given a present from the "New Zealand Tea Towel Collection" bearing the motif "New Zealand No Longer Down Under", and showing the world with south at the top and the meridian running through New Zealand. The only towns named were six in New Zealand and the only islands named were all in the Pacific. This captures the degree of choice involved in habitual conventions – in this case placing north at the top and the meridian through Greenwich – and the extent to which this can be challenged.

Furthermore, we are quite ready to extend mapping to fictional worlds, such as Middle-earth in JRR Tolkien's book *The Lord of the Rings*. This mythic epic involves a journey, which is made more concrete by providing a map. The map of "A Part of the Shire" in the first book of the trilogy helped to underline the domestic character of the Hobbits' life. Use of the map was taken further in *The Two Towers* (2002), the second part of Peter Jackson's film trilogy, where the strategic position in the confrontation with the forces of evil was shown on a map which employed similar conventions to those of the Western tradition and was being used in a similar way.

One definition that simply will not do, therefore, is that a map is a representation of reality. It is fairer to argue that it is a depiction of spatial relationships. This definition accepts the range of what is "mapped" and the variety of ways in which such relationships can be represented. It also captures the extent to which mapping is not necessarily the process of producing permanent works, those we generally term "maps". Instead, there is an important element of the transient in mapping, whether in the realization in one's head of the route that has to be followed, its depiction in speech or in a sketch (maybe drawn in the sand or in mud), or its presentation on screen as information that will be deleted at the press of a button. This last raises the question, which is the transient image? Is it the map or the centre that contains the information and can depict it? But it has to be the former, as the latter definition would extend to human (and animal) brains as much as to computer information systems.

The distinction is regularly blurred in works of fiction. For example in *Suicide Hill* (1986), author James Ellroy, a brilliant depicter of the dark side of Los Angeles, has his villain Duane Rice show a detailed knowledge of the city's neighbourhoods and roads. Brain/map language is employed: "Coming out of a long driveway, Rice turned his brain into a map and calculated two blocks to Silver Foxes", and, again, "He tried to make his brain into a map like he did in Hollywood".

Using the term "spatial relationships" beg the questions, "What spaces?" and "Which relationships?" For example, the World Values Survey run by the University of Michigan since the 1970s organizes and depicts its results in terms of two categories, one from traditional to "secular-rational" values, and the other in terms of survival values (those held when the struggle for survival is foremost) to "self-expression values". Countries can then be plotted on a chart where the axes are these categories. The resulting diagram can be

↗ Medieval World Map to accompany *Liber secretorum fidelium crucis*, a treatise by Marino Sanudo (1270–1343) calling for another crusade to regain the Holy Land that Sanudo presented to Pope John XXII in 1321. The map was by the Genoese Pietro Vesconte who also provided plans of Acre and Jerusalem, and a map of the Holy Land for the treatise. Sanudo called for the conquest of Egypt to be followed by an overland advance on Jerusalem. The scheme was not pursued.

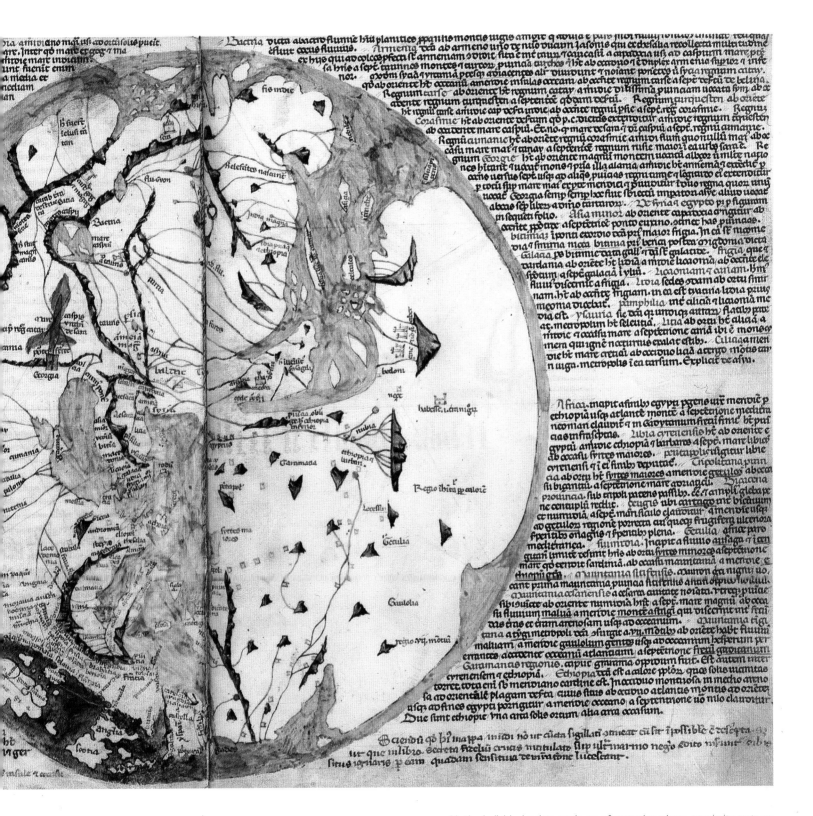

seen as a map, with the individual points made up of countries whose proximity rests on values rather than geography. The locations can also be grouped to produce a series of "continents" that are different to the conventional list: Asia, Africa, and Latin America are similar, but Protestant Europe, Catholic Europe, Confucian, and the English-speaking group – which includes Ireland (for some reason not with Catholic Europe), Britain, Canada, Australia, and the United States – are based even more clearly on value systems. The central issue is whether the diagram can be seen as a map. It is certainly a spatial representation, and if it reconfigures space that is what all maps do. At the same time, this is an approach that would have many electrical wiring diagrams deemed maps.

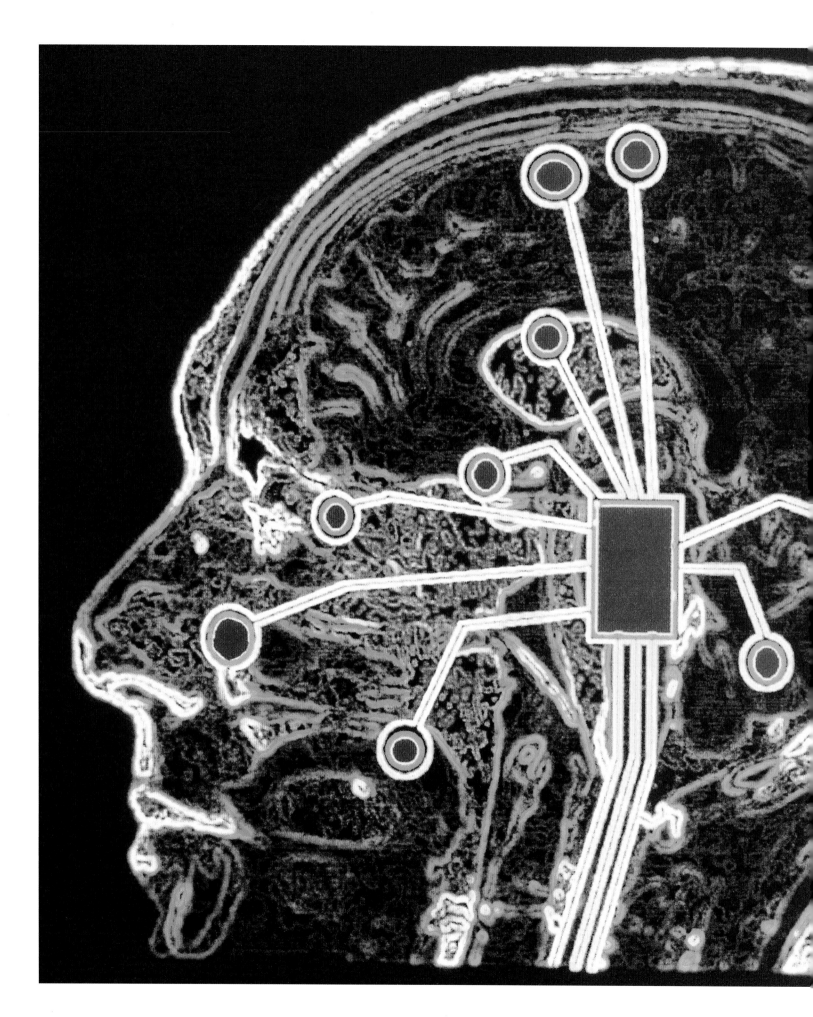

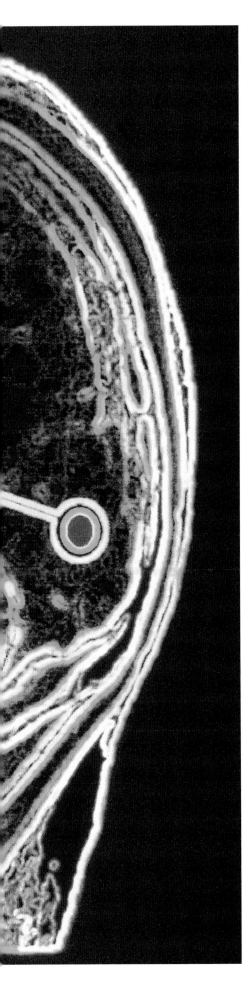

The politics of mapmaking

In recent decades, discussion about the nature of mapping has frequently been accompanied by a critique of cartography as a Western knowledge system falsely claiming scientific precision and used to "appropriate" the rest of the world in the service of Western interests. Many of these comments were somewhat simplistic, reflecting an inherent suspicion of authority, government, the notion of objective truth, established views on cartography, and the role of Western power, knowledge, and culture in world history, but they do raise the important issue of objectivity. More generally, the theory that knowledge is constructed offers only limited guidance to the processes and problems of map creation, not least the needs and compromises that characterize the collection of data and the decision of what can be mapped.

In politicizing these processes of choice, writers searching for conspiracy simplified a complex situation, replacing "can", as in what can be mapped and what can be seen in a map, by "should", or argued that the question of what can be mapped was determined by cultural and political suppositions. In fact, maps are selective representations of reality – they have to be. The subject of a map reflects choice, as do its scale, projection, orientation, symbolization, key, colour, title, and caption. To imagine that there is a totally objective cartography is to deny the element and nature of choice and to neglect the assumptions present in choices. Most map users, however, see cartography as a science, a skilled, unproblematic exercise in precision, made increasingly accurate by modern technological advances. This approach is misleading. The limitations of the map medium are more than technical and non-controversial; the questions involved are more than merely a matter of which projection or scale to select, and also embrace much wider issues.

Even if maps were to be life-size photographs they would be distortions of reality: a three-dimensional, spherical object, such as the globe, cannot be presented in two dimensions without its essence being altered, and this problem also affects the mapping of parts of the globe. Even if life-size photographic maps were produced in some futuristic virtual-reality technology, there would still be the question of how the photography/cartography should be presented. For example, what perspective would be employed? Would there be shadows? Would the map be in darkness, and, if not, why not? A landscape in twilight or darkness, the human presence etched in light, is as realistic as the total vision of unclouded daylight seen in most maps. Derived from satellite photography, weather maps are the most obvious exception to this, although when they predict the weather the connection is indirect.

In fact, maps are not life-size; they are models not portraits, let alone photographs, of life. Most are minute compared with what they depict, and the use of scales make this readily apparent. Even when scales are not explicit, they are part of the mental mapping that readers bring to maps.

As a result, mapmakers have to choose what to show and how to show it, and, by extension, what not to show. What is shown is real, but that does not imply any completeness or entail any absence of choice in selection and representation. This process of choice also rests on the problems of establishing and representing information. These are real problems, not the products of conspiracies, but they also reflect values and interests that have changed across the centuries.

◄ The map as science. This image, showing a chart indicating sensory and motor centres, superimposed over a magnetic resonance imaging (MRI) scan of the brain, depicts the use of a diagram to explain what is otherwise unclear, the diagram or key being integrated, in a dynamic fashion, into the image. In this sagittal "slice", the brain is shown folded and coloured blue/green. The cerebrum (top) controls intelligent thought and memory; at ear level, the cerebellum coordinates muscle action and posture; yellow lines and red spots indicate areas of the central nervous system which carry sensory information to, and motor information from the brain – these connect at the the top of the spinal cord (centre).

The World through Ancient Eyes

Thirty years ago any account of mapping would have concentrated solely on Europe, starting with the geographical knowledge amassed by the Greeks, then moving on to describe Roman mapping, before considering maps of the world, both known and imagined, by medieval Europeans.

Nowadays we seek to give due weight to other mapping traditions which are no longer regarded as inherently weaker than those of Europe. This is partly due to the widening of the definition of maps and mapmaking. Mental maps and the maps depicted in oral culture are seen as being just as valid as their manuscript and printed counterparts. Even if we focus just on printed maps, there are still other cultures to consider.

Early Chinese cartography

The most important of these cultures is that of the Chinese. They had an active map-using tradition from early on, although their development of cartography had little impact elsewhere in the world. The first map in China dates from about 2100 BCE (Before common era, that is before Christ) and appeared on the outside of a *ding* (an ancient cooking vessel). Early Chinese maps continue to be discovered: for example, a map of a graveyard produced between 323 and 15 BCE was uncovered in a tomb in 1977. Nevertheless, maps in China only became relatively common under the Western Han dynasty (206 BCE–9 CE), although very few have survived from before the 12th century CE. Chinese mapping was in no way inferior to that of the Middle East and Europe; during the later Han period (25–220 CE), for instance, topographical maps were already being drawn to scale.

Much of the difficulty in judging mapmaking developments in China is caused by the limited range of the surviving evidence. Among the Chinese maps that have disappeared is the *Yü Küng Ti Yü Thu* (Map of the territory of the Yugong) of Phei Hsiu/Pei Xiu (224–71 CE), the founder of scientific mapmaking. Appointed minister of works in 267, Phei Hsiu presented his 18-sheet map to the emperor, who kept it in the secret archives. Hsiu's Six Laws of Mapmaking were: the use of graduated divisions; a rectangular grid; pacing the sides of right triangles to ascertain the distance; the levelling of high and low; the measuring of right and acute angles; and finally the measuring of curves and straight lines. However, it is unclear to what extent these are an accurate account of his views and how they affected mapmaking.

Nevertheless, by the first century CE the Chinese were possibly employing both the scaling of distances and a rectangular grid system. Subsequently they were also to adopt the mariner's magnetic compass and the printing of maps, before these were introduced into Europe.

From the 12th century CE, maps were used frequently in China in documents such as administrative works and histories, which may have reflected a move towards a spatial rather than a cosmological definition of how China was envisaged. Certainly much information was available that could be used to produce maps; in particular, the government was assiduous in collecting reports from envoys.

Already, an edict of 780 had ordered that "maps with explanations" be submitted every three years. From the 12th century, if not earlier, numerous *fangzhi* – gazetteers of various parts of China – were compiled, normally with maps of the district, prefecture, or province described. The practice was originally used by court-appointed officials to familiarize themselves with the history, economy, flora and fauna, and important families of the area that they had been sent to govern. These local gazetteers also gave travelling distances and often included maps of some of the cities or of the entire district.

The routes and methods by which ideas and techniques of mapping spread are difficult to establish and assess. Certainly, the bold arrows that are often used on modern maps to indicate the spread of influences and innovations would be inappropriate. Chinese advances, such as printing by engraving on wood blocks, were, it appears, adopted by Islamic traders and thence passed to Europe. Thus the Western mapping of the last half-millennium, with its Eurocentric assumptions and its relationship with the spread of European power, drew, at least to a degree, on Chinese roots.

Despite this, and the changes in Chinese mapping, China did not play a continuing key role in the world history of cartography. Although Chinese travellers reached India, initially overland, from the fifth century, and Chinese or Japanese boats may have reached the west coast of North America in the 17th century, if not before, the Chinese had limited interest in the outside world.

Nomadic attacks

China's long-standing relations with the peoples of the steppe lands to the north and northwest did, however, encourage a search for information, if only out of necessity; China sought to recruit them as allies in order to remove their threat to her borders. Much of the information accumulated was ethnographic in character; it also had a spatial component, but it is unclear how far this was given map form.

Part of the *World Map* of 1459 by Fra Mauro showing Cathay and the Empire of Ghengis Khan. The original map was lost, but a copy was preserved in Venice, and today it is considered a masterpiece of cartography.

This Chinese star chart dates from the Tang dynasty (618–906 BCE). It depicts the night sky seen from the northern hemisphere and is divided according to the stations of the planet Jupiter into 12 sections.

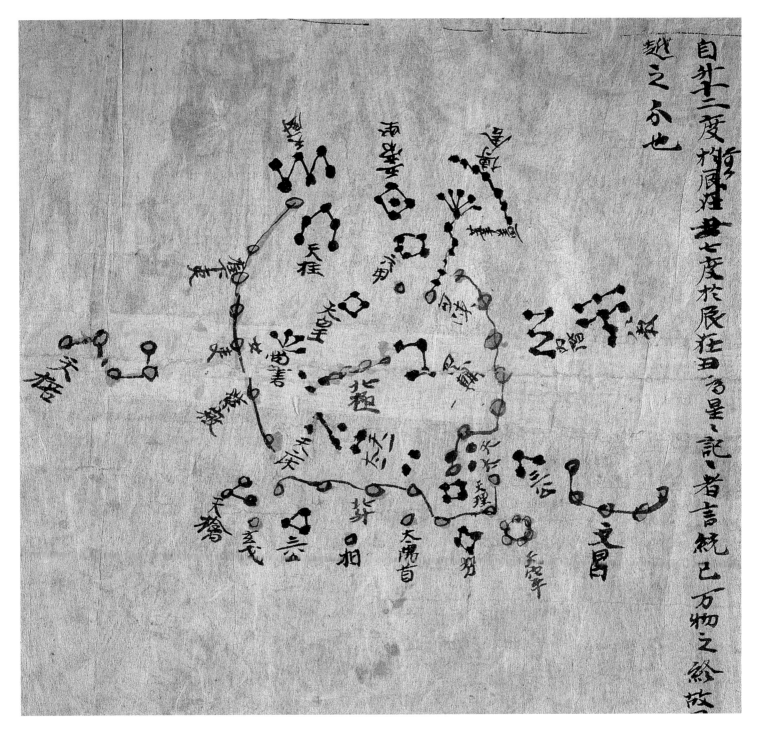

The same is true of Chinese colonization. This was closely linked to defence against nomadic attacks and led to the establishment of military colonies in the Tarim Basin and even the construction of walls, which relied on an understanding of topography and invasion routes.

As in other periods and societies, China's military imperatives greatly influenced the way she sought to understand the land. Until the institutionalization of military cartography in the West, however, the resultant mapping was ad hoc and episodic, and few, if any, records were left. For example, the plan of an ambush or a fort might be drawn with a stick in the dirt. The degree of spatial depiction at the strategic level is less clear, but pre-modern armed

forces certainly carried out complex operations that would have required a foreknowledge of terrain.

Mongol invaders

Chinese nautical mapping originated at the latest in the 13th century. For example, Zhu Siben's 14th-century world atlas included maps showing the Philippines, Taiwan, and the East Indies. However, the chart based on the voyages of Zheng He as far as the Red Sea and East Africa in the early 15th century is a pictorial representation that could not be used to establish distances. China's major episode of Indian Ocean exploration in the early 15th century brought her little or no benefit, unlike the massive

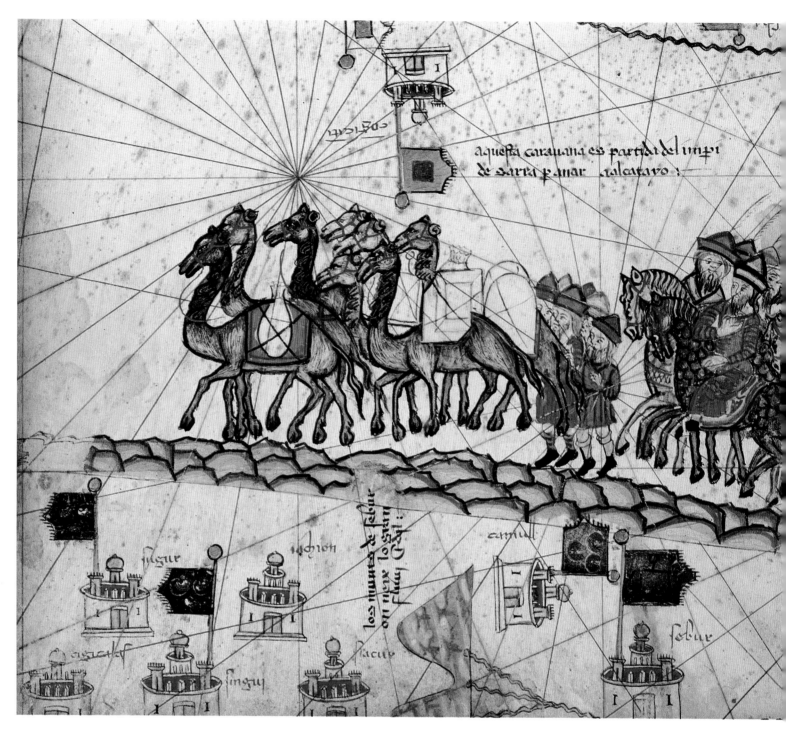

aquesta carauana es partida del imp̄i
de sarra panar ...alcatayo :

los montes de sabur
on nex̄ lo span
ffluuy Regi :

expansion in cartographic knowledge that the Europeans gained from their explorations from the 15th century onwards. China was central to the Chinese world view, and other peoples were very much on the fringe – it was not an attitude that encouraged any deep engagement with the outside world.

After its conquest by the Mongols, China had been part of a system that spanned Eurasia. Other Mongol forces during the 13th century had overrun Persia, captured Baghdad, invaded Syria, and advanced into eastern Europe. This expansion might have served as the basis for a long-standing Mongol federation within which geographical knowledge could have developed, but the Mongol world rapidly fractured.

The Mongols drew on the different cultural traditions of the societies with which they came into contact, and the Mongol world served as an intermediary between China, the Islamic world, and Europe. This was important in the dissemination and exchange of some technologies and practices, but not, it appears, for mapping.

Little is known of Mongol mapping, but the absence of either an ecclesiastical and educational equivalent to the Christian church, or of a bureaucratic and educational equivalent to the Confucianism of Chinese administration, helped to ensure that the extensive geographical knowledge which must have existed did not lead to a map culture. There was no need to fit this

⌃ A camel train from the *Catalan Atlas* (1375). The Western focus on the accumulation of knowledge has been on maritime exploration, but much, in fact, was gained from overland travel. The journeys of Nicolo, Maffeo, and Marco Polo brought back much information, and the *Catalan Atlas* was the first map in which this was clearly incorporated.

knowledge into systems of received wisdom. Instead, it could remain specific to the military tasks that the Mongols required.

Compared to China and the Islamic world, South Asia has a modest pre-modern cartographic record, little of which survives. Incised potshards carrying plans of monasteries exist from the second or first century BCE, but the first clear map dates from no earlier than 1199–1200 CE: a bas-relief in stone depicting a mythical continent.

Religious culture, particularly Hinduism and Jainism, was the dominant theme in Indian mapping. This was linked to astronomy and required the development of astrolabes and celestial globes. As a result, astronomical painting was a prime form of early Indian mapping. Religious and symbolic themes dominated the Indian presentation of the world. The world depicted as a lotus, with the petals representing land masses, was one important theme. In both the Puranic and the Jain views of the human world, India was seen as the southern continent.

More conventional mapping was influenced by other cultures, first Islam – Indians produced copies of world maps of Islamic origin – and then by Europe. Other Indian maps included roads or river routes shown in strip form – maps of pilgrimage routes, for example. Indian navigational charts from the 17th century have also been discovered.

Indian mapping conventions differed from those in Europe: the maps did not carry a scale as size was considered in terms of importance, not distance; few had compass roses or a geographic grid; and there was no standardization of symbols. The reproduction of landscape with geometric exactitude was not regarded as the goal of mapmaking. Religious issues were more important. However, research on Indian mapping is limited, and our understanding of it will only improve as more maps are found.

Drawing from native memory

Mapping in traditional African, American, Arctic, Australian, and Pacific societies is not easy to study. Surviving maps are relatively few and are often damaged or very fragile. The problems of analysis require the perspectives of anthropologists, archaeologists, art historians, geographers, and historians.

Maps survive in many forms: as rock paintings and engravings; stone arrangements; bark paintings; the exposed white wood of blazed trees; decorated weapons; painted buffalo hides; ceramic vessels; and many more. However, aside from the map forms designed solely for immediate use – for example, drawings in the dirt – many others, such as those on North American birchbark, are intrinsically ephemeral.

The survival of native maps often depended upon Westerners deciding to copy them onto paper, or on the natives being asked by Europeans to draw their maps. For example, the *Sketch of the River St Lawrence from Lake Ontario to Montreal by an Onondaga Indian* was copied in 1759 by Guy Johnson, the commander of a unit of British rangers. No scale was given, and the place names were in the native language. In 1828–9, while she was in a Beothuk Institution founded by William Epps Cormack (who had walked across Newfoundland in 1822) and where she died of tuberculosis, Shanawdithit, the last known member of the Beothuk tribe of Newfoundland, drew maps that recorded key episodes in recent Beothuk history. These ran together episodes from different periods and places, and there was no clear scale. Instead, the crude drawings presented figures and routes. These, however, were rare occurrences, and it would be many years before the value of preserving native maps came to be appreciated.

In judging the spatial values and practices of a great variety of cultures, it is important to treat them as neither superior nor inferior to Western mapping culture. They have a different language, and this needs to be understood.

Maps made in traditional cultures do not incorporate the abstract projection, coordinate geometrics, and measured space that we now associate with mapping. The landscape was approached in terms of values different to modern cartographic quantification. Traditional maps share a common geometry in which concepts of linearity, centre and periphery, contiguity, and connectedness are far more relevant than coordinate locations in an abstract, infinite plane. Native maps were drawn mainly from memory, and, as they were not based on surveys of the land, lacked the characteristics and values of this latter, more western approach to mapping.

A high proportion of traditional maps were in the form of linear itineraries. Sacredness was especially important; landscape and universe were not distinct or separate from the spiritual, but fused. Religious foundation myths ensured an interest in spatial relations, and in the Pacific island of New Caledonia, for example, the well-developed sense of mental mapping included the mythological place from where man originated and the entrance to the subterranean country of the dead.

Mental maps existed not only in the mind, but also in forms such as sand paintings and carvings. That such maps were not reproduced by natives in manuscript or print in no way decreases their accuracy or their symbolic potency, although printing does make the creation of a readily repeatable image far easier.

This form of mapping presented the way in which the spiritual and physical worlds interacted, and this is a concept which must be grasped in order to understand the purposes and resonances of maps. Part of this purpose is the very creation of the map: this creativity is a journey in search of knowledge and fulfilment.

Aboriginal rock painting

In Australia, Aboriginal maps depict ancestral stories and traditional relationships with the environment, although the symbolism is often difficult to interpret. Many different media were used, including decorated tumuli, bark paintings and drawings, and rock paintings and engravings. Decorated weapons and utensils probably also had totemic or territorial designs, but the relationship between such designs and local religious geography is frequently unclear.

It is also necessary to stress that there was no single Aboriginal culture, but a large variety. This emphasized the degree to which representations were made by and for local people and therefore could draw heavily on local meanings. Rock paintings and engravings were identified with mythic beings particular to specific rocks. These rocks focused the character of landscape as home and thus as possessing a sacred character that spanned the generations. Places such as rock formations and water holes were both physical and supernatural entities and were given a dynamic character by the idea that "dreamings" (ancestral beings) travelled along paths between them.

Aboriginal images of country were perpendicular (ie. aerial, from above) rather than landscape in viewpoint, giving them a similarity with modern maps; however, a very different spatial culture underlay them and their use. Aboriginal mud maps and sand drawings have a less iconic value, concentrating as they do on linear images of landscape with walking stages and key points shown.

From the Andes to Polynesia

In the Andes, pre-Inca societies had their own sense of how best to express spatial knowledge. The organization of signs and icons into radical, parallel strip or grid-like geometries appears to have reflected geographic realities.

Conventional Western mapping, however, would have been of only limited value to the Incas as they carved out their far-flung empire in South America during the 15th century. Their frontiers varied considerably in nature, as military, political, economic, and cultural perimeters did not match well. It is awkward to record the influence of such societies in space under these circumstances.

The degree to which the extensive Inca road system stemmed from, and contributed to, a map culture is unclear. Nevertheless, without conventional maps, or, indeed, writing, Incas were able to structure space, for example, by aligning *huacas* (mountain-top shrines).

In Central America, early cartographic forms depicted journeys and historical narratives. The Aztecs used maps to chart paths and to organize space visually. Maps guided travellers, outlined property, and were important in encoding history.

The Aztecs and other Central American people also kept close watch on the movements of planets and constellations – they were particularly interested in the movements of Venus – and this led to attempts at celestial maps. The Spaniards were in fact able to use Aztec maps in preparing some of their own maps.

In New Zealand, Maori mental maps embodied abstract, mythological, and religious concepts; a strong tradition of story-telling was also based on an understanding of geography and landscape. Many Maori names could only be understood through their connection with other names and places. Such connections

commemorated events such as journeys and related to an oral world of stories. The relationship between people and the natural world was central to the understanding of space.

In 1793, the British persuaded two Maori whom they had abducted to draw a map of New Zealand. This was very different to European maps of the period, as scale depended not on a geometric representation of distance, but rather reflected the interest of the mapmaker. Thus, the North Island was shown at a larger scale than the South Island in which the source of greenstone, the most important item for North Islanders, was similarly emphasized. The Maori did not, in fact, produce maps such as this prior to contact with the Europeans; however, this demonstrated the attitudes that conditioned their mental mapping.

There has been extensive debate about the navigational methods and knowledge of Polynesians and other Pacific Islanders, and how far these permitted navigation across hundreds of miles of open ocean. Recent attempts to re-enact Polynesian sea voyages suggest that navigational errors that resulted from the islanders' methods may have cancelled each other out. In other words, the navigator's sense of where his craft was may not have been too far from where it actually was. Furthermore, it has been argued that their use of the star compass to establish a position by dead reckoning meant that they did not need to concern themselves unduly over distance.

When sailing offshore, the Polynesian sailors could read the changes in swell patterns caused by islands, such as the Marshalls, and thereby fix their position. They recorded this pilotage information in the form of stick charts which were studied by mariners before undertaking their journeys.

The arrival of the Spanish

In North America, although the native languages did not include terms equivalent to "map" until the 19th century, maps were used in every part of the continent from the earliest period of encounter with Europeans onwards. It has been argued that adults of both sexes, and probably all tribes, already possessed the ability to communicate by means of maps, although it is unclear for how long this had been the case. The evidence from rock art, for example, is inconclusive and hard to date.

The first recorded finding of an indigenous map in North America was in June 1540 when Francisco Vásquez de Coronado, the governor of the frontier province of New Galicia, found a Zani painted skin that he took to be a map of the seven cities, or *pueblos*, of Cibola.

The earliest definite evidence of a native producing a map for a European occurred two months later when a Yuma made one of the lower Colorado River for another Spaniard, Hernando de Alarcón. In return, the Yuma asked Hernando to let him have a map of de Alarcón's homeland, and one was duly produced. In the same year, the French explorer Jacques Cartier was shown part of the St Lawrence River system in the form of a stick diagram.

➤ The World Map by Fra Mauro was commissioned by Alfonso V, King of Portugal, and finished in 1459. The extant copy was made at the request of the Venetian government. Working in a monastery on the island of Murano, Mauro was an experienced cartographer who drew from portolan charts, Ptolemy's *Geography*, and news of discoveries in Asia, including those by Marco Polo. He also claimed to have Portuguese charts in his possession. The circular format is a clear sign of the map's medieval roots.

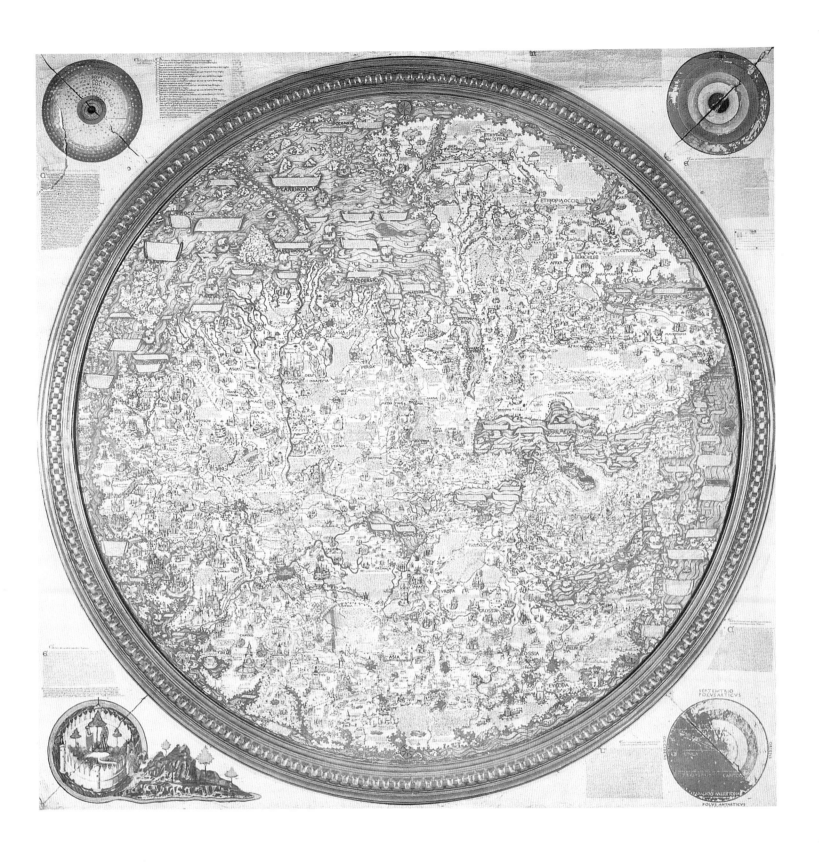

◄ The *Babylonian World Map*, from about 600 BCE, depicts the relationship between the Babylonian world and the legendary regions beyond the oceans. Babylon is shown as an elongated rectangle, and the parallel lines running to and from it represent the River Euphrates. The circle represents the salty ocean. Within the circle, cities and regions, such as Assyria, are depicted.

Rivers played a prominent role in all North American native mapping, for example, in the maps by Blackfoot natives collected in 1800–2 by Peter Fidler, a surveyor for the Hudson's Bay Company. Thus, Ac ko mok ki's 1801 map of the western half of the continent, as redrawn by Fidler, showed the Missouri and Saskatchewan river systems, the Rockies, and two rivers to their west, as well as a list of tribes and the number of their tents.

In his map of 1802, another Blackfoot chief, Ki oo cus, or Little Bear, depicted tracks across the prairie, with "sleeps" marked by circles in order to show the length of journeys, and the line to take between open grasslands and the woods.

Our understanding of much of the world's traditional maps and mapping, particularly from New Guinea, the Philippines, and Madagascar, is still limited. Surprisingly, although the Norse sailed widely, including across the North Atlantic, and wrote sagas describing their voyages, there are no signs that they produced maps. Indeed, like Old English, Old Norse also does not appear to have had a word for map.

Clues to a lost world

Ancient peoples were anxious to understand themselves and surrounding regions – although, disappointingly, a limited amount of material exists, it is difficult to analyse. The greater willingness to search for spatial representation is an important development, but does not greatly lessen the weight of these two limitations. The destruction of remains that might have cast light on notions of representation – those of the Druids in Britain, for example, and of pre-Christian culture in Ireland (and more generally) – is especially unfortunate.

The few surviving cartographic fragments show, unsurprisingly, that perceptions of the world centred on their cultures or origin. A clay tablet from about 600 BCE that depicts the Babylonian world map has Mesopotamia surrounded by the ocean; beyond this there are signs of legendary lands. Babylon had been destroyed by the Assyrian king, Sennacherib, in 689 BCE. The Assyrian Empire fell in 612 BCE as the Chaldeans, who had taken control of Babylon in 625 BCE, destroyed the Assyrian capital Nineveh. Under Nebuchadnezzar II (605–562 BCE), Babylon was rebuilt, and the Babylonian empire took over most of the former provinces of Assyria, including Syria and Palestine, destroying Jerusalem in 587 BCE. The map's essentially circular form was one also seen in other cultures, such as China and India.

The process by which information inspired such maps is unclear. Little is known either about most early exploration or about how maritime knowledge was spread. In the case of some cultures there is a dearth of material, and this is particularly true of the Phoenicians. They sailed beyond the Mediterranean into Atlantic waters, both south along the coast of North Africa and north towards Britain – indeed, the historian Herodotus claimed that they sailed round Africa – however, there is no indication that the Phoenicians used maps.

Two greats: Alexander and Ptolemy

The Greeks, who also voyaged and traded extensively, in contrast, left more information about their knowledge of the world beyond their shores, based on scientific interpretation of facts gleaned from returning travellers. These early reports largely reflected the Greeks' prowess as maritime traders; however this knowledge was greatly expanded by the conquests of Alexander the Great (334-23 BCE) who took surveyors with him.

Alexander aimed not only to conquer the Persian empire, but also to reach the eastern ocean, believed to lie to its east. Having marched to the Indus, Alexander returned overland through southern Persia, but sent his admiral, Nearchus, to sail from the Indus to the head of the Persian Gulf in order to explore the maritime route. These travels produced information that was eagerly used by Greek geographers, contributing towards a mapmaking tradition that was not restricted in its scope to Greece.

Hecataeus of Miletus, a pioneer Greek geographer and historian who worked in the sixth to fifth centuries BCE, argued that the Earth was a sphere. Greek thinkers made globes and applied mathematical models to the information and rumours brought back by travellers, and tried to estimate the size of the Earth. Greece took a central place, and the world – Europe to the north, Asia to the east, and Africa to the south, all three of which were very imperfectly realized – was surrounded by an ocean.

When Eratosthenes (c. 276–194 BCE), a Greek astronomer who became the chief librarian at Alexandria, calculated the Earth's circumference, he was, we now know, less than 76km (50 miles) out. This enabled the Greeks to advance a geographical perspective very different to anything previously proposed by the Chinese and other cultures.

The realization that their known world was only a small portion of the globe meant that the Greeks appreciated that the world needed exploring and mapping. Eratosthenes' account of the world was also more informed than that of Hecataeus, especially in the eastward expansion of what was known in Asia.

Subsequent travels increased the knowledge available, and the geographical writings of Strabo (c. 64 BCE–23 CE), Ptolemy (Claudius Ptolemaeus) (c. 90–c. 168 CE), and others synthesized this information, much of which was lost with the decline of the classical world and not rediscovered until the 15th century.

Writing in about 15 CE, Strabo described the Greeks' interpretation of geographical thought as developed by, and under, the Romans. Strabo, who had himself explored the Nile Valley, wrote about Crates of Mallos, a Greek Stoic philosopher. Crates, in about 150 BCE, had made a large globe in Rome at least 3m (10ft) in diameter that depicted four balancing continents, one in each quarter of the world, but all separated by water: Strabo wrote: "Crates, following the mere form of mathematical demonstration, says that the torrid zone is occupied by Oceanus, and that on both sides of this zone are the temperate zones."

Ptolemy, a Greek subject, geographer, and astronomer – the conjunction was typical – who worked in Alexandria in the second quarter of the second century CE, drew up a world gazetteer that included an estimate of geographical coordinates. Latitude and longitude based on astronomical data could perhaps be calculated for some sites, allowing others then to be located with reference to them – although this approach was probably responsible for errors.

This method provided information that could be mapped for North Africa, Europe, and much of South Asia, although accuracy diminished towards the boundaries of the then-known world, for example, in the upper valley of the White Nile. This reflected the composite nature of Ptolemy's sources and the difficulty of judging them. For example, he followed earlier writers in presenting Taprobane (Sri Lanka) as too large and India too small.

As the surviving copies of Ptolemy's gazetteer *Geography*, which date from the 12th century and later, do not contain copies of his maps, it is unclear whether they indeed ever included any, but it has been argued that Ptolemy must have drawn them in order to help the compilation.

Ptolemy's improvements can be judged by comparing his information on Britain – which was not too far out on actual size and made an effort to produce a detailed outline (with limited success in Scotland) – with the far less accurate sizes and shapes offered by earlier writers who generally used the earlier Greek depiction of Britain in terms of a triangle that was larger than the country's size. This had continued as a pattern even after reliable information became more available as a consequence of Roman expeditions and, from 43 CE, conquest.

Ptolemy's information about Britain highlights the problems of working from multiple sources. Apart from our ignorance of how he compiled his material, it is probable that his sources have not survived. These included military maps and the work of the Phoenician geographer Marinus of Tyre (who lived around 100 CE).

The Roman sense of scale

The mapping of the known world in the classical period and the accompanying development of large-scale mapping served a number of purposes: for depicting the size and extent of estates, in engineering plans and itineraries, and for military use.

This type of mapping began in Mesopotamia and Egypt, but was developed by the Greeks, who applied their mathematical knowledge, and by the Romans, who were prolific surveyors and capable of drawing to scale. There was a close connection in the Roman world between mapmaking and imperial conquest and rule, and between what purported to be world maps and pretensions to world power. The value of display was captured by the large-scale plan of the city of Rome, the *Forma Urbis Romae*, which was incised on a wall for public view.

The Romans benefited from the advances of those such as Ptolemy, although they utilized one of the less accurate Greek

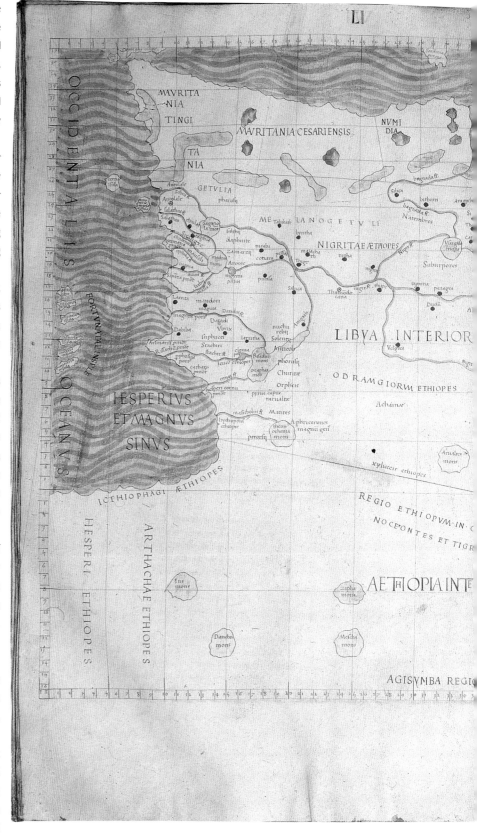

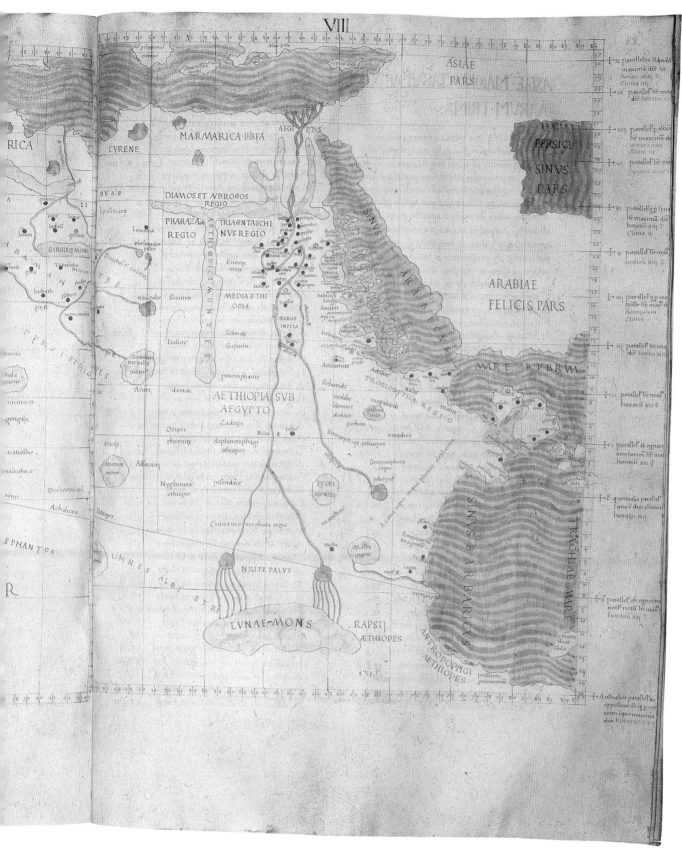

East Africa and the Eastern Mediterranean based on Ptolemy's *Geography*. Like others, Ptolemy was interested in depicting the source of the Nile, the life-river of Egypt. The Blue Nile is correctly traced to Abyssinia, but the White Nile is given an imaginary source in the Mountains of the Moon. The depiction of the East African coast is inaccurate, and the presentation of the Indian Ocean as an enclosed sea even more so. It is possible that the Phoenicians had considerable knowledge of the coastline of West Africa, and there have even been suggestions that they circumnavigated Africa; however, if so, they left no maps that could be used by Ptolemy. Nonetheless, there were trade routes across the Sahara, especially from Sijilmassa to the Niger, and the coastline of West Africa down to the Senegal valley was known. The Romans themselves, however, ruled no further south than Mauretania, a province that included much of modern Morocco.

∧ Al-Idrisi drew on
Ptolemy's world view,
which meant that India
and East Africa were
inadequately mapped.
China's coast, however,
was depicted. The map
had south at its top.

estimates of the circumference of the world. The Romans' accumulation of information reflected the range of their military and governmental systems. It was necessary to understand the empire if it were to be administered effectively. Flavius Vegetius – the author of the fourth century CE *Epitoma Rei Militaris*, a summary of the art of war – stated that a general must have "tables drawn up exactly which show not only the distances in numbers of steps, but also the quality of the paths, shorter routes, what lodging is to be found there and the mountains and rivers". The quest for this information cannot be compared to the systematic mapping of imperial Britain in the 19th century, but maps as well as lists were used to represent similar kinds of information.

The *Tabula Peutingeriana* is a 12th century copy of a fourth century Roman road map. It was a route planner, not a topographical map, and therefore adopts a strip form. It provided an indication of distances and of the size of places. The *Tabula Peutingeriana* is the most frequently reproduced of Roman maps – although, while it certainly shows an important achievement of Roman cartography, it does not display its full range.

A less well known source is the *Ravenna Cosmography*, a list of more than 5000 place names covering the Roman Empire, drawn up in about 700 CE by an anonymous cleric at Ravenna, the last capital of the Western Empire. It has been suggested that the compiler had access to a range of official maps. No fewer than three map sources have been discerned for the British section of the *Cosmography*. None survives.

Gone, too, are the maps that may have helped in the compilation of the *Notitia Dignitatum*, a late-Roman collation of administrative information that is known through a now lost 11th century copy, the *Codex Spirensis*. This included crude illustrations that show, for example, bird's-eye views of Britain; however whether it is helpful to see these as proper maps is debatable: they were representational only in presenting Britain as an island.

Stars of Islam

In the Islamic world, classical knowledge, in the shape of Greek geographical information and ideas, survived and was expanded by information flooding back from far-flung lands through Islamic conquests, trade, and travel. Caravan routes linked the Orient to the Middle East and also crossed the Sahara, while Arab traders using a star compass sailed the Indian Ocean and the Mediterranean. There is no evidence that they used charts.

The Islamic world was studied by Arab geographers. Indeed, this practice was actively encouraged by a number of rulers. The Caliph al-Ma'mun (r. 813–33) sponsored scholarship, leading to the production of a large map of the world. This has not survived, although it was described by al-Mas'udi (d. 956) as a representation of "the world with its spheres, stars, lands, and seas, the inhabited and uninhabited regions, settlements of peoples, cities, etc. This was better than anything that preceded it". It is unclear how far this map relied on the Greek inheritance. Al-Ma'mun also had the length of a degree on the arc of a meridian measured in Mesopotamia. New geographical knowledge was also used by Arab geographers, some of whom, such as al-Qazwini, were very active travellers.

The *Book of Roger*

The great triumph of Islamic mapmaking was the world map of al-Idrisi, finished in 1154 for King Roger II of Sicily and engraved on a silver tablet, which was destroyed in 1160. Al-Idrisi also produced a geographical compendium ("The book of pleasant journeys into faraway lands"), also termed the *Book of Roger*, which included a world map, as well as 70 sectional maps. He explained that Roger wished that he should accurately know the details of his land and master them with a definite knowledge, and that he should know the boundaries and routes both by land or sea … together with a knowledge of other lands and regions in all seven climates, whenever the various learned sources agreed upon them.

Al-Idrisi drew on Ptolemy's map and thus failed to map East Africa and India adequately, but he did extend his map to include China's coast. Following Ptolemy, al-Idrisi tried to describe the world in terms of seven "climates" and located places by their supposed coordinates. The map was oriented with south at the top.

The failure to map East Africa and India, both of which were known to Muslim merchants, indicates the difficulty of transmitting information – al-Idrisi worked in Sicily – and the competing claims of classical knowledge and new information. Furthermore, although less dramatically than in Europe, where classical knowledge of geography had been lost during the Dark Ages following the fall of the Western Roman Empire in the fifth century CE, it is inappropriate to think that "later" necessarily means "better". For example, although al-Idrisi's 12th-century map is less stylized and represents far more of an effort to locate place than that of al-Istakhri, produced in 934, the geographical knowledge of India is inferior to that of the 11th-century astronomer al-Biruni. He produced a now-lost world map in 1021, as well as a list of latitudes and longitudes.

The grid of reference, used by al-Idrisi and drawing on Ptolem, was also employed by al-Qazwini (d. 1283), a Persian of Arab ancestry. He produced a synthesis of geographical knowledge ("Monuments of the lands") and a cosmography ("Marvels of things created and miraculous aspects of things existing"), and world maps appeared in copies of both.

Islamic mapping was diverse and included celestial globes and world maps centred on Mecca, the destination of pilgrimages, as well as bird's-eye views of cities. There appears, however, to have been less of an emphasis on the more practical uses of such maps, unlike those developed in Europe by the 15th century.

The world map is the most important continual preoccupation of cartography. It reflects iconic and symbolic attitudes and values alongside those regarded in the modern age as more objective and scientific. Indeed, objectivity and science are important to the symbolic values of our culture. For example, the transition from the Hereford *mappa mundi* (page 30) to Fra Mauro's World Map (page 21) reflects changing values and methods of obtaining and placing information in the late Middle Ages.

The Mapping of the Middle Ages

By modern standards, there were very few maps in the Middle Ages; there is none for England between the late seventh and 12th centuries. Notions of spatiality played a role in the ninth-century division of the Emperor Charlemagne's inheritance and, in England, in the definition of the boundaries of bishoprics and shires. This was also true of the burghal (town) policies of Alfred the Great of Wessex (r. 871–99) and his successors, but it is unclear how these notions were advanced or implemented. There are occasional references to maps and plans. For example, in his *Life of Charlemagne* (written between c. 829 and 836), Einhard stated that the emperor had plans of Constantinople and Rome – the centres of imperial resonance – engraved on tables of gold and silver. But there are few sources from the so-called Dark Ages, and there has not been a systematic study of the cartographic role of the Byzantine (Eastern Roman) empire.

Classical mapmaking culture was kept alive in Byzantium, and there was also influence from the Islamic world, although the practical uses of mapping seen earlier in the Roman empire seem to have declined during this period.

The Bible appears to have been a significant inspiration for cartography in medieval Europe. There was interest in the location of places mentioned in it, and also the wish to construct a geography that could encompass Eden. It is possible that early Church fathers, including Eusebius in the early fourth century and Jerome in the late fourth and early fifth centuries, drew maps to further their investigation of biblical toponymy.

A now lost map of the Holy Land, perhaps by Eusebius, may have been the first to show the divisions of the 12 tribes of Israel. The copy of Jerome's works that includes maps is far later – a 12th-century manuscript that comes from Tournai and which may also have been made there. There is nothing to suggest the maps are Jerome's; it is much more likely that the copyist simply added maps from some other source, thinking that they would be an appropriate accompaniment to the text. If so, that is a significant indication of changing attitudes.

The maps that survive from the Middle Ages cover a variety of forms ranging from maps of the (known) world to estate maps. The most famous, the great *mappae mundi* (world maps), conveyed geographical knowledge in a Christian format, offering a combination of belief and first-hand observation.

These *mappae mundi* employed a tripartite internal division with a T-O shape depicting three continents – Asia, Europe, and

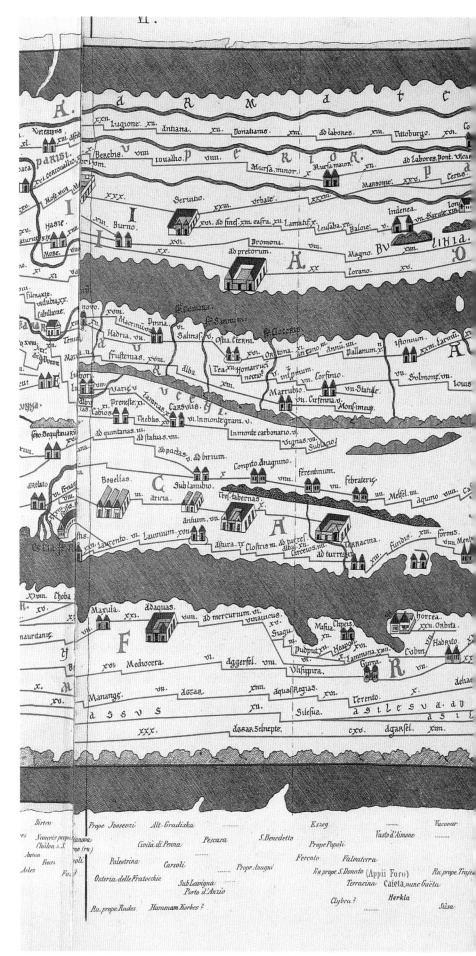

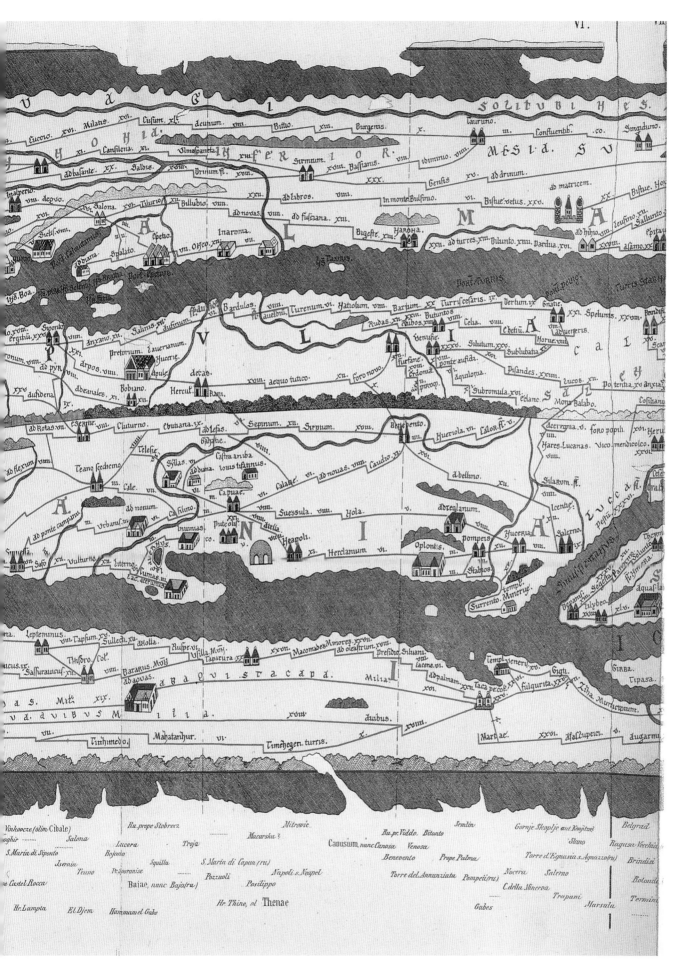

◁ The *Peutinger Map* (*Tabula Peutingeriana*) was originally a long, narrow parchment roll. It was transcribed in the 12th century from a Roman map of between 335 and 366 CE, which probably drawn on a papyrus roll. The map showed main roads, as well as other features including mountains (pale brown), rivers (green), forests (groups of trees), and staging posts. The map's proportions ensure that distances north–south are represented at a much smaller scale than distances east–west . These were calculated by adding the mileages between staging posts.

Africa – all contained within a circle, the O, with the horizontal bar of the T representing the rivers separating Asia from the other two continents. The T was a symbol of the Christian cross. Jerusalem came at the centre of the world, and maps such as that of Hereford were full of religious symbolism.

Monsters with men's heads

As with other *mappae mundi*, the Hereford map depicted monstrous races that derived from Greek accounts of mythical peoples in distant areas. The Hereford map depicted the dog-headed Cynocephati, the Martikhora – four-legged beasts with men's heads – and the shadow-footed Sciopods. The prototype of the Hereford map is believed to be a lost work, the *Agrippa World Map*, produced during the reign of the Emperor Augustus (*r.* 27 BCE–14 CE). Races depicted on other maps included the mouthless Astomi, the Blemmyae (who had faces on their chests), the one-eyed Cyclopes, the Hippopodes (who had horses' hooves), and the cave-dwelling Troglodytes.

In these world maps, the sense of place meant not only geographical space, but also location in terms of the Christian story and the universe. Indeed, Christian clerics, and particularly the English, played a major role in the mapping of this time. The *mappae mundi* of the 13th and early 14th centuries produced in the English or closely related north French traditions – the Ebstorf, Vercelli, Hereford, and Duchy of Cornwall maps – sought to order the entire known world. Maps of the world drew heavily on the geographical knowledge inherited from the classical world.

There was also a Jewish cartographic tradition. It has been suggested that a map may have accompanied the *Book of Jubilees*, written in the second century BCE, and it is possible that there was a cartographic tradition in Hebrew biblical commentary. Maps of the Holy Land survive in manuscripts dating from the 13th to the 15th century; these stemmed from originals probably drawn by Rashi (rabbi Solomon ben Isaac). The Jewish tradition of mapmaking influenced its Christian counterpart. The commentaries of Nicolas of Lyra, *Postillae litteralis super totam Bibliam*, written between 1323 and 1332, drew on Rashi and included a number of maps that were subsequently influential.

European mapmaking faced the challenge of deciding how best to incorporate reports from travellers, such as Marco Polo, who, in 1271–95, crossed Asia to China and travelled in the Orient, before returning to Europe.

Distance was a particular problem with travelogues, many of which described it simply in terms of numbers of days travelled. The 11th-century Islamic astronomer al-Biruni noted: "As for the distances between the various parts of India, those who have not themselves actually seen them must rely upon traditions; but unfortunately it is such a nature that already Ptolemy incessantly complains of its transmitters and their bias towards story-telling".

Maps were seen as a way better to understand human history. Roger Bacon, a Franciscan friar who taught at Oxford and

described a system of coordinates, argued in his *Opus Maius* (*c.* 1268) that, "if one does not understand the physical form of the world, history is apt to become a stale and tasteless crust … But if he can picture to himself what the places named [in scripture] are like, and has learned their positions, their distances, their distance up or down, their length and breadth… then… history will fill him with pleasure, and he can easily and confidently advance to a realization of its spiritual sense".

The boundaries of Europe

There were also maps of Britain, more particularly England, notably the Matthew Paris and Gough maps. Paris, a Benedictine monk, produced four versions of a map of Britain in *c.* 1255–9. North was at the top, but Scotland was depicted as an island. The Gough map of about 1360, named after the antiquarian Richard Gough (1735–1809), appears to have followed the same approach of beginning with an outline, partly from a portolan chart and partly from a world map, then inserting information, probably from an itinerary.

The Gough map shows routes, although the reason for their selection is unclear. In his *British Topography* (2nd edition, 1780), Gough stated that the map could "justly boast itself the first among us wherein the roads and distances are laid down". It has been suggested that the Gough map was one of a type and that it may have been intended to help governmental officials.

At the other extreme, mostly from England and Italy, were local maps covering towns and some estates. These maps included drawings – for example, of buildings and bridges – indicating the extent to which maps contained elements of pictograms. Most local maps date from after 1100, suggesting that mapping was playing a role in local disputes as people sought to demonstrate the boundaries of landholdings. While up to the mid-14th century, the overwhelming use of maps appears to have been in scholarship, from that period onwards there was an increase in the numbers made for practical purposes. Nevertheless, written surveys remained more common than maps or plans.

Maps were slowly used to delineate some European frontiers from the 15th century. Maps helped to make the understanding of frontiers in linear terms, rather than as zones, easier, and this came to play a role in frontier negotiations.

Henri Arnault de Zwolle, councillor of Duke Philip the Good of Burgundy, produced in 1444 a map of a contested region between France and Burgundy. This was seen by Philip as part of a process by which French enclaves could be defined and eliminated in order to simplify the frontier. However, there were problems in mapping frontier lines. In his treatise *De Fluminibus seu Tiberiadis*, Bartolo de Sassoferrata had to consider the difficulties of mapping meanders, changes of river course, and new islands in rivers.

Marco Polo, by contrast, assumed that he had travelled 16,000 miles from Venice to Beijing, instead of 7000 miles, and this helped

◄ The Hereford *mappa mundi* ascribed to Richard of Haldingham was made in the 1290s, probably in Lincoln (although it can now be seen in Hereford Cathedral). The map was drawn on vellum parchment with a circular world and flanking drawings. The Holy Land is at the centre of the map, and east is at the top. The Mediterranean is the prominent sea forming the upright of the T. Christ sitting in majesty at the Day of Judgement is at the apex of the map outside the frame.

lead to a misunderstanding of the distance from Europe to China across the Atlantic.

The veracity of Polo's account has been challenged by some scholars, but it certainly had a major impact on European knowledge about the Orient. Furthermore, the account testified to the Mongol peace and its impact on facilitating journeys along the Silk Road from the Orient to Europe.

Polo claimed to have left Venice in 1271 and to have reached Kublai's summer palace at Shangdu (Xanadu) in 1275. In 1292, he was given, he claimed, the task of escorting a Mongol princess from China to Hormuz on the Persian Gulf, and from there he returned home in 1295. Marco Polo was not alone. William of Rubruck crossed Asia in 1253–5 travelling on behalf of Louis IX of France to the court of the Mongol Khan at Karakorum.

Guiding the mariners

A different form of map was provided by portolan charts, derived from the Italian word *portolani* meaning written sailing directions. It was believed that these charts were used alongside the directions; although that theory is now questioned. The charts offered coastal outlines in order to help navigation and were covered in rhumb lines: radiating lines resembling compass bearings.

The charts were a guide to anchorages and sailing directions, and were a testimony to the importance of trade links within the Mediterranean. Many of those that survive are attractive works that may have been designed for consultation ashore rather than to be taken to sea.

These charts became more accurate with time and were most accurate for areas where navigation was most common. New discoveries could be incorporated into this format as improvements in navigation made it easier to record voyages accurately. Nautical charts were part of a developing map culture. By the end of the Middle Ages, nearly every major map type known today had an equivalent.

The Nuremberg geographer Martin Behaim's globe of 1492, the most up to date available, depicted only islands between Europe and China. His information was derived largely from Ptolemy, Marco Polo, and the Portuguese explorers who had sailed down the west coast of Africa, first rounding its southern tip in 1488. Behaim also showed a large island called Antilia between Africa and China, an island that since 1424 had been linked with the long-held belief that seven bishops and their flocks, who had fled the Moorish invasion of Portugal in the eighth century, had established seven islands, or cities, beyond the Atlantic horizon.

Some maps showed a Saint Brendan's Island. This was based on the reputed voyages from Ireland in about 570. The saint was reported to have encountered icebergs, pack-ice, and volcanoes, as well as to have celebrated Mass on the back of a whale.

Ptolemy's legacy

Ptolemy's *Geography* was translated from Greek into Latin in 1406, and maps drawing on the coordinates from this translation appeared over the following two decades, with printed versions being produced after 1475. Fifteenth-century editions of the *Geography* generally included 27 maps. The Indian Ocean was shown as enclosed, with Africa below the equator stretching east to join a land mass that stretched south from Southeast Asia.

Although Ptolemy's *Geography* was supplemented in 1427 by Claudius Clavus's map of northern Europe – Clavus was a Dane who had visited Norway, Iceland, and southern Greenland – subsequently, the Greek's work was to be further supplemented and then superseded by accounts of what were, to Europeans, discoveries in every direction.

Nevertheless, the ideas Ptolemy expressed had considerable influence. His *Geography* included material about three projections and thus encouraged the idea that the world could be seen through different projections. Ptolemy's tables of latitudes and longitudes furthered an emphasis on the mathematization of location, and thus on accurately measured data, while the use of latitude and longitude led to an emphasis on recording data with reference to a graticule; this grid was to become a central feature of Western mapping.

In search of riches

Portuguese exploration rapidly affected European geographers. From 1482, editions of Ptolemaic maps were updated to include recent discoveries. The manuscript book *Insularum Illustratum*

(*Illustrated Islands*), written *c.*1490 by the Florentine-based German cartographer Henricus Martellus, included knowledge of Dias's voyage rounding the Cape of Good Hope, in both text and map.

Like Columbus, others set sail in search of riches. A chart of 1413 by Mecia de Viladestes depicts the "river of gold" that would provide a trading route from the Atlantic to the African interior, a potential source of gold and ivory for European trading nations. Indeed, the Portuguese sent expeditions along the coast of Africa in search of riches, as well as to undermine their Islamic opponents.

Prince Henry the Navigator (1394–1460) was the major patron of this activity, and it led to a huge increase in information about African waters which, in turn, led to improved mapmaking. Islands off Africa – Madeira, the Canaries, and the Azores – were sighted. Then, thanks to more voyages, their number, correct

∧ Produced in about 1360, the Gough map, named after a later owner, depicted the whole of Britain, including nearly 620 settlements. Eastern England is presented with more accuracy than the West and, in particular, Scotland. The map may have been compiled for official use; it provided an effective route map.

The Catalan Atlas

The Catalan Atlas, hand-drawn on vellum in 1375 and now preserved in the Bibliothèque Nationale in Paris, is a unique document that offers unparalleled insights into the early motivations of the great explorers. It was one of the most accurate maps of its time.

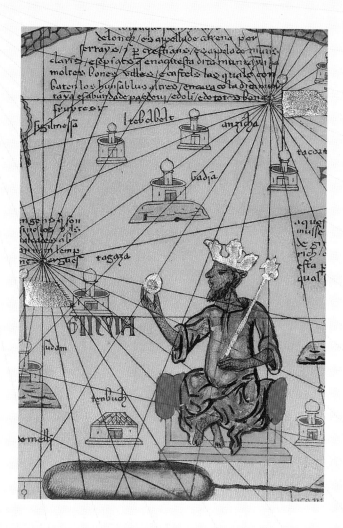

This remarkable atlas is believed to have been the work of Abraham Cresques, a leading figure of the famed Majorcan cartographic school that dominated 14th-century European mapmaking. His expertise in cartography had earned Cresques a brilliant reputation and privileged status in the court of King Juan of Aragon, who commissioned the Catalan Atlas as a gift for Charles V of France.

If Cresques was indeed the author of the atlas, then he excelled himself. He drew on known facts, where these were available, to provide outlines of countries and features in the landscape, and he embellished his work with images drawn from a mixture of myth, history, and stories reported by the early travellers.

The atlas comprised just six leaves of vellum (prepared animal hide), folded in the centre to form pages. Texts on astronomy and astrology were presented in the early pages, including such details as tips for sailors on measuring the passage of time at night and a table showing the movements of tides. The map proper took up several pages and identified cities, seas, ports, and other features. It drew on the developments in mapmaking seen in maritime charts, in that it was orientated to the north and depicts compass lines.

Tales of wonder

Biblical references abound among the Catalan Atlas's illustrations – indeed, Jerusalem marks the centre of its eastern section. Further to the east, into China, lie tantalizing hints of the abundant riches described just a century earlier by Marco Polo. The information about Asia in the atlas is largely drawn from Marco Polo, although not all of his knowledge is presented.

The explorer visited the East Indies and sailed via the Straits of Malacca, but the map neglects southeast Asia. Polo's reports of silk, spices, and other exotic goods had been met with incredulity back in Europe, but similar reports from later travellers – and, no doubt, images in documents such as the Catalan Atlas – helped to fuel Western Europe's interest in Far Eastern trade and the endeavours that followed. It was the quest for gold – made legendray by tales about Mansa of Mali, who was depicted in the Atlas – that inspired the first Portuguese voyages along the African coast. "So abundant is the gold which is found in his country that this lord is the richest and noblest king in all the land" read the text. And it was in pursuit of a westerly route to the Far East that Christopher Columbus set sail in 1492 and accidentally bumped into the Americas.

The Catalan Atlas happily combines the real with the imaginary, resorting to the depiction of myths and legends for those areas where reliable evidence was not yet available. One such exotic legend illustrated in the Atlas is that of the pearl-divers in the Indian Ocean who, as if by magic, were protected from sharks. Another has diamond-seekers who threw meat into mountain clefts; the diamonds stuck to the meat, which was brought down to them by birds.

⋀ Among the illustrations on this African portion of the atlas was a depiction of the fabled King of Mali, Mansa Munsa. Legend had it that Mali possessed dazzling quantities of gold, its precise location a closely guarded secret. Prester John, a mythical Christian king, also featured in many maps. He was located in Ethiopia in Carignano's chart of about 1307 and in India in the Vesconte and Sanudo world maps of about 1320.

➤ The Catalan Atlas was a multi-sheet *mappa mundi* that showed how the Mediterranean-centred civilization of Europe was expanding. Thus, information from Marco Polo and explorers along the African coast was included.

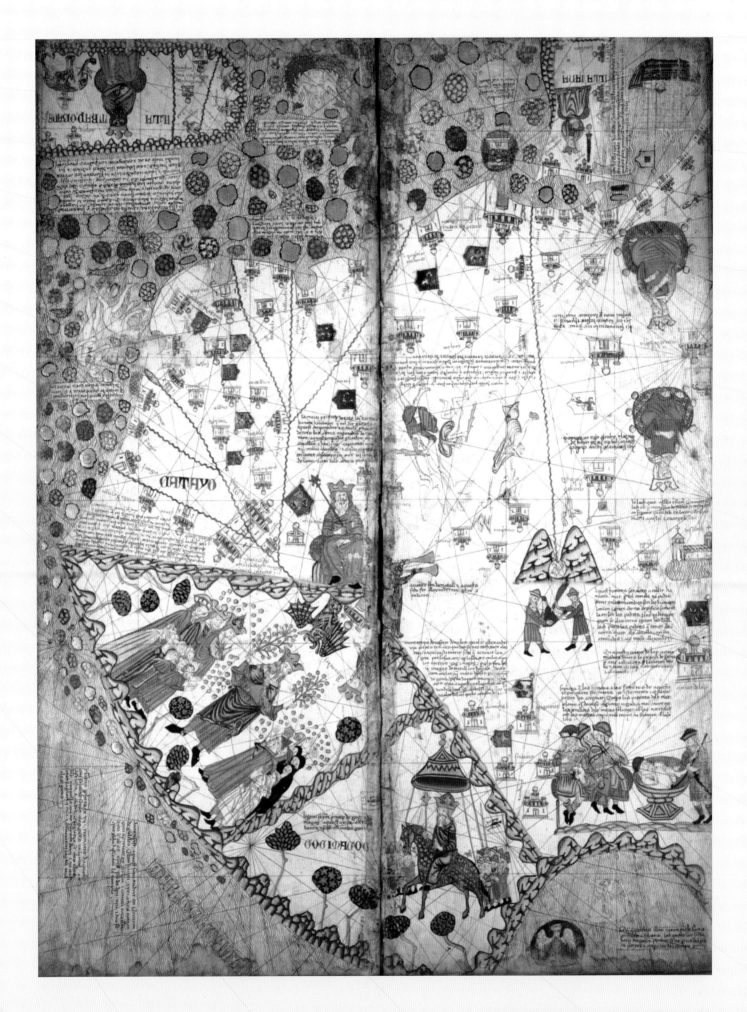

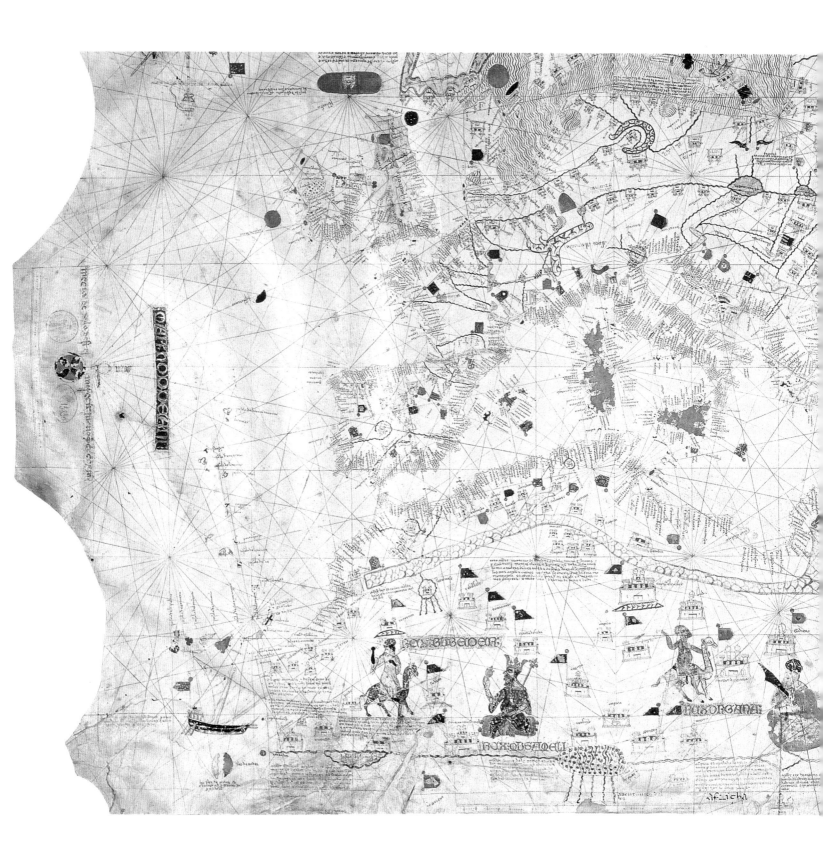

orientation, and true positions were all mapped. This was achieved between 1339 and 1452, so that maps such as the Venetian Andrea Bianco's of 1448 offered a less stylistic and more realistic account than their predecessors.

As exploration led to a greater understanding of the shape of the world, Cresques's *Catalan Atlas*, with its mysterious blank spaces and alluring illustrations, would be out of date as a summary of European knowledge within a century.

Maps: myth and magic

There is a long tradition of treating pre-modern and non-Western mapping as primitive. The former's depictions of mythical creatures, such as men with faces in their chests or with a large foot that could be used as a sunshade, were cited as evidence of a tendency to treat the outside world as fabulous and to prefer an irrational to a scientific approach. This interpretation also displayed scant sympathy for religious themes, in both Western and non-Western mapping, treating them as further manifestations of this non-scientific approach. Instead, the path of progress was seen as leading from the Greeks to the modern era via a rediscovery of Greek knowledge as part of the 15th-century European Renaissance.

This analysis rested, however, on a failure to appreciate the role of religious considerations in the knowledge systems of societies and, in particular, their need to map the Earth as part of a more general cosmic understanding. Furthermore, the "big bang" approach to cartographic history, the rediscovery of Ptolemy in the 15th century, underrated the incremental nature of change in the intervening period.

Underlying our entire assessment, in this chapter, of a period which covers the majority of human history, is the central lesson of historical research: the need to consider the nature of the evidence, especially its limitations and variety. It is particularly difficult to assess the likely reality for ages for which map survival is nonexistent or fragmentary, but it is likely that map use was more than occasional.

This is especially the case in the Middle Ages, as maps had been in use previously. Aside from evidence of maps, there is also the issue of indications of how they were used and understood. It is all too easy to assume that modern practices provide the guidance to these or at least to best practice. This is mistaken. The study of early maps requires the comprehension of the culture within which they were produced and considered.

⋏ This 1413 map by Mecia de Viladestes, classified as a compass maker 12 years earlier, reflects the expansion of knowledge of West Africa as European explorers moved south. According to one commentator, the Cape Verde islands were marked, although they are usually given as having been discovered in 1455–6. This map also reflects interest in trading into the West African interior to obtain gold and other goods without the intermediary of North African Muslims.

In the Wake of Columbus

Drawing on the up-to-date geographical knowledge of the late 15th century, Christopher Columbus set sail in 1492, bound, he thought, for Japan. Using Ptolemy's maps as a guide, he had expected the voyage from Europe to be a distance of around 2400 nautical miles; in reality, he would have had to travel some 10,000 miles to reach his Asian goal. When Columbus made landfall, he presumed that Asia was what he had indeed found. He was, in fact, in the West Indies. His subsequent voyages identified other Caribbean islands, solved the riddle of Cuba, and allowed him to view the coast of South America stretching to the horizon.

This new world was rapidly mapped. Columbus's pilot on his second voyage, Juan de la Cosa, is usually held to have produced the first map to show the discoveries, but it may, it is argued, have appeared later than the traditional date, 1500. His map certainly showed North and South America as a continuous landmass. In 1502, the Cantino map revealed Columbus's discoveries as well as those in both North and South America, the coast of Brazil being depicted rather vaguely, complete with trees and parrots. The coast of West Africa is revealed in greater detail.

Four years later, the Contarini map had a greater impact because it was printed. This map by the Italian Giovanni Contarini indicated the variety of ways in which new discoveries could be assessed. Cuba and Hispaniola were shown, but Newfoundland and Greenland were presented as parts of a peninsula stretching northeast from China. Between them and the West Indies lay a large body of water giving access between Europe and China. South America was shown as a separate continent. This approach was also adopted in a map published by the Dutch cartographer Johann Ruysch in 1507 or 1508, although more detail was offered for Newfoundland, possibly reflecting the benefit of a voyage there.

In 1507, the German cartographer Martin Waldseemülle, produced a world map, printed from 12 woodblock engravings, in which he named the New World "America" in honour of the Italian explorer Amerigo Vespucci. It was not until the Fleming Gerhardus Kramer's (Latinized as Mercator, 1512–94) 1538 map that the names North and South America were differentiated.

Images of the New World spread rapidly. The Ottoman empire benefited from the capture of Columbus's cartographic sketches, and this led to the production of the Piri Reis map in 1513. In 1520, the *mappa mundi* of Schoener depicted the New World as a separate continent between Europe and East Asia, but showed a marine route between North and South Africa. In addition, the Pacific was depicted as being far smaller than was subsequently revealed by the first circumnavigation of the world in 1519–22, begun by Ferdinand Magellan, who was killed in the Philippines in 1521. This expedition was the first (in late 1520) to round the southern point of South America and achieved the first recorded crossing of the Pacific; although Polynesian travellers had made long voyages across that ocean.

This circumnavigation made the globe a more obvious tool for understanding the world, and thus emphasized the need to give greater attention to the projections used in depicting that world. By drawing attention to the size of the Pacific, the circumnavigation also clarified not only the size of the Earth, but also how much remained to be mapped by Europeans: the larger the Pacific, the more extensive its shores.

Magellan's expedition had taken a route across the ocean; it had not followed its shores. The voyage also left open plenty of possibilities that land masses may lie to the north or south of the route. Like the Greeks, the European mapmakers were faced by the need to fill in the gaps that they were certain existed. The sense of flux and uncertainty was similar to that of the mapping of the sky which, in the 16th and 17th centuries, was to be challenged by new concepts and new information.

America through Spanish eyes

In the 1570s, Philip II of Spain commissioned an extensive survey of his territory, the *Relaciones Geográficas*, partly with the aim of elucidating the political boundaries or tribute-reach of pre-Conquest states. Indigenous artists were, in the main, responsible for the maps that emanated from New Spain in response to Philip's commission.

This mixture of native and European mapping conventions and symbols marked a transition stage that reflected the syncretic character of Spanish imperialism: its ability to adopt and adapt as part of its rule, seen, for example, in the way in which native religious cults were given a place within Christianity. The Spaniards, however, became increasingly concerned with having standard European-style documentation to support titles to land and other claims, and this contributed to the decline of native mapping.

Further north, the process of European settlement was to be accompanied by the destruction of native American people. At the same time, the Europeans' maps gradually obliterated native place names and replaced them with their own. This was a long process, and the mapping of the New World was not completed until the 19th century.

Alongside the mapping of settled areas came that of regions where settlements had not yet been established. This involved both inland mapping and that of coastlines, and can be seen with each of the European imperial powers. Thus, in 1516, the explorer Amerigo Vespucci's nephew Juan was instructed to produce a *padrón real* (official royal chart), a work that was frequently updated to take note of new reports from navigators.

◄◄ A map of America from 1686, a copy of an atlas by Joan Blaeu, (1596–1673). Dutch cartography was at its height in the 17th century. The Dutch drew on earlier mapping, but also benefited from information provided from their colonies in North America and the West Indies, as well as from their attempt to conquer the Portuguese settlements in Brazil. The Dutch base of New Amsterdam on Manhattan Island was captured by the English in 1664 and renamed New York.

➤ Commissioned by Alberto Cantino, the envoy at Lisbon of Hercules d'Este, Duke of Ferrara, for the duke, this map includes details of Portuguese discoveries and accompanied the account of the second voyage of Gaspar Corte-Real to American waters in 1501. The map, which is known as the Cantino planisphere, was produced in 1502. The brightly coloured parrots appear in Brazil.

Visions of Plunder

The conquest of a new world brought Spain and Portugal into contact with the mapmaking traditions of native peoples. On the whole, they paid little attention to them, but, as with the spread of Christianity, there was a native contribution to the culture created by the conquerors.

In 1519, Hernán Cortés made landfall in Mexico, visions of plunder in his mind. The first people he encountered, the Toltecs, led him to their powerful masters, the Aztecs, whose capital was the island city of Tenochtitlán, on Lake Texcoco. The location and founding of the city are portrayed in pictorial Aztec maps. One reproduced in the *Codex Mendoza*, a manuscript book of about 1541 – presumably made for Antonio de Mendoza, the Spanish viceroy from 1535 to 1550 – used symbols to depict not only the social layout of the city, but also its history.

The map is dominated by an eagle alighting on a cactus, testifying to the mythic origin of Tenochtitlán; it also depicts the clan leaders who founded the city in response to this divine signal. The map shows the quadrants of the city in which the Aztecs settled and, below, it showed the conquests initiated from it. This contrasted with the European mapping of the period, not least because the latter was focused only on space, with no suggestion of a timescale.

A European map of Tenochtitlán (woodblock printed in 1524) to accompany the printing of a letter from Cortés to the Emperor Charles V was different to the Mendoza map, not least because it was printed. It sought to offer a representation that was accurately pictorial and non-symbolic, although it has been suggested that the map also drew on native ideas.

The mapping of Central America changed as a result of Spanish conquest, not simply because Spain was now the imperial master, but also because the Meso (or Central) Americans swiftly began to follow Spanish practices. For example, they replaced hieroglyphs with alphabetic writing, which transformed the way in which information could be recorded.

Native maps thus became easier for the Spaniards to understand, and this was important if the maps were to play a role in litigation. More generally, the landscape was increasingly understood in European terms, with an abandonment of Mesoamerican abstraction in favour of the imagery of European maps. The use of perspective spread.

The Mendoza map provides no key to the recent Spanish conquest. Cortés had about 500 Spanish soldiers, 14 small cannon, and 16 horses when he landed at Vera Cruz. His initial welcome owed much to the Emperor Montezuma's conviction that Cortés was the god Quetzalcoatl, but in 1520–1 Cortés still had a fight on his hands.

Earlier Aztec expansion had left conquered peoples ready to ally with the Spaniards. The Totonacs and the Tlaxcalans welcomed Cortés, and he made an alliance with the Totonacs at the coastal city-state of Cempoala, then under Aztec dominion, in 1519. This native support was essential in order to match the massive numerical superiority of the Aztecs.

Tenochtitlán was captured after three months of bitter fighting on the causeways. The city was sacked and a large proportion of the indigenous population was massacred. Thirty years later the Spanish Royal Cosmographer Alonso de Santa Cruz made a map of Tenochtitlán (now Mexico City) and its environs (see pp 60–1).

⋏ Name glyphs for groups of towns in the Lake Texcoco region, north and south of Tenochtitlán, taken from the *Codex Mendoza*. This map, by depicting both the mythic origin of the city and its current organization, collapsed the boundary between time and space. These name glyphs were gradually superseded by European names and alphabetic writing in the mapping of the area.

➢ This map used symbols to depict the social layout of the Aztec capital, Tenochtitlán, and illustrates the eagle that in myth marked the site where the great city should be built.

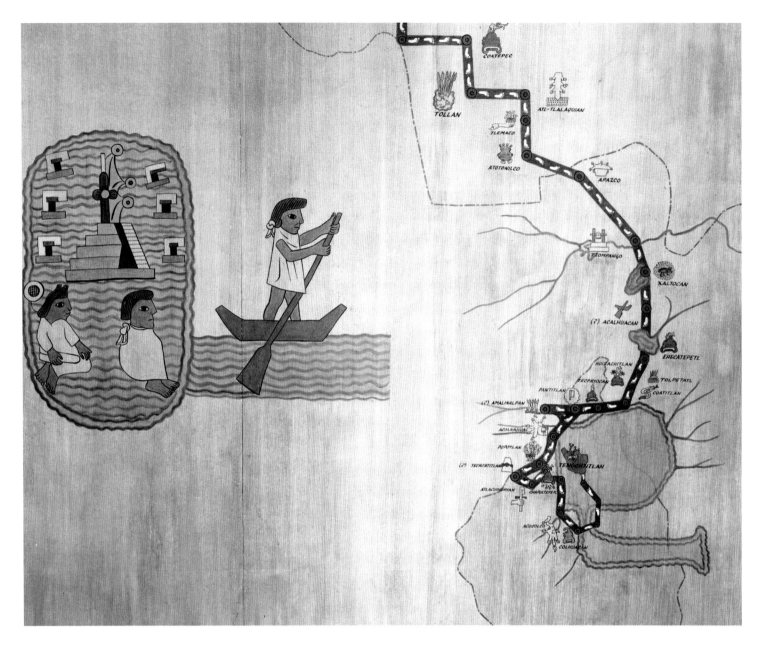

⋏ The Chichimeques founding Tanayuca in 1224. This map was part of a pattern of Mesoamerican migration maps in which the cartographic structure is provided by the journey, rather than by landscape.

A manuscript map of the world that he produced in 1526 survives and it shows how Spanish knowledge of coastal waters rapidly increased. Thus successive estuaries on the coast of North Africa were recorded, while the outline of some of the American islands, especially Cuba and Hispaniola (but not Jamaica), was considerably more accurate than in earlier maps.

Exploration caused major changes in the world of maps. It led to the overthrow of the authority of the classical maps and geographers. Ptolemy's maps, for example, became simply curiosities, historical sources – although classical texts long continued to be cited in accounts of Asia.

The 1513 Strasbourg edition of Ptolemy's *Geography* was the first to separate modern from ancient maps. In 1578 Mercator issued the Ptolemaic maps alone, without modern supplements, so it could stand as an unrevised atlas of the classical world.

The mapping of the New World is the pre-eminent development in this period, but the arrival of voyagers in Asian waters – such as Pedro de Covilham, a Portuguese explorer who had sailed down the Red Sea in 1487, subsequently to India, and from there down the east coast of Africa to Sofala in modern Mozambique (1489) – also led to major changes in knowledge about the Indian Ocean and East Asia. Bartholemeu Dias, who rounded the Cape of Good Hope in January 1488, produced a map depicting the lands he explored. And fellow Portuguese navigator Vasco da Gama reached Calicut in India in 1498, at the end of the first all-sea journey there from Europe.

The Portuguese rapidly followed up by travelling on from the Indian Ocean to China and Japan, and other Europeans followed. New maps were supplied not only by individual mapmakers, but also by institutions created to train navigators. These navigation schools, which were linked to the Casa de Contratación at Seville (the organization established to control trade with the New World) and the Almazém de Guiné India (Storehouse of Guinea and the Indies) at Lisbon, organized the production of charts.

In Lisbon, a hydrographic office was established in the *Almazém* at the close of the 15th century in order to control, as well as ensure, the flow of information. The office was responsible for the issue of charts to pilots and also for securing their return. It also oversaw the production of nautical charts and globes; those deemed unacceptable were destroyed, and it was illegal to possess charts and globes that had not been approved. In order to improve accuracy, returning pilots were expected to submit their charts and logbooks for scrutiny.

In about 1502, India was recorded on the "Cantino planisphere", a secret copy of the official record in Lisbon on which all Portuguese discoveries were recorded. The Contarini map of 1506 showed the coast of Africa with considerable detail, but there was less accuracy in its coverage of South Asia. In 1513, Waldseemüller produced an atlas in which the Ptolemaic world maps appeared alongside updated ones. The latter included a less inaccurate account of South Asia, with India more elongated than on the Ptolemaic map, although the depiction of the coast to the east was full of error.

Thereafter, mapping improved – both Portuguese cartography and mapping based on the travels of other nationalities. For example, in 1518, Pedro Reinel, the leading Portuguese chartmaker with official status, was responsible for a map of the Indian Ocean in which he drew on the expedition to the Moluccas five years earlier. Portuguese expeditions to these waters produced their own information and obtained copies of charts from native pilots, as with the 1511 expedition to Java and the Moluccas. The charts of the Indian Ocean produced by Sebastião Lopes in his portolan atlas (Lisbon *c.* 1565) reflected a growing awareness of the coastline – for example, of Sumatra – although the Philippines were only poorly understood.

The Portuguese base of Goa developed as a centre of mapmaking. Aside from nautical charts, there was also, from 1580, the mapping by Manuel Godinho de Eredia (1563–1624), of parts of Asia as a whole, in order to replace what were seen as inaccurate maps. From the 1590s, a series of plans of Portuguese positions in Asia was produced.

Translation of travellers' accounts spread knowledge. Thus the account of Jan Huygen van Linschoten (who had been a secretary to the Bishop of Goa), which included a good map of South Asia, was published in Dutch in 1596 and translated into English two years later. The first map of India to be drawn by an Englishman – William Baffin – was produced in 1619, based on information from Sir Thomas Roe, who had been envoy there. In 1625, Samuel Purchas published in England the rutter (advice for pilots) of Joao de Castro describing the routes he took in the Red Sea in 1541. In turn, de Castro had relied on the charts of Arab and Gujarati pilots.

Mapping: the mother of invention

Another major change came from printing. Maps were first printed in Europe in the 1470s. All types of maps found in England

in the Middle Ages, except *mappae mundi*, continued to be made and used, although not all were immediately translated into print. The first map to be printed in England was a simple T-O diagram from English printing pioneer William Caxton's *Mirror of the World* (1480 or 1481); a copperplate map of London, printed in the city, was reported in 1497. It was Venice, Antwerp, Frankfurt, and Amsterdam, however, that dominated the 16th-century map world.

Manuscript maps continued to be produced – for example, in Venice from 1536 to 1564 by Battista Agnese – but printing was now central to most map production, although not for nautical charts. Thanks to printing using woodblocks, maps could be more speedily produced and more widely distributed. From the mid-16th century, woodblocks gave way to engraved copper plates as they were easier to correct and revise, both important factors in a mapmaking world that emphasized novelty and precision.

As a result of printing, most mapmakers had more, and more recent, maps to which they could refer. Printing facilitated the exchange of information, and the processes of copying and revision that were so important for mapmaking. Hand copyists, in contrast, were prone to variations and thus to corruption.

Printing also led to an emphasis on the commercial aspect of mapmaking and to a wider public interest in maps, and thus to a new dynamic for the production of maps and the propagation of mapmaking. Increased map use was therefore related to social change, especially the expansion of literacy.

Technology played a part. In place of the screw press came the rolling press, which was used for printing from copperplates and which offered speedier output and greater uniformity. Eventually, the copperplate replaced the woodcut.

Earlier maps were generally itinerary or picture maps, and were not drawn to a consistent scale. However, in England in the 1540s (earlier in Germany, Italy, and the Netherlands), scale was introduced to topographic maps, and by the end of the century maps drawn to scale were well established. Meanwhile, new techniques in drafting and presentation were discovered and adopted. The increasing use of the compass in surveying and mapmaking from the late 15th century was reflected in a growing tendency to draw local maps with north at the top, except where (as in South Germany) compasses had south-pointing needles.

The growing sophistication of some mapping was shown in the atlas of Bavaria produced in 1568 by Philipp Apian, a professor of mathematics at the University of Tübingen. He had recorded distances using an odometer and bearings with a compass, and his atlas included an index map that indicated by numbers the order and content of each of the sheets in the atlas. North was at the top, and the map showed rivers, mountains, bridges, and towns. It was framed by a scale and appeared between the decorative crests of the Bavarian towns.

In Europe, triangulation was introduced, the plane table and the theodolite invented, and a more consistent and sophisticated use of uniform conventional symbols in place of pictures on maps, for example, to signify towns, arose. In place of impressionistic, symbolic, or spiritual landscapes, more emphasis was placed on producing a scaled-down image of the physical world.

Triangulation, the system of measurement discussed in simple terms by Gemma Frisius in 1533, in England by William Cunningham in *The Cosmographical Glasse* (1559), and others later in the 16th century, then advanced in 1615 by Dutch mathematician Willebrord Snell (Snellius), is the only way to measure a straight line over the Earth's curved surface. It required the accurate measurement of a baseline; the theodolite (see p.102), allowed the surveyor to ascertain the angles between this baseline and the third point visible from both ends. Trigonometric tables could be used then to calculate the lengths of the other sides of the triangle; this process could be repeated.

Printing did not simply banish the old order in maps. Religious themes continued to be of some importance and indeed were accentuated by the Protestant Reformation. The Protestants sought to spread knowledge of the Bible, making its printing a major priority, and maps were the obvious way to communicate biblical geography and thus to establish and illustrate its truth. In his *Lectures*, Martin Luther revealed his wish to have "a good geography and more correct map of the Land of Promise". Maps were published as illustrations to biblical commentaries and explanations from the 1520s, the first being a version of Lucas Cranach's map of the Exodus in the 1525 edition of the Old Testament published by Christopher Froschauer. A map illustrating the Exodus appeared in England in 1535.

Later in the century, Bibles printed in Europe included maps of such subjects as Eden and the division of Canaan among the 12 tribes of Israel. Biblical maps were updated to incorporate developments in astronomy and cartography, but Paradise and the Garden of Eden continued to be located in many maps. The first printed Jewish map of the Holy Land appeared in 1560.

As mapmaking was driven increasingly by non-religious motivations, and undertaken by secular cartographers, so the ecclesiastical mapmakers and the religious inspiration to their work fell into abeyance. Printers therefore tended to focus more on new secular works. Maps came to play a greater role in Europe in a number of secular fields, for example, in diplomatic negotiations as frontiers were both defined and contested. A map was used in the diplomacy that led to the Anglo-French Treaty of Ardres of 1546, although the discussions were not without serious difficulties. Before the treaty, William, Lord Paget and a French emissary went with several guides to examine the source of a boundary stream and fell into a serious dispute over which of five springs it was.

Monarchs of all they survey

A number of monarchs were interested in their frontiers, not least as active expressions of their power. Henry IV of France

(*r.* 1589–1610) decided in 1607 to have a map of his coasts and frontiers produced. Royal surveyors were appointed for the frontier provinces, and triangulation was employed in the preparation of the maps. This mapping provided the basis for small-scale maps of the entire kingdom and, in 1651, for French cartographer Nicolas Sanson's *Théâtre de France.*

However, the devices of printed linear boundaries, different colouration, and textual specification were introduced slowly and were sometimes of limited applicability. In the French (1695) and the Dutch (1696 and 1700) editions of Sanson's popular French world atlas of 1658, lines on plates contradicted the colouring, and there were discrepancies between the national and European maps. The treatment of Alsace, Franche-Comté, and Roussillon in these editions varied. Similar inconsistencies can be found in the maps produced by Pierre Du Val between 1663 and 1684.

Nevertheless, there were innovations, such as the common practice, in use by the end of the 17th century, of distinguishing between traditional provincial borders and contemporary international frontiers by marking the latter within historically united provinces which were in fact divided between rulers.

This cartographic advance accorded with the general trend towards more defined frontiers, which made it increasingly possible to draw maps that corresponded to political reality. In contrast, across much of the world, shifting peoples posed problems for the notion of fixed frontiers. Instead, it was more pertinent for many (although not all) areas around Europe to think in terms of overlordship – a concept that is difficult to map – or in terms of maximal and minimal control.

Maps also played a growing role in legal disputes. By the end of the 16th century, estate maps were well established, whether supplementing or replacing written surveys. These maps were then used in court cases over disputed lands or boundaries.

Maps for the military

Military purposes, especially fortification, accounted for the mapping of certain localities. The increased role of artillery demanded the planning of defensive sites, the better to deploy optimum firepower to cover enemy attack from all sides. For example, the first maps drawn to scale by English mapmakers date from about 1540 and related to attempts to improve the defences of Guines, near Calais.

The geometric style of fortification encouraged the use of plans and of drawing to scale. The polygonal bastion developed from the 1450s was then spread across Europe by Italian architects. In a new defensive system known as the *trace italienne*, bastions, generally quadrilateral, angled, and placed at regular intervals along all walls, were introduced to provide effective flanking fire. Alongside the need for geometrically perfect shapes, fortification techniques had to be adapted to terrain and topography. These goals, and the cost of such building projects, made the ability to produce accurate scales crucial.

➤ The Middle East from the world map by Juan de la Cosa, Columbus's pilot on his second voyage. It has been argued that the map appeared later than the traditional date, 1500. The presence of pictures on maps as seen in this example was to become less common.

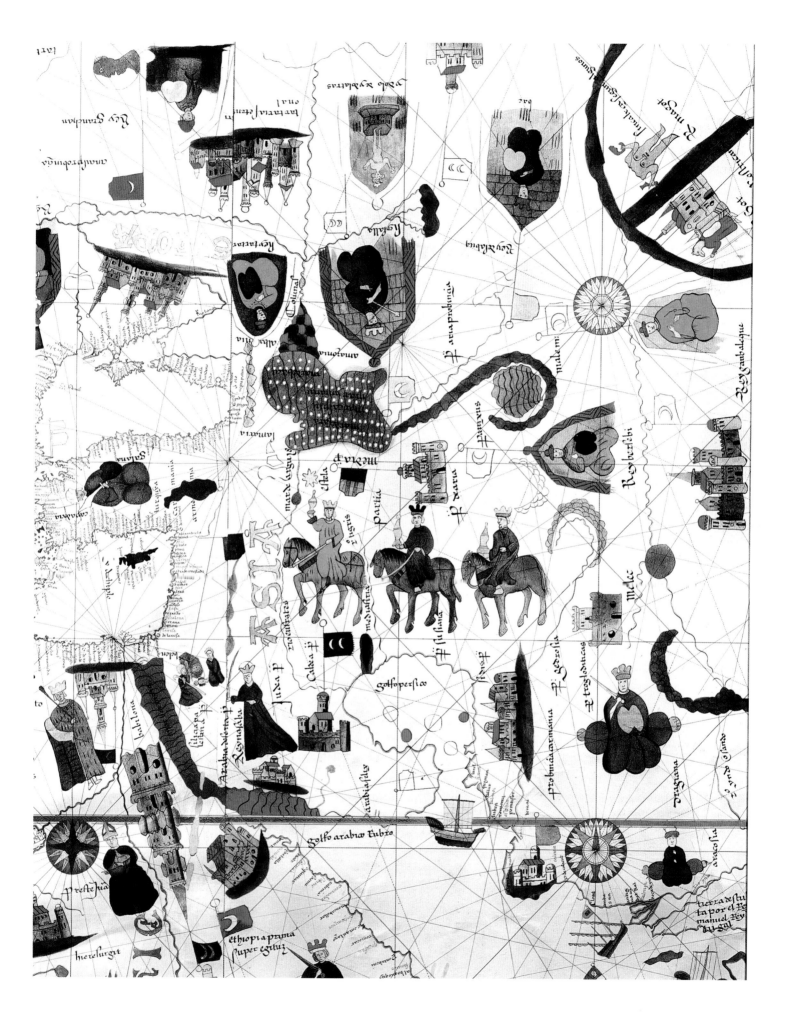

Maps were also used to plan, assist, or explain the movements of military units. Thus, the English invasion of Scotland in the 1540s was accompanied by mapping, while maps of Franche-Comté were produced in order to help plan the route for Spanish units moving through the province en route between Italy and the Low Countries in the late 16th century. The maps showed relief features, which crucially affected routes and timing along part of the so-called "Spanish Road".

A map of Ireland survives in the French archives showing the major military moves made in the campaign there in 1690. By then, the French had established a permanent collection of maps for military purposes, the *Dépôt de la Guerre* being founded in 1688. The records of fortifications included the *Recueil des plans des places du roi,* also known as the *Louvois Atlas,* of 1683–8.

Maps were also used, although far less commonly, by opponents of the state. In 1682, William Hack, a London mapmaker, dedicated his map of Jamaica drawn on a sheepskin to the pirate Bartholomew Sharp, who operated around the coast of Jamaica in 1684. In general, however, mapping served the cause of government and order, rather than their opponents.

Some medieval Christian maps had been centred on Jerusalem, but in the 16th century the world was rethought. Remember that this was the century in which the world was first circumnavigated, and this by Europeans, so it is not surprising that many of the charts they then produced used a projection that made most sense for compass work, pilotage, and navigation – especially in the mid-latitudes. Europeans needed to be able to sail great distances if they were to exploit the commercial opportunities and trading possibilities of distant possessions.

Mercator puts Europe centre stage

In 1569, Mercator produced a projection that treated the world as a cylinder, so that the meridians were parallel, rather than converging on the poles. The poles were expanded to the same circumference as the equator, although in 1569 Mercator produced a separate map of the Arctic, presenting it as a rock surrounded by a large body of water from which four channels crossed a continent dividing it into four islands. Beyond that there was a continuous ocean to the north of the various continents.

The maps that used Mercator's projection greatly magnified the temperate land masses at the expense of tropical ones. Taking into account the curvature of the Earth's surface, Mercator's projection kept angles, and thus bearings, accurate in every part of the map. A straight line of constant bearing could thus be charted across the plane surface of the map, a crucial tool for navigation. This was a huge achievement, unmatched by the Arab traders of the Indian Ocean, who were unable to use a grid of latitude and longitude in order to create practical navigation charts.

To achieve the navigational goal, the scale was varied in the Mercator projection, and thus size was distorted. This was not a problem for European rulers and merchants keen to explore the

➤ Portuguese exploration in the Indian Ocean rapidly led to an account of its northern shores that was correct in the general outline. This map comes from a Portuguese nautical atlas of about 1519. In detail, however, there were many errors, not least a lack of knowledge of the shape of Burma.

possibilities provided by exploration and conquest in the middle latitudes to the west (America) and to the east (South Asia). The Mercator projection highlighted the imperial world of Portugal and Spain. It was, therefore, an appropriate prefiguring of the Spanish success, under Philip II, in creating the first global empire with the establishment of a settlement in the Philippines, : the first empire on which the sun literally never set.

Mercator placed Europe, which, to a European, seemed both most important and the easiest to map, at the top centre of his world map. It gave the northern hemisphere primacy over the southern, not only by treating the north as the top, but also by giving the southern less than half the map. However, a Mercator projection need not necessarily include more of the northern hemisphere than the southern, nor place Europe at the top centre. A Mercator projection might just as easily have the North Pacific in its top centre, with Europe split between left and right extremities, and it might just as well have the south at the top.

Mercator's activities reflected not only intellectual enquiry, but also the commercial opportunities presented by widespread interest in mapping. His works included a wall map of Europe in 1554 and a map of the British Isles in 1564. An English edition of

Map of Europe, 1554, by Mercator, a Flemish mathematician, also skilled in making printed globes. Mapmakers had earlier concealed uncertainties by choosing projections that placed the known world in the centre.

his atlas, originally published in three parts in 1585–95, was published in 1636.

Like all projections, that of Mercator involved distortion. A projection is a flat (two-dimensional) representation of the (three-dimensional) curved globe. There can be no such thing as a "correct shape" on a map projection, not least because maps have "cuts", which occur along the edge of the map. Distortion increases with the area covered.

Mercator and others provided rectangular representations of the map. These reflected the nature of printing and are appropriate for the atlas or double page. However, rectangular maps deprive the world of its circularity: they make each parallel and meridian appear as straight, instead of circular, and give the world the misleading visual character of right-angled corners and clear edges.

Globes were important as they presented a truer picture of the universe and the world. Celestial globes were joined by a new development: terrestrial globes. These required a system of projection that worked both in the sense that it looked accurate and that it did not entail too much deformation.

As globes were more accurate in their portrayal of the world than flat maps, they seemed especially valid once the world had been circumnavigated. Furthermore, it seemed possible on globes to follow explorers and to integrate their discoveries with existing knowledge. In his painting *Three Scholars with a Globe* (c. 1670),

(see p.001) the Dutch painter Cornelis de Man (1621–1706) depicted two men studying a terrestrial globe, while the third has a hand resting on a map on the table, a map that has been identified as that of the Arctic published in 1598 by Cornelis Claesz and designed by Willem Barents. Barents had led three expeditions to find a northeast passage, dying, in 1597, on the last.

Globes, both terrestrial and celestial, were found in libraries – such as that of Philip II of Spain at the Escorial – and educational institutions – for example, the library of Queen's College Oxford in the 18th century – but they lacked the ability of flat maps to provide information at all scales. Globes did, however, serve to help explain concepts of time and of the relationship between the Earth and other bodies in the solar system. The terrestrial globe was a model not only of the Earth but also of the sphere of the sun, showing with its accessories – a movable meridian ring, a fixed horizon ring, and an hour circle with pointer – the motion of the sun around the Earth.

Saxton and Tudor cartography

"Come, here is the map; shall we divide our right" says the Welsh leader Owen Glendower to his fellow conspirators in William Shakespeare's *Henry IV, Part 1* (1597). In practice, they would not have done so in 1405, when the conspiracy took place: maps were not widely used and were of insufficient quality to enable the detailed comments attributed to the conspirators by Shakespeare. Nevertheless, to his late 16th-century audience, it is perfectly credible that the conspirators refer to a map. Harry Hotspur is angry about the impact of the River Trent's course on his share:

> Methink my moiety, north from Burton [on Trent] here,
> In quantity equals not one of yours.
> See how this river comes me cranking in,
> And cuts me from the best of all my land
> A huge half-moon, a monstrous cantle out.
> I'll have the current in this place damm'd up,
> And here the smug and silver Trent shall run
> In a new channel, fair and evenly;
> It shall not wind with such a deep intent
> To rob me of so rich a bottom here.

Thus, the map was to be linked to a reordering of nature. Such references to maps and to spatial considerations occurred more frequently in 16th-century society, and the map grew in potency, both as symbol and as reality.

The visual splendour of the maps of the period, which can be grasped from surviving examples, reflected the appeal of mapping and encouraged their display on walls. Maps also began to feature in portraits. The authority of maps was enhanced when one of the Holy Land was printed in the 1535 English translation of the Bible, while religious reformer John Calvin used maps in the editions of the Bible printed in the Calvinist centre of Geneva.

The development of mapmaking in Europe in the 16th century can be seen in the attractive maps produced in England by Christopher Saxton. Little is known about his early life. Born in about 1542–4 in Yorkshire, Saxton learned surveying and was commissioned by Thomas Seckford, Surveyor of the Court of Wards and Liveries, to produce his county maps. Seckford was close to Elizabeth I's leading minister and secretary of state, William Cecil, Lord Burghley, who had a substantial collection of maps – some annotated in his own hand – and Saxton's project was presumably backed by the government.

Saxton's sources, including earlier maps, are not known, but he carried out surveys that led to the engraving of 34 county maps. That of Norfolk (1574) may have been the first of the Saxton county maps to be printed. Most of the maps covered a single county, such as Northumberland, although some covered several. Kent, Surrey, Sussex, and Middlesex appeared on one map published in 1575, and Northamptonshire, Bedfordshire, Cambridgeshire, Huntingdonshire, and Rutland in another of 1576. The coastlines indicate the extent of subsequent change as, on the map for Kent, Sheppey and Thanet appear as islands.

The scale of Saxton's maps varied, as did the degree of pictorial detail – woods, bridges, and hills were drawn in – but not roads, which must have affected the maps' value to travellers. The level of accuracy, however, was high, although there were some significant errors, such as the shape of Cornwall. The prominence given to the scale affirmed the mathematical surveying values underlying the map.

Saxton also produced, in 1579, the first printed atlas of the counties of England and Wales. His large general map of England and Wales was printed in 1583, and, like the atlas, bore the royal arms. Such maps were an aspect of majesty, a proclamation of the extent of the state and its unity in and under the crown. Marcus Gheeraerts the Younger (1561–1635), for example, painted Elizabeth standing on a rendering of the 1583 Saxton map, and she was pictured on the title page of Saxton's atlas. Burghley was sent proof copies of the county maps, which formed the core of his personal atlas. He added his own notes to the margins, recording, for example, possible enemy invasion sites on the map of Dorset.

Lowlands and highlands

Saxton's maps were copied with few, if any, changes for two centuries, largely because the cost and effort of new surveys seemed redundant not only for commercial reasons, but also due to the authority of the Saxton maps. As a result, map publishers took over from mapmakers. Saxton's surveys were the basis for maps by cartographers, such as John Norden (1548–c. 1625), Surveyor to the Duchy of Cornwall, William Smith (d. 1618), and John Speed (d. 1629), who further helped to consolidate the visual image of counties. This was an aspect of the extent to which particular images were propagated in introducing maps to a wider public and encouraging map use.

Norden planned a series of county maps and descriptions, the *Speculum Britanniae*. Middlesex was published in 1593 and

Estate Mapping

Surveying and maps were an important aspect of the social stratification or division of knowledge. This can be seen readily in England. Surveying was seen as a tool with which landlords controlled their estates and introduced agrarian change. Maps were regarded as a way of recording this information, as well as a display of pride in possession. For example, Sir William Cordell commissioned a survey of his Suffolk manor of Long Melford in 1580. It hangs in Melford Hall, every field named.

Surveys were certainly important not only for recording ownership, but also for facilitating agricultural changes. As such, they challenged traditional assumptions about agricultural practice. Thus, they were linked to enclosure in England and to water management in the Netherlands and the Italian Veneto region.

In John Norden's *The Surveyors Dialogue* (1607), the surveyor offered an inclusive view of economic change: "Surveys are necessarie and profitable both for Lord and Tenant", only to meet with the farmer's claim "oftentimes you are the cause that men lose their land". The surveyor's view – "the faulty are afraid to be seen... the innocent need not fear to be looked into" – would have convinced few.

Norden's work included estate plans in more than 20 counties, for instance, a manuscript atlas showing the Suffolk estates of Sir Michael Stanhope, as well as maps of several counties. Another surveyor, Edward Worsop, noted "The common people for the most part are in great fear when survey is made of their land". At the same time, it is important to note that the equation landlord power = survey/map = agricultural change is overly simplistic. Much change, for example, with the introduction of new crops, occurred without surveys or maps, and much, indeed, stemmed from initiatives by peasants.

Surveying revealed different ideas about space. The idea of the "estimated acre" – the folk equivalent of surveying – remained potent into the 18th century and was usually the preserve of the old men of the parish who could remember older apportionments of land. Land surveyors developed appropriate conventions in the way they recorded information so that estate maps from different areas could be compared. The estate map of the Cornish estate of Cotehele that probably dates from the 1550s lacks a sense of scale and is, in part, diagrammatic. In contrast, the maps of Cotehele (1731 and 1784) were reliable as to scale and distance.

Charles, second Earl of Radnor and owner of the Cornish estate of Lanhydrock, commissioned Joel Gascoyne's *Land Atlas* of 1694–9, a masterpiece of the estate surveyor's work. It depicts more than 40,000 acres of his Cornish estates in colour on 258 parchment maps. Gascoyne also produced a nine-sheet *Map of the County of Cornwall newly Surveyed* (1699) on a scale of about one inch to one mile, as well as the *Stowe Atlas* for the Grenville family. The quality of the mapping was superior to that at the beginning of the century, for example William Senior's, 1610 map of the estate at Hardwick. Although, in England, the Land Surveyors' Club, the forerunner of the Institute of Chartered Surveyors, was not founded until 1834, guides to surveying appeared much earlier, including William Leybourne's *The Compleat Surveyor* in 1685.

➢ A portrait by Michael Dahl (1656–1743) from 1685, of Charles Robartes (1660–1723) second Earl of Radnor. He commissioned Joel Gascoyne's *Land Atlas* of 1694–9, which surveyed his Cornish estate of Lanhydrock.

➢ Estate mapping at its finest. A map of part of the Bodardle estate from Joel Gascoyne's atlas for the Robartes family. This depicts more than 40,000 acres in colour on 258 parchment maps. A table compares the customary with the actual acreages.

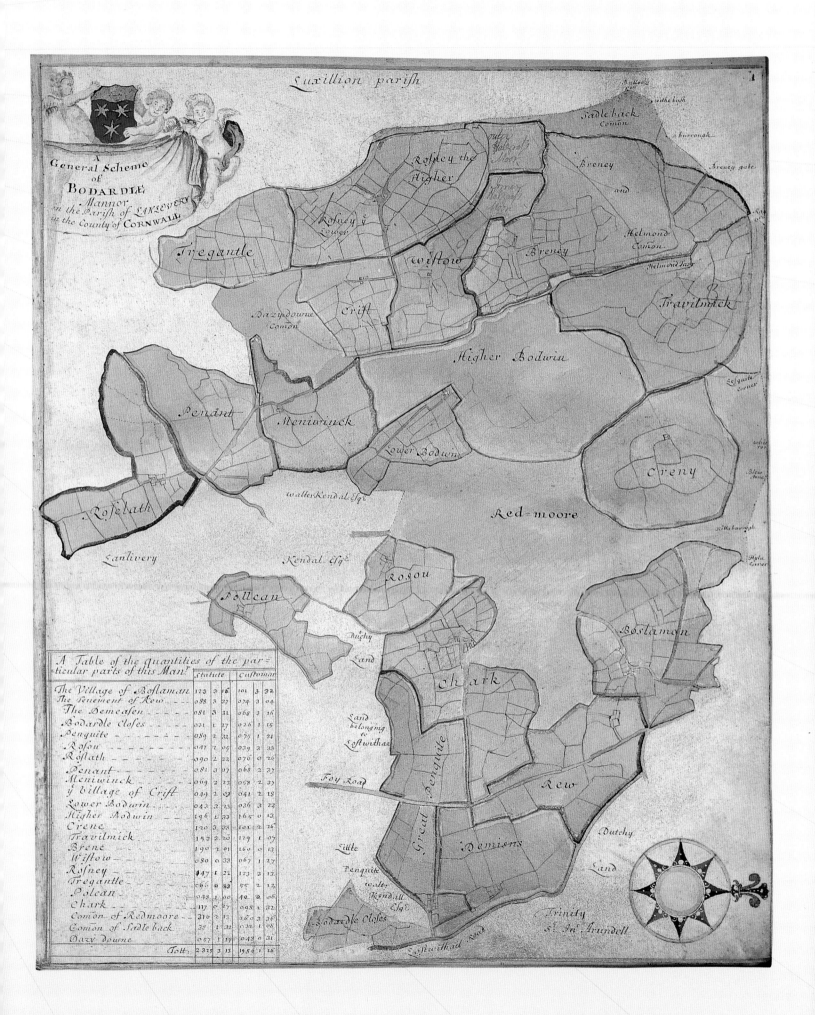

Luxillion parish

A
General Scheme
of
BODARDLE
Mannor
in the Parish of LANLEVERY
in the County of CORNWALL

Sadleback
Comon

Rosney the
Higher

Breney

and

Rosney y
Lower

Helmond
Comon

Tregantle

Wistow

Breney

Helmond Tart

Crift

Travilmick

Dazy downe
Comon

Higher Bodwin

Penant

Meniwinck

Lower Bodwin

Creny

Roselath

Walter Kendal Esqr

Red=moore

Lanlivery

Kendal Esqr

Rosou

Pollean

Boslamon

Duchy

Land

Chark

Land
belonging
to
Lostwithael

Great Penquite

Rew

Foy Road

Demisns

Duchy

Little
Penquite
walt:
Kendill
Esqr

L Bodardle Closes

Land

Lostwithael Road

Trinity
Sr Jnᵒ Arundell

A Table of the quantities of the par=ticular parts of this Man.!	Statute			Customari		
The Village of Boslaman ___	123	3	16	101	3	32
The Tenement of Rew ___	088	3	37	074	3	04
The Demeasen ___	081	3	31	068	3	16
Bodardle Closes ___	031	1	17	026	1	15
Penquite ___	089	2	32	074	1	21
Rosou ___	047	2	09	039	3	33
Roslath ___	090	2	22	076	0	26
Penant ___	081	3	07	068	2	37
Meniwinck ___	069	2	23	058	2	37
y Village of Crift ___	049	2	03	041	2	18
Lower Bodwin ___	043	3	13	036	3	22
Higher Bodwin ___	196	1	32	165	0	12
Crene ___	120	3	38	101	2	26
Travilmick ___	153	3	00	129	1	07
Brene ___	190	2	01	160	0	13
Wistow ___	080	0	38	067	1	27
Rosney ___	147	1	22	123	2	13
Tregantle ___	666	0	33	557	2	17
Polcan ___	048	1	00	40	2	06
Chark ___	117	0	27	098	1	32
Comon of Redmoore ___	310	2	13	260	3	36
Comon of Sadleback ___	38	1	32	032	1	08
Dazy downe ___	057	1	17	048	0	31
Tott.	2325	3	13	1954	1	26

Hertfordshire five years later, but no other maps were published in his lifetime. Unlike Saxton's, these maps indicate roads and include distance tables and a key, but the project was abandoned leaving a few other counties in only manuscript form. Other county maps included that of Kent in 1596 by Philip Symonson. This took the pictorial image further by depicting churches with spires as opposed to churches with towers. Saxton's copper plates were reused, but with alterations, for example, by William Webb in 1645, and Philip Lea in about 1690. Roads were added to Saxton derivatives, notably in Smith's and Lea's maps.

The popularity of Saxton and Saxton-derived maps reflected the desire for images drawn to scale in which crucial physical outlines – coastlines and rivers – were precisely marked. North was at the top of these maps. Saxton's maps also reflected the increased use of uniform conventional symbols to depict, for example, forests and hills. In 1573, Humphrey Llwyd, an MP and a noted antiquarian, produced the first map of Wales with a considerable degree of accuracy.

Mapping of Scotland also improved. In the mid-16th century, John Elder and Lawrence Nowell both produced maps, and others followed in the 17th century. A more accurate depiction of the Scottish coastline emerged, although the Highlands remained poorly mapped, as can be seen in the map of Scotland by the English mapmaker John Speed (1542–1649).

Timothy Pont (c. 1565–1614), who sought to emulate Saxton, faced a much tougher task in Scotland. The pressing commercial imperative found elsewhere was missing, however, as indicated by the fact that his manuscripts were not published in his lifetime. Instead, they proved the basis of the maps of Scotland in a Dutch work, Joan Blaeu's *Atlas Novus* (1654). Blaeu presented his role as that of rescuing material that was otherwise at risk of being lost "like sacred objects from a shipwreck … deposited … with us in the safe harbour of Amsterdam, where we engraved them for the use of posterity, to live again (in case they should perish) in copper". A similar process characterized much map publication, but, in most cases, information about sources is lacking.

Speed and commerce

Speed, whose maps were published as an atlas, the *Theatre of the Empire of Great Britain* (1611), was quick to see the commercial value of maps. He printed town maps as insets on his county maps. Speed's town maps indicate the importance of local topographical features, as in the 1610 map of Newcastle. The maps in the *Theatre* were reissued in 14 editions up to 1770.

The differences between the mapping of England and Scotland reflected the greater wealth, central government, and stability of England, and this contrast was more generally seen within Europe. Thus, neither England nor Spain in the late 16th century saw civil conflict on the scale of that in France. Nicolas de Nicolay was able to carry out a number of surveys, but nothing on the scale of Saxton. This situation was to change when France was brought under stronger governmental control during the reign of Louis XIV (r. 1643–1715).

The desire for geometric precision that helped to define the character of Western mapping was linked to a major shift in European culture. Scientific developments, particularly those undertaken by the Dutch in optics during the 17th century, emphasised *sight* as the sense through which God reveals his creation most clearly to mankind. This affected both art and maps.

Cartographer, artist, polymath

Dutch cartography has been linked to Dutch painting, as both attempted the description of physical reality. Fascination with the sense of sight led painters to describe the world as they viewed it – although in this process the Dutch were preceded by the Italians, and it is instructive to note the close links between mapmaking and painting in Renaissance Italy.

Cartographers such as Cristoforo Sorte (c. 1506–94) were also artists, while some artists, such as the polymath Leonardo da Vinci (1452–1519) also drew maps. This reflected the precision required by both disciplines. The linear perspective then becoming important in landscape painting mirrored cartography in its attempt to offer a scientific view. In both paintings and maps, there was an emphasis on accurate, eyewitness observation, faithfully reproduced.

A greater value came to be placed on geographical realism in cartography, rather than on the older stylized maps which did not depend on accurate topographical description. Whereas mapmakers had been primarily concerned with noting the existence of features, a purpose often achieved by means of pictures, now there came a stress on recording their accurate shape and course. Saxton's individual maps had a particular scale and represented a major advance on bird's-eye views. With his, and other maps, pictorial features were located on scale maps.

Another major shift from the medieval mental world occurred as a result of a change in the notion of time. Whereas some early maps had located events separate in time in the same image – all part of a world that was fallen as a result of human sin and that awaited the millennium – this was now rendered invalid by an approach that stressed change in human time, with the past as a separate sphere. In the Western imagination, as opposed to those of some non-Western people, time was seen as an experience of duration with no necessary connection to spatial movement. For Westerners, time was therefore marked by clocks and predicted in almanacs.

Geographical realism was developed within a set of cultural and political assumptions. Thus, the purpose of the maps described in the section on Saxton was, obviously, not that of highlighting problems. Instead, there was the idealizing vision seen also in maps of cities with their presentation of an ideal image and/or an ideal geometric plan. This has its present-day counterparts in maps of cities such as Nairobi that neglect or underplay the presence of shanty towns.

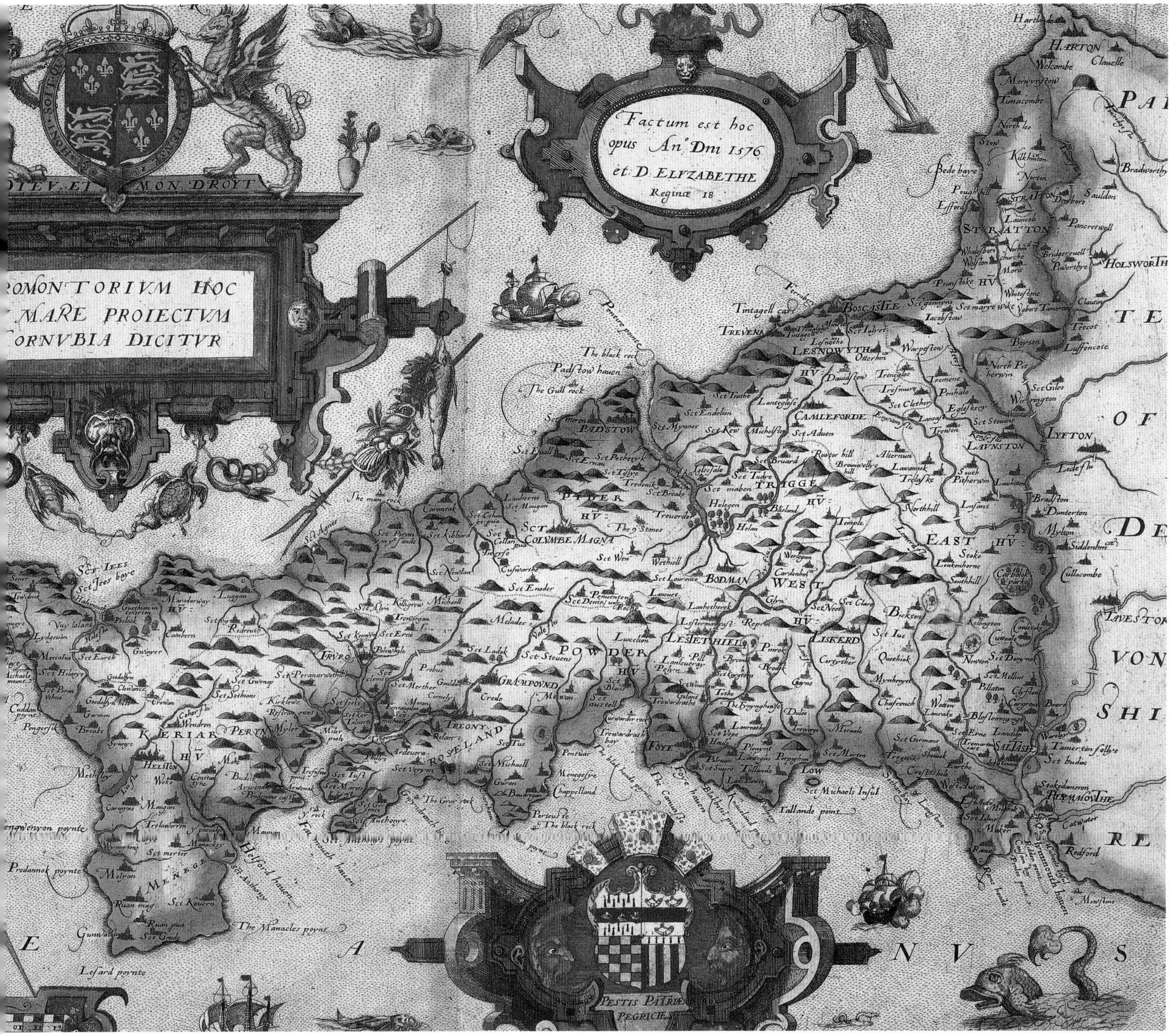
Factum est hoc opus An° Dni 1576 et D. ELYZABETHE Reginæ 18
…ROMONTORIVM HOC … MARE PROIECTVM …ORNVBIA DICITVR
…DIEV ET MON DROYT
BOSCASTLE
LESNOWYTH
CAMLEFORDE
PADSTOW
PYDER HV
BODMAN
TRIGGE
LAVNSTON
EAST HV
WEST
POWDER
LESTETHIEL
LISKERD
TRVRO
GRAMPOVND
TREGNY
ROSELAND
KERIAR
PERYN
HV
HELSTON
MENEGE
FOYE
LOW
SALTASH
PLYMOVTHE
HARTON
PESTIS PATRIÆ PEGRICIES
N V S

> Cornwall from Christopher Saxton's map of the county. The elaborate cartouche and the sea monsters create a different impression to the precise scale. The indentations of the coastline were captured with greater accuracy than the alignment of Penwith (the "big toe" of Cornwall).

At the same time, maps were increasingly being hung on walls as a form of domestic decoration, and the fashionable appeal of this practice was enhanced as maps were shown in paintings of interiors. Wall maps represented a domestication of the more splendid publicly displayed maps of the 16th century, such as Kaspar Vopel's 12-sheet woodcut map of Europe (1555).

More generally, the concept and use of maps spread. They were increasingly used for general reference. In England in 1675, for example, John Ogilby brought out *Britannia, Volume the First*, the initial part of what was intended as a multivolume road map. His strip maps covered 7500 miles of road and used a scale of one inch to one mile, a scale that was to become the dominant one in general use. The map of London to Highgate is a reminder of how much of Middlesex was still countryside. The maps offered considerable detail, including the material from which bridges were made, the existence of gates across roads, landmarks, the direction of slope, whether roads were enclosed (by walls, hedges, or fences) or open, and the destination of crossroads. *Britannia* sold well, and pocket-sized versions appeared in 1719 and 1720.

Ogilby was not alone. Richard Carr's sheet map *Description of all the Postroads in England* was published in 1668, as were comparable maps by Wenceslaus Hollar (1607–77) and Robert Walton. Other route maps included William Berry's *The Grand Roads of England* (1679), John Seller's *A New Map of the Roads of England* (*c.* 1690), and George Willdey's *Roads of England* (1713). Bound into the front of *Britannia*, there was a single-sheet *New Map*

... *Whereon are Projected all ye Principal Roads Actually Measured and Delineated.* This provided guidance to the entire network.

There were also maps of towns in a variety of forms, including bird's-eye views and pictograms of towns. The six volumes of Braun and Hagenberg's *Civitates Orbis Terrarum* (1572–1617), which were seen as a counterpart to Abraham Ortelius (see p.59), were followed, in the 17th century, by numerous town plans, in Europe and under European control. Thus, in 1659, a large-scale map of Batavia, the Dutch base in Java, was published.

Maps were also increasingly used by governments. For example, mapmakers employed by the British Crown played a prominent role in Ireland, where they depicted administrative boundaries and their maps were used for military purposes. Similar goals were also pursued elsewhere in Europe. Ireland was mapped in the late 16th century and the 1600s, a period of greatly increased royal control as well as of British and Scottish settlement.

The sense of mapping as a vital aid to national defence was seen in England in 1681 when the government appointed a naval officer, Captain Collins, commander of the *Merlin*, "to make a survey of the sea coasts of the kingdom by measuring all the sea coasts with a chain and taking all the bearings of all the headlands with their exact latitudes." It was finished in 1688 and led to the publication of *Great Britain's Coasting Pilot* (1693).

This was the first systematic survey of these waters and the first marine atlas to be printed in London from original surveys. However, although an improvement on what had gone before, there were many problems with this survey, due to the speed with which it was accomplished, the limited manpower available, and the lack of an available comprehensive land survey of the coastline as a basis for the marine survey. Nevertheless, it helped to break the Dutch monopoly of such printed works. Collins's atlas was reprinted frequently, finally appearing in 1792.

Drawing the battle lines

The role of the market was shown when maps were produced in response to events. In 1590, for example, a sense of popular topicality was displayed when the publication of an English translation of an account of the defeat of the Spanish Armada in 1588 included a set of 11 maps by Robert Adams showing the successive stages of the campaign on a background of scale-maps of the Channel. Maps covering events in the immediate news, particularly battles and sieges, also appeared. In 1635, one such depicting Dutch conquests in Brazil and Curaçao was published in The Hague by Hendrick Hondius (1563–1612). It provided both details of particular sites, such as Recife, and a large-scale map of Brazil on which the general campaign could be followed.

It is interesting to look at old maps of where we now live, but to understand them it is necessary to appreciate a very different world. Space and distance are apparently established and measured by the scale, a comforting suggestion that the past is but a prelude to the present. But they are not the same. Maps of

➢ The road from London to Bristol from John Ogilby's *Britannia*, published in London, 1675. The illustration depicts the first page of the map. The section west of London was infested by highwaymen. The value of the Ogilby maps diminished greatly in the mid-18th century, as turnpiking became more common. Under the statute for Mending of Highways of 1555, each parish was responsible for road upkeep. However, as the resistance of the surface, usually loose and rough, to bad weather or heavy use was limited, there was a need for frequent repair. Costly in both money and manpower, this duty was generally not adequately carried out, certainly not to the standard required by heavy through-traffic.

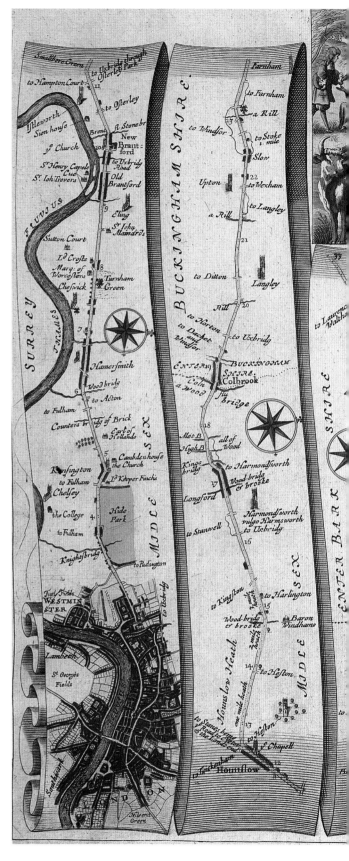

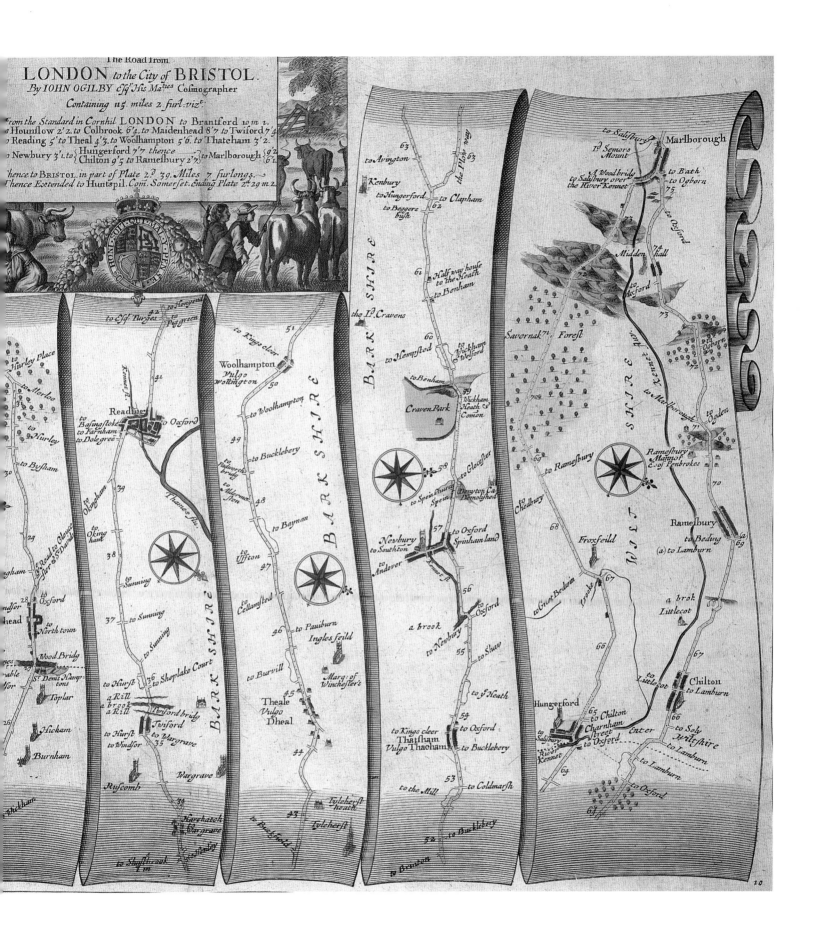

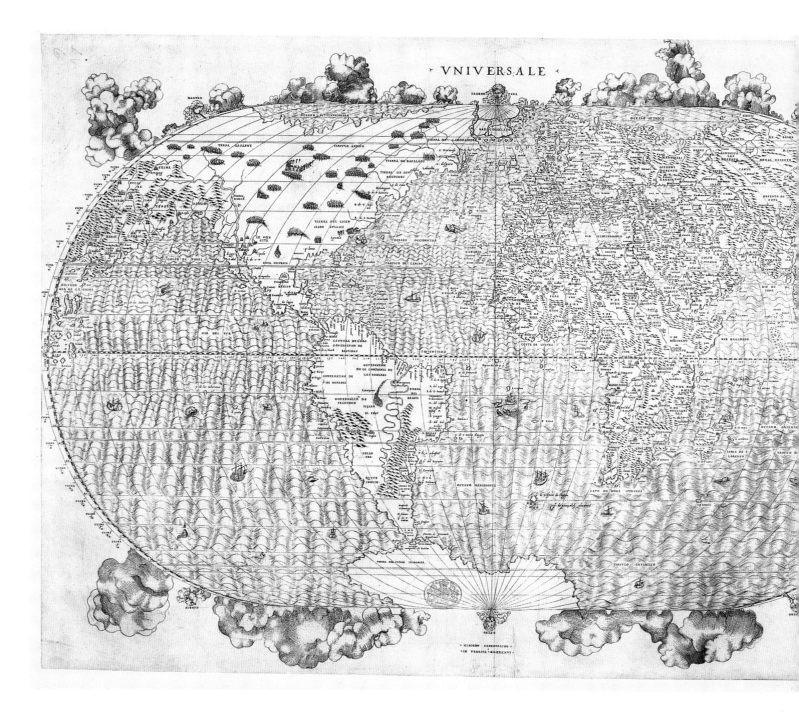

VNIVERSALE

countries such as England in 1700 and today may employ the same projection, alignment, and scale, but they cover different experiences of space and contrasting meanings of travel. Space and distance are not just a matter of the number of hours it takes to get from, say, Ipswich to Exeter, but also the attitudes of mind that are created by the nature of travel and the effects of these attitudes on how distance is perceived.

Concepts of time and space formed parameters to our ancestors' mentalities, just as they do to ours. Thus, in 1700, travel overland was far more unpredictable, slow, and hazardous than it is today. Unreliable road surfaces, greatly affected by rain, were poorly maintained. Bridges were few, and whether or not they were indicated on maps could be important. And this was made more complex by the extent to which many rivers were crossed

not by bridges, but by ferries, which, in turn, were affected by the weather, for example, by spring spate, summer drought, and winter freeze. Ferries were not shown on most maps.

More generally, travellers were still dependent on horses or, at sea, on wind-powered sailing ships. The role of the wind ensured that travel at sea was even more unpredictable than that on land. The information that maps did not convey included the limited nature of harbour facilities and the consequent difficulty of landing people and freight.

The ability of explorers to provide new information helped to enhance a sense that the European world view was correct and should shape the world. However, it also created problems about how best to integrate this information with existing material. The mapping of the New World made this abundantly clear. Indeed,

Giacomo Gastaldi's World Map of 1546 shows North America merging into Asia; in later maps he separated the two continents. Gastaldi had a prodigious output, and is thought to have made more than 200 maps between 1544 and 1565. As official cosmographer to the republic of Venice, Gastaldi helped to make Italy the leader in map production in the 16th century.

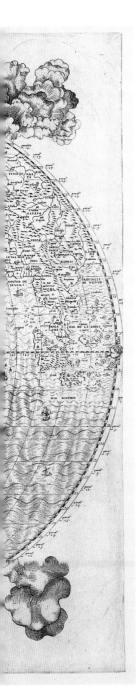

Shakespeare in *Twelfth Night* (1602) has the duped Malvolio "smile his face into more lines than is in the new map with the augmentation of the Indies" (III, ii).

Many of the additions were inaccurate, sometimes because they included material from explorers who had not understood what they saw. An important example occurred in 1524 when Giovanni de Verrazano, a Florentine explorer in the service of Francis I of France, followed the coast of North America from Georgia to Nova Scotia. He thought, when sailing off the Outer Banks, that he was seeing "an isthmus a mile wide and about 200 long, in which from the ship, was seen the oriental sea … which is the one without doubt, which goes about the extremity of India, China and Cathay". This was shown in the world map of 1529 by his brother Gerolamo da Verrazano, and this erroneous idea was adopted by other mapmakers.

Filling in the blanks

In his *Universale*, or world map, of 1546, Giacomo Gastaldi (c. 1500–c. 1565), a leading Venetian mapmaker, captured the eastern seaboard of the Americas and the western seaboard of South America with some accuracy, but he had Asia and North America as a continuous land mass, with the "join" no mere land bridge, but as wide as Europe. This was an influential model for other maps of the period, although growing knowledge of North Pacific waters, in particular as a result of voyages to Japan, led to an abandonment of the land link in many maps by the late 16th century. Thus, Edward Wright's map of the world, published in the second edition of Richard Hakluyt's *The Principal Navigations, Voyages, Traffiques and Discoveries of the English Nation* (1599), a map drawn on Mercator's projection, left the coastlines of the North Pacific blank. However, it was not until Vitus Bering's voyages in the early 18th century that the idea of a land link could be conclusively rejected.

The leading Antwerp cartographer Abraham Ortelius (1527–98), in his map-book, the *Theatrum Orbis Terrarum* (*Theatre of the World*), published in 1570, presented a large northwest passage between Canada and an Arctic land mass to the north. This work was very popular, and about 40 editions had appeared by 1612: translations from Latin, for example, into Spanish in 1588 and into English in 1606, increased the appeal. It expanded to include new information. The 1595 edition included a map of Japan based on the work of the Portuguese mapmaker Luis Teixeira. The relationship between China, Korea, and Japan was not captured in the map. The 1584 edition had included a map of the Azores, also by Teixeira.

The concept of a map-book or atlas was an important advance. The idea of maps systematically produced to a common purpose was very much a "modern" project, in the sense of a fusion of utility and the consequences of the technology of printing, including predictability and quantity. In addition, an atlas could be perceived as having an authority which surpassed that of individual maps.

Reaping the Rewards

There were rewards for cartographic entrepreneurship. Ortelius was able to purchase a new house in Antwerp in 1581. Antwerp was well placed to be a cartographic centre, not only because of its role in publishing, but also because it was ruled by the kings of Spain (also kings of Portugal) from 1580 until 1640 and had access to information about their dominions.

Like Mercator, Ortelius captured the idea of mapping as a continuous process, rather than the proclamation of a complete body of knowledge. Ortelius's *Theatrum* made reference to the sources used for its maps, a practice that carried with it the implication that new information would lead to new maps. Mercator was similarly committed to using new sources rather than familiar images, and his range of correspondents extended to the cartographic centre of Goa in India.

In 1564, Ortelius had shown Canada as an island. When it came to the western coast – although a voyage by the Spaniard Francisco de Ulloa in 1539 to the head of the Gulf of California had revealed that California was a peninsula – the belief grew, based in large part on a 1625 map by the English mapmaker Henry Briggs, that it was an island. Thus Nicolas Sanson's *Amerique Septentrionale* (1650) and Nicolas de Fer's *L'Amerique* (1698) showed California as an island. This was not refuted until a 1701 map based on the travels of a Jesuit missionary, Eusebio Francisco Kino, was confirmed by the voyage of Father Fernando Consag round the Gulf of California.

British maps followed suit. The map of the world in John Seller's *Atlas Maritimus, or a Book of Charts of the World* (London, c. 1670), also showed California as an island. Seller, hydrographer to both Charles II and James II, also offered an outline of the northern, western, and much of the southern coast of Australia, although the east coast was not marked, and only a fraction of the coastline of New Zealand was presented; further south came *Australia Incognita*. Seller's work drew heavily on Dutch maps, and, in some cases, this borrowing extended to the use of Dutch plates with the substitution of an English title.

It proved somewhat easier to give detailed shape to coastlines than to the interior of continents. Diego Gutierrez's 1562 map of South and Central America, for example, offered a complete account of the coastline, which captured the general configuration, although with many detailed errors. The interior, however, was poorly covered. Apart from areas of settlement, European maps offered relatively little for the interiors of other continents. This reflected the precedence taken by navigational requirements.

In Amsterdam in 1614, Prince Johann Ernst of Saxony was impressed in the meeting room of the East India House by the large chart in which "the Asian navigation with all winds and harbours was depicted, beautifully drawn on parchment with pen and partly painted". The East India Company had no need for similar maps of overland routes in Asia, and this was true of other mappers. For example, French cartographer Etienne de Flacourt's map of Madagascar (1666) was largely accurate for the southeast

➤ This is one of only two maps that gives a fully accurate picture of Mexico City (Tenochtitlán) and its surrounding regions in the mid-16th century. It was made by Alonso de Santa Cruz, who was appointed Royal Cosmographer to Charles V of Spain in 1536. The map shows Tenochtitlán surrounded by water with canals between its buildings. The roads that are drawn over the mountains to other parts of the country enable us to retrace the steps of the Spanish *conquistadores*. The map gives ethnographical information and depicts the flora and fauna of the region. People are shown engaged in a range of activities, such as canoeing, hunting, and fishing, and Indians can be seen transporting heavy loads along the roads, driven by their Spanish masters.

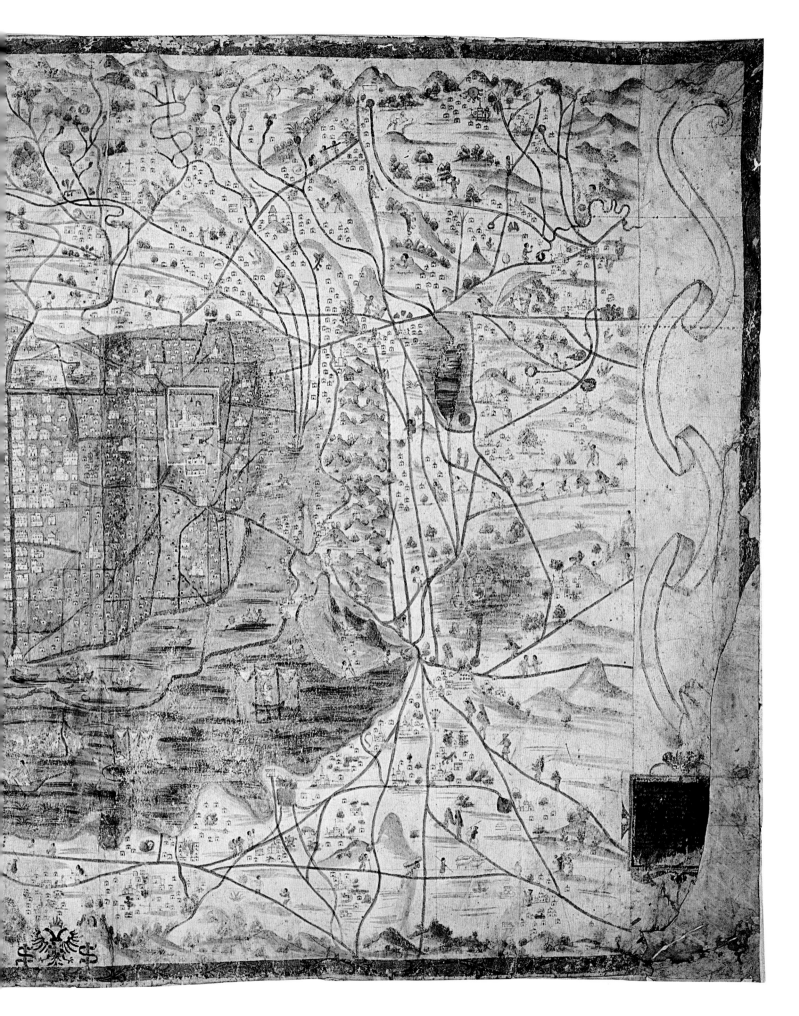

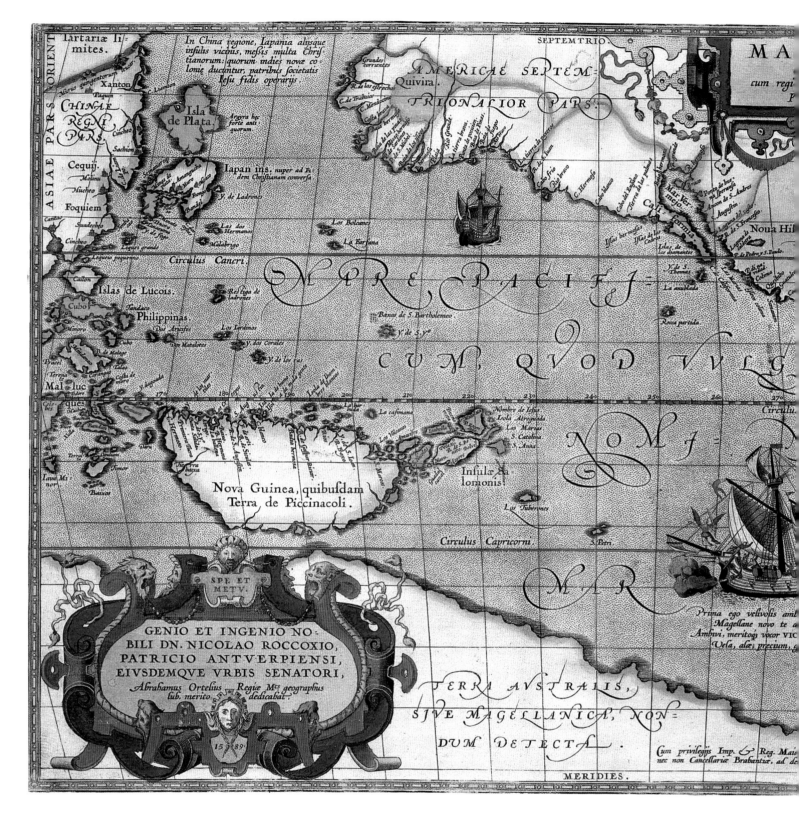

of the island, where the French had established Fort Dauphin in 1642, but not for other parts.

The English geographer Robert Thorne's world map of 1527 depicted a large lake in the Libyan Sahara from which a river flowed to the Mediterranean. Similarly, alongside those that did (and do) exist, such as Lake Chad, fictional large lakes appeared in Giacomo Gastaldi's eight-sheet map of Africa published in Venice in 1564. Based on recently published travellers' accounts, this was the largest map of Africa yet to appear. The coastline was captured well, and the mapping of the interior in part reflected journeys such as those of the Portuguese into Abyssinia.

They were also used as a source for Ortelius's map *The Empire of Prester John* (1573), although this exaggerated the extent of Abyssinia, which was seen as an ally against Islam. The *Descrittione dell'Africa* (Venice, 1550) by the Arab scholar known as Leo Africanus, who had travelled extensively in North Africa in

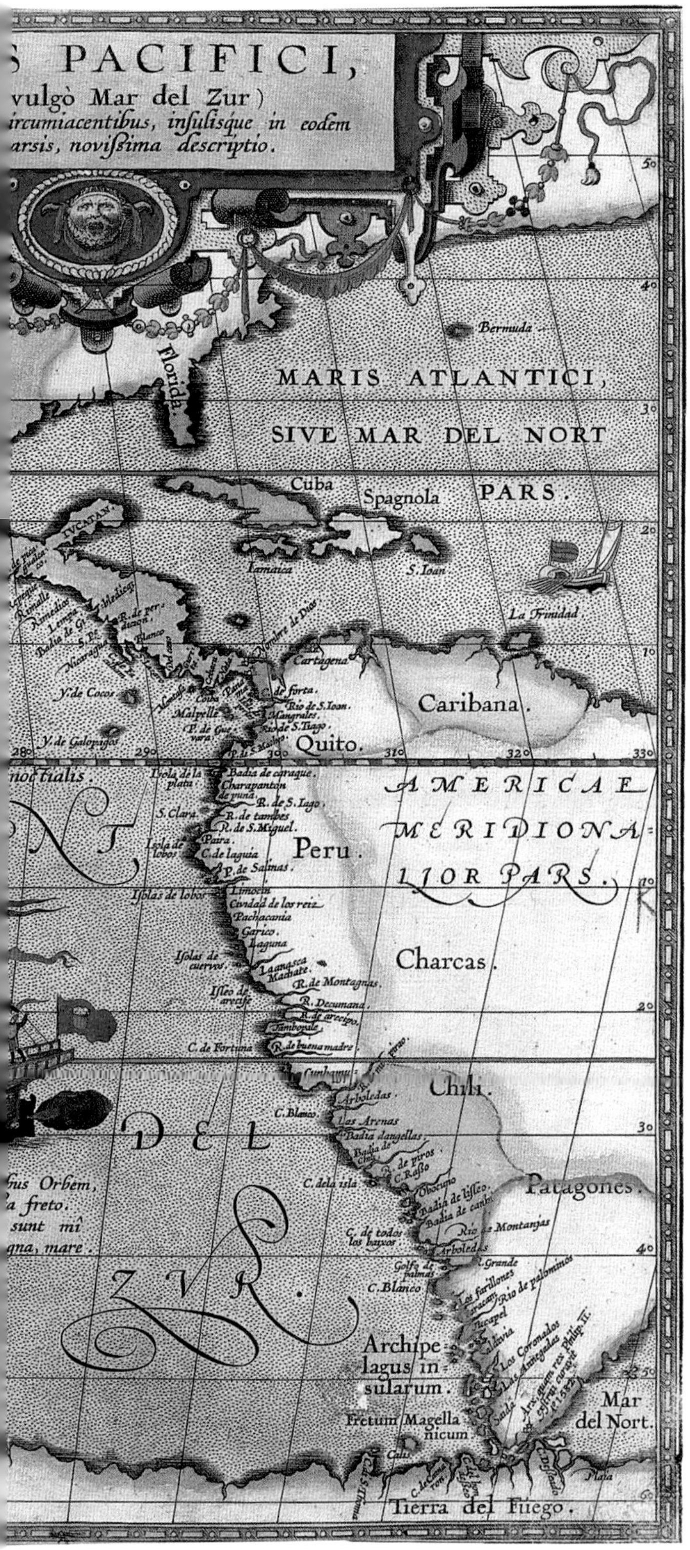
PACIFICI,
vulgò Mar del Zur)
ircumiacentibus, insulisque in eodem
arsis, novissima descriptio.
Florida
Bermuda
MARIS ATLANTICI,
SIVE MAR DEL NORT
PARS.
Cuba
Spagnola
Iamaica
S. Ioan
La Trinidad
Caribana.
Quito.
Peru.
AMERICAE
MERIDIONA
LIOR PARS.
Charcas.
Chili.
Patagones.
Archipe lagus in sularum.
Fretum Magella nicum.
Mar del Nort.
Tierra del Fuego.

◄ *The Pacific* from *Theatrum Orbis Terrarum* (*Theatre of the World*) by the Antwerp cartographer Abraham Ortelius (1527–98), which was published in 1570, showed both Magellan's voyage in the *Victoria* and the great southern continent. The North Pacific is also depicted, albeit inaccurately.

the 1510s, was an important source for European mapping, but his errors included the notion that the Niger flowed westwards, a belief linked to the conviction that a large lake must be its source.

The map of India in Joan Blaeu's *Atlas Major* (French edition, 1667) contained much error for the interior, including very inaccurate alignments of the Ganges and Indus rivers, the movement of the hills of the Western Ghats far inland, and a failure to mark in the Himalayan range. On the other hand, Blaeu's 12-volume atlas contained nearly 600 maps, an indication of the amount of cartographic information that was available.

Looked at slightly differently, mapping reflected the density of information available, and this receded as you moved away from coasts and areas of European settlement. This was true not only outside Europe but also of the parts of Europe controlled by the Ottomans. Thus, in the map of Hungary in Frederic de Wit's *Atlas* (Amsterdam, 1671), Hungary west of the Danube was far better covered than the area to the east.

There were also many problems in mapping the interior of the Americas. The manuscript map of South America by Battista Agnese (1514–64), which appeared in about 1550, misplaced the axis of the Amazon, having its headwaters further south of the Plate estuary. The shape of the continent was also wrong, not least with Patagonia and Chile tapering insufficiently. The map of "La Florida" – in fact of the southern states of the modern United States – published in the 1584 edition of Ortelius's *Theatrum*, misleadingly shows the axis of the Appalachians as northwest to southeast (in fact it is northeast to southwest). It also inaccurately depicts a river leaving the Rio Seco and having an estuary at a considerable distance from the estuary of the latter.

Many maps erroneously showed a large lake in northern Georgia. The *Atlas Contractus* (1671) by Dutch cartographer Nicolas Visscher (1618–79) was typically far more detailed about the Atlantic coast of North America than the interior. Frenchman Louis Hennerin's *Carte d'un très grand Pais nouvellement découvert dans L'Amerique Septentrionale* (1697) showed the Mississippi and its tributaries, but, due to the difficulty of relating the course of the river to the Gulf of Mexico, put its mouth too far west.

Even coastal regions were often poorly mapped. Blaeu's *Atlas Major* showed Australia, New Guinea, and the Asian coast north of Korea only sketchily, although China was depicted more accurately than hitherto, with a reduction of the northeastern Asian land mass. This was as a result of the inclusion of the atlas of China and Japan compiled by Martinus Martini (1614–61). This Dutch Jesuit priest had resided in Beijing and been captured by the Dutch East India Company, who had made a translation of his work. Martini's information corrected that derived from Marco Polo.

The Trouble with Longitude

Until the American Arctic explorer Robert Peary (1856–1920) explored its northern extremes in 1882 and 1895, it was not demonstrated that Greenland was an island. Furthermore, because there were no clocks accurate enough to gave a ship's meridional position, and longitude could not be checked by observation while at sea, many islands were placed too far to the west or the east.

The Venetian Vincenzo Coronelli's *Route maritime de Brest à Siam et de Siam à Brest* (1687), which was based on the Jesuit mission sent to Siam (Thailand) by Louis XIV in 1685, carried a note saying that the map used two sorts of longitudinal marking: those generally agreed and those based on Jesuit information.

Nevertheless, thanks to the accumulation of information, the Europeans knew far more about the world than other cultures. A synergy existed between overseas expansion, navigation, and mapping. In the case of the Dutch East and West India companies, ship's pilots began to keep logbooks and to produce reconnaissance charts employing sheets of paper with pre-drawn compass lines. Company ships were provided with navigation instruments, and an East India Company mapmaking agency was established in Amsterdam from 1616. The companies also regarded surveys with information on crops and town plans as essential instruments for management and planning.

Similarly, in Dutch Brazil and elsewhere in the territories of the two major trading companies, engineers and land surveyors were present to map, plan, and remodel fortresses, settlements, and agricultural areas. In every settlement founded by the Dutch West India Company, a land registry was established where large-scale cadastral maps and ledgers were updated regularly.

Oral information obtained from sources such as the native population, reconnaissance expeditions, and the mapping of settlements and plantations were all integrated into medium-scale topographic maps of the colonies. Thus, a map of Surinam, the Dutch colony on the northern coast of South America, was printed in 1671, and a new survey of all plantations began in 1684.

Maps for profit

This was mapping for economic benefit, a major theme of Western cartography. But this was not the only theme. The directors of the companies also ordered highly decorative charts and maps to demonstrate their new position as actors on the global stage. There was also a wider public dimension. And maps were bought by citizens of the United Provinces (Dutch Republic) who were interested in the global dimension of Dutch trade and the struggle with Spain.

The maritime role of the United Provinces enhanced Amsterdam's position as a cartographic centre. It also benefited from the economic decline that affected Antwerp and many German cities in the 17th century. It is no accident that the United Provinces was the centre then of both mapping and the development of newspapers. With few exceptions, newspapers did not include maps (or, indeed, many illustrations) until the 19th century – although news maps in the shape of plans of sieges and battles were published as separate items, for example, Claes Visscher's map of the successful Dutch siege of Breda in 1637.

Aside from access to information, it benefited cartography that the United Provinces was relatively unregulated both politically and economically. Dutch map production was driven by the search for profit. This was a sphere in which, by contemporary European standards, entrepreneurship was little constrained by the need to seek government permission or to operate only within the constraints set by guilds. As a result, entrepreneurs were able to respond to the demand for information.

Dutch production of maps was dominated by competing publishing houses, especially those of the Blaeu and Hondius families. In their competition, they drew on maps from any source they could, benefiting from the absence of any real sense of copyright, and this competition helped to ensure a constant process of updating. Thus, maps of the East Indies by Portuguese mapmakers were published by the Dutch. The map of the East Indies designed by Petrus Plancius and published by Cornelis Claesz in 1592, which ranged to include New Guinea and the Solomon Islands, drove home the image of commercial value by adding pictures of nutmeg and sandalwood.

Dutch supremacy challenged

In addition, the search for profit led to the spread of Dutch atlases abroad, either by direct sale or through foreign editions. Thus Joan Blaeu also produced a French edition of the world atlas he published in Amsterdam. The cartographic role of the Dutch, however, was to be challenged by their two major foes in the late 17th century: France and Britain.

In the case of France, maps were seen as an important way in which to glorify Louis XIV (r. 1643–1715), as well as to provide information that would help French overseas expansion. The globe was seen as a particularly potent symbol of French royal power – potent because it suggested a range of lordship without being dependent on expression in words.

Louis XIV had Vincenzo Coronelli (1650–1718), Italy's most prolific globemaker, make the two immense globes of Marly, one terrestrial and the other celestial. They depicted the position of the planets and stars at the birth of the king in 1638, and thus suggested that this was the most important moment of celestial history. Like its press, French cartography was uneasily balanced between a world of permission and government controls and that of opportunity and entrepreneurial activity.

In the long term, although she was important during the 18th century, France was not to succeed in becoming the dominant map producer. Instead, it was to be Britain, or, more specifically, London, that took over the role. Its commercial freedom was similar to that of Amsterdam, and, like that of the Dutch, the British mapmaking world benefited from an expanding global system of trade and activity.

In the early-modern period, maps were increasingly seen as crucial if Europeans were to understand their place in the world. Areas of settlement were the best mapped. The Virginia Company established a base at Jamestown in the Chesapeake in 1607. In 1624, John Smith produced a map of Virginia, with the Atlantic to the south. Thus, and as was frequently the case with the mapping of America, the lesser known side was to the north. The map showed how bays and rivers aided English penetration.

A similar approach was taken in the English writer John Ferrar's (also spelt Farrer) *Map of Virginia* (1651). This also sought to attract settlers; Virginia was positioned and its appeal enhanced

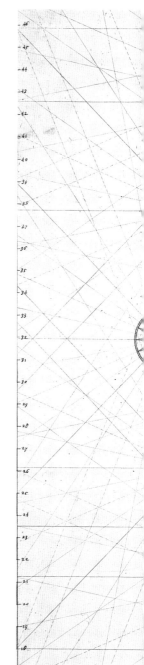

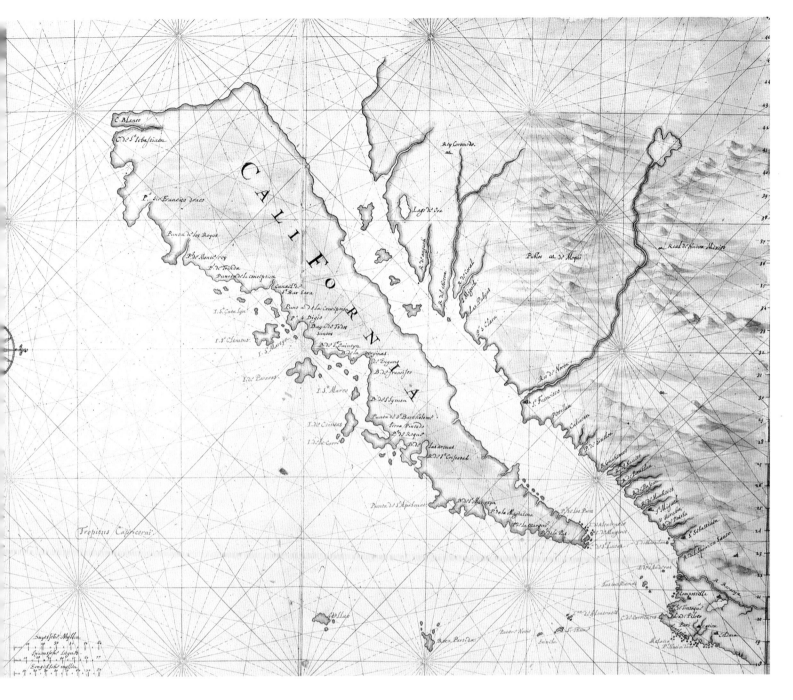

The following text appears on the map:

C. Blanco
C. de S. Sebastian
CALIFORNIA
P. Sir Francisco drace
Punta de los Reyes
P.de Monterrey
P. de Trinida
Punta de la conceptio
I. S. Catalyn
Canal de S. Barbara
Puno de la Conception
P.ª S. Diego
Bay de Todos Santos
I. S. Clement
B. de S. Quintyn
I. S. Martyn
B. de la Virginas
P. de Engaño
B. de Francisco
I. S. Marc
B. de S. Symon
Punta de S. Bartolome
Sierra Pintado
I. de Crinias
B. de Roque
I. de S. Carro
B. de las arenas
B. de S. Cristobal
Tropicus Capricorni
Punta de S. Apolmat
B. de S. Malarya
P. de la Magdalena
P. de los Pinos
A. ley Coronado
Lago de Oro
R. Tocuyuch
R. de Silveron
R. del Coral
S. Miguel
Las Polgas
P. S. Clara
R. de Norte
Pueblos de Moqui
Real de Nuevo Mexico
R. de Francisco
S. Francisco
Pitirlake
Culiacan
P. de Sinaloa
R. Guachara
S. Miguel
V. Horcada
Sv. Puebla
S. Sebastian
R. de Spiritu Sancto
S. Andreas
Los vustiones
Compostella
Sv. Intaqui
L.d.S. Piloto
Port le grion
S. Luna
Malacu
Puerto Nuevo
B. les Parida
I. de Lupo
Bahia Parida

Suydsche Myllen
Spaanssche Leguas
Eengelsche mijllen

by suggesting that the New Albion discovered by Sir Francis Drake on the Pacific was close by on the other side of the Appalachians. The map proclaimed that it could be reached in 10 days' march "from the head of the James River, over those hills and through the rich adjacent vallies beautified with as profitable rivers, which necessarily must run into the peaceful Indian Sea, maybe discovered to the exceeding benefit of Great Britain".

Thanks to the animals depicted on shore and in the sea, North America seemed exotic, but it also appeared an easy prospect. Bays and rivers gave passage, no natives were depicted, and although there was reference to Swedish and Dutch settlers they were to one side. Similarly, Samuel de Champlain's *Carte Geographique de la Nouvelle France* (1612) showed how the St Lawrence River gave access to a great inland lake.

Rulers sought to have their territories mapped, Charles II of England ordering the Council of Plantations in 1670 "to procure maps or charts of all … our … plantations abroad, together with the maps … of their respective ports, forts, bays and rivers". Other rulers issued similar instructions.

Missionaries, traders, and others who pushed forwards the boundaries of the European presence played an important role in accumulating knowledge that served mapmakers. Missionaries were particularly important, as they were more committed than traders to putting down information on paper. Thus, in South America, although the southward advance of Spanish rule in Chile was stopped near the Biobio River, missionaries travelled further south, mapping the coastline and, to a lesser extent, the interior. The Franciscans Antonio de Quadramito and Cristobal de Mendo

◢ Looking much like a portolan chart, complete with rhumb lines, this map of 1639 by Johannes Vingboons depicts California as an island, a common misconception in the 17th century. Some features will be familiar, such as San Diego and San Clemente. Others, such as the Lake of Gold, are not.

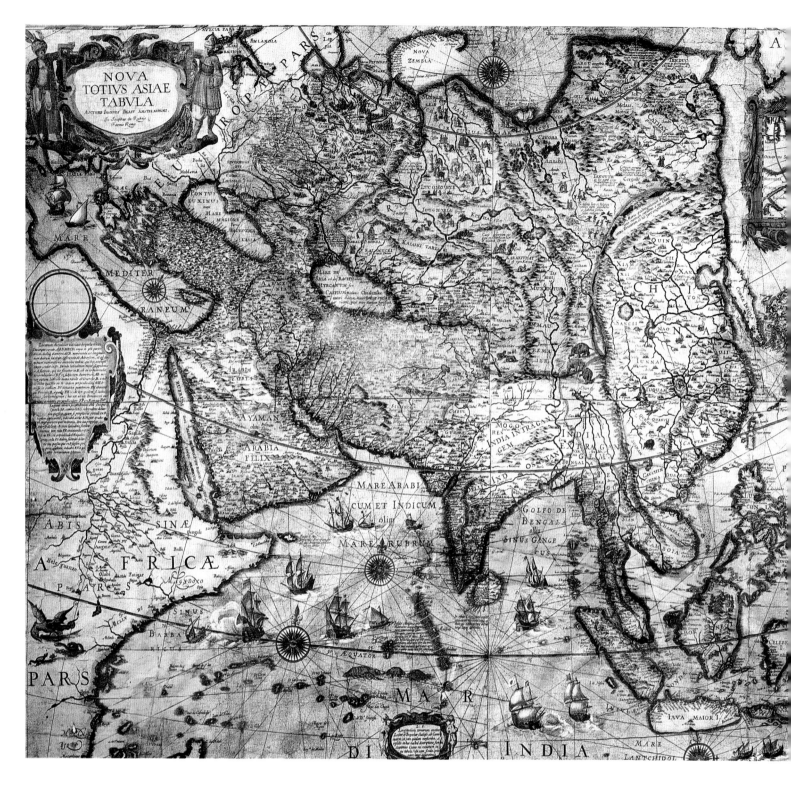

NOVA
TOTIVS ASIAE
TABVLA

Map of Asia from an atlas by Johannes Blau, 1686. The coastline north of Korea is particularly wrong, while the lake shown north of Burma from which major rivers flow does not exist.

were important in the former in 1574–81, while Norberto and Felipe Sánchez helped in the latter in 1679–80. Their travels are a reminder of the far-flung character of European exploration.

Missionaries were also influential elsewhere. Father Paul Klein, a Jesuit in the Philippines, produced a map of the Caroline Islands based on reports from castaways. Another Jesuit, Juan Antonio Cantova, based on the island of Guam, in 1722 drew another chart reliant again on information from castaways.

The history of mapping from the late 15th century is generally told in terms of European mapping – understandably so, as it was

European enterprise on sea and land (most obviously in Siberia) that led to greater knowledge and understanding of the world. A society that could circumnavigate the globe could know it more effectively than any other. This does not imply Western triumphalism: although other societies had their own views of their world, these did not span the globe. For instance, a cosmological view, and mapping that reflected that view, was not of much use for any secular exploitation of that world.

Yet, the mapping that was carried out by Europeans was, in part, dependent on native contributions. This took a variety of

forms, including not only the provision of information, but also that of personnel. The willingness of European mapmakers to draw on multiple sources for maps was important to this process, but so was their desperate need for information.

The process is difficult to follow because the originals of native maps used by the Europeans prior to the 18th century have not generally survived. Nevertheless, the results can be seen in the contents of European maps, as well as in the way in which information was shown. It has been pointed out by the scholar Louis De Vorsey that it is possible to note native American influences on European maps through the treatment of rivers. Without acknowledgement, European mappers often adopted the way in which natives depicted transport routes, but misunderstood them to be simply rivers. In fact, the natives were in the habit of showing communication systems as a whole and not distinguishing between rivers and portages.

Triangulation

European mapping was transformed by the discovery of triangulation. In 1679–83, thanks to the work of Jean-Dominique Cassini, the head of the Paris Observatory, who had advanced a new way of determining longitude by the sighting of Jupiter, the French Académie worked out longitudinal positions in France. As a result, a geodetic survey of France was carried out; its 180 sheets were based on a triangulation network with 800 triangles.

An improved ability to calculate longitude, combined with the use of triangulation surveying, made it necessary to draw new maps, as old ones seemed redundant. The Dutch-born, London-based geographer and cartographer Herman Moll noted in the *Atlas Geographus* (1711–17) that "the curious, by casting their eye on the English map of France, lately done and corrected according to the observations of the Royal Academy of Sciences at Paris, may see how much too far Sanson has extended their coasts in the Mediterranean, the Bay of Biscay and the English Channel". Nicolas Sanson (1600–67) was the major French cartographer of the 17th century who produced an atlas of the world in 1658–9. However, errors in assessing angles led to errors in measuring surface area.

In China in 1708–17 the Jesuit Jean-Baptiste Régis supervised the first maps there to be based on triangulation. This dependence on the Europeans was to be a more general feature of the period. Other cartographic traditions do not appear to have developed in a comparable fashion to that of Europe, not least because of the Europeans' application of advances in mathematics, instrumentation, navigation, and an understanding of the globe – although there is still need for much research on this point.

In the Ottoman (Turkish) empire, the use of maps was far more restricted. The panegyric Ottoman royal histories produced by the official court historians contained some illustrations from the 1530s, and several of these were maps. The works were in manuscript, however, and their wider impact was limited.

In addition, the Ottomans came to be influenced by (Christian) European printed views and maps; printing aided the dissemination of cartographic images, models and techniques to foreign states and cultures. The Ottoman cartographic tradition was found wanting from the late 17th century and replaced by borrowings from Europe. A plan of Buda produced shortly after 1684 on the European model appears to be the first instance of this shift.

It is unclear how far this process was seen elsewhere prior to the late 19th century when non-Western powers that sought to retain their independence adopted Western methods. In cartographic terms, this was a necessary response to their territorial demands and pretensions.

In the late 17th century, this process still largely lay in the future. However, as a sign of what was to become increasingly common, in 1699–1701, Austrian and Ottoman commissioners were forced to deal with the ambiguous and contradictory wording of the Peace of Karlowitz (1699) on such matters as the "ancient" frontiers of Transylvania, the status of islands where the rivers Sava and Maros formed the new border, and the course of the frontier where it was defined as a straight line. The treaty stipulated that the commissioners were to survey and agree on the new frontier, and the Austrian commissioner was instructed by his government to produce a definitive map.

As far as East Asia is concerned, there are signs of developments in China and Japan. For example, the *Guang yutu* (enlarged terrestrial atlas) by the Chinese geographer Luo Hongxian (1504–64) is the oldest known printed Chinese set of maps using a grid system, although not triangulation. The employment of a grid system can be traced back to Pei Xiu in the third century. There is still need for a careful comparative study of the situation in Europe and elsewhere, but, for the 15th and 16th centuries, China's culture appears to have been less focused on maps and on changes in their content and use.

"... to beautify their halls ..."

John Dee (1517–1608), a leading English mathematician and cartographer who had studied with Mercator was a keen advocate of England's imperial expansion, and in 1570 published a translation of Euclid's *Elements*. In his preface, Dee captured some of the range of contemporary interest in maps: "Some to beautify their halls, parlours, chambers, galeries, studies, or libraries … some others to view the large dominion of the Turk, the wide Empire of the Muscovite … some other for their own journeys directing into far lands, or to understand other travels".

This sense of a demand-driven interest in maps captured a distinctive aspect of European cartography. Alongside the role of government came a desire to have and to use maps, which was important to the particular trajectory of European mapmaking. The Europeans were not the only imperial powers, but, within both Europe and their transoceanic possessions, map use was most pronounced.

The Age of Enlightenment

The great adventure of the 18th century was the exploration of what was, to Europeans, the dark side of the Earth – the Pacific – an account of which must come first in any discussion of a period in which European mapping was to span the seas of the world. However, important advances in mapping both within European colonies and in Europe itself were also being made. No other culture saw comparable activity, although the Chinese cartographic tradition continued with Zhang Xuecheng (1738–1801) and Hong Liangji (1746–1809) both producing sets of maps of China. It has been argued that Chinese cartography and ethnography developed in parallel in this period, moving to a similar form of representation, rather than the Chinese borrowing from Western developments. However, insufficient work has been carried out to demonstrate this thesis.

Nevertheless, there were certainly important Chinese maps being produced at this time, for example, those of the Kangxi atlas (c. 1721). Jesuit missionaries also produced maps of China which drew on Chinese sources, but it is unclear whether (and unlikely that) China witnessed the developments in local and national mapping seen, for example, in Britain, British North America, and France, particularly the growth of a robust entrepreneurial cartography. What is clear is that the Chinese cartography lacked the global reach and techniques of its European counterparts.

Making sense of the Pacific

The mapping of the Pacific by Europeans was full of error at the start of the 18th century. In his *New Set of Maps Both of Ancient and Present Geography* (Oxford, 1700), Edward Wells, an Oxford academic, showed California as an island and, more generally, knew little of the northern Pacific. English mapmaker John Senex (1719–95) made a map of Asia (1711) depicting a large island, Yedso, to the north of Japan, where Hokkaido is, but far larger. Another, Compagnia, close to the east of Yedso, could have been a misrepresentation of part of North America. The map was further confused with further evidence that the cartographer was speculating without hard evidence. For example, to the north of Compagnia appeared the legend "these parts remain as yet undiscovered" while along the inaccurately portrayed eastern coast of Siberia was written: "It is not known where this chain of mountains ends or whether they are not joined to some other continent". The islands mapped were based on the voyage of Maartin Fries in 1643, but a mixture of his own misjudgements and the misleading interpretations of later mapmakers had led to an inaccurate account of the northern Pacific.

In 1748, the Hudson's Bay Company commissioned a map of North America for use in response to a planned attack in the British Parliament on its monopoly. Aside from showing Jedso and Compaignes Land, the latter being part of a big island in the North Pacific that stretched from near Kamchatka to near North America, the map still depicted California as an island. It also showed no Northwest Passage. America was joined by land to an Arctic land mass that included Greenland. The map also offered a route for the voyage of Bartholemew de Fonte. Dated to 1640, this had been described in *Memoirs for the Curious* (1708), and was usually explained in terms of a strait from the Pacific coast of America to Hudson's Bay. This route influenced a number of 18th-century maps, but there was no basis to the report.

At a different scale in 1687, the buccaneer Edward Davis had allegedly discovered "Davis's Land" in the Southeast Pacific between the Galapagos Islands and South America. The printed account of the expedition spread the news, "Davis's Land" was recorded on maps, and it was suggested that this was the outlier of Terra Australis (southern land), the vast continent in southern latitudes that was believed to balance the land masses of the northern hemisphere and which was marked in Ortelius's map of the Pacific in 1589. Later explorers searched in vain for "Davis's Land", which the buccaneer had probably taken to be the small island of Sala-y-Gómez. This, and a cloud bank to the west, had suggested a larger land mass.

Alongside such mistakes, many maps were obliged to note a lack of information in a way that would not be seen today. In Robert's map of the *Archipel des Indes Orientales* (1750) a caption reading "the end of this Gulph is not well known" appears for the coastline of the Teluk Tomini in the Celebes (Sulawesi). *The Carte plate qui comprend l'Isle de Ceylon* (1775) includes the captions "Laccadive Islands of which the detail is not exactly known" and "neither the number, size or respective situation of the Maldive Islands are known".

A determined effort was made, however, to improve the basis for navigation. The English astronomer Edmund Halley, who explored the South Atlantic, produced his chart of trade winds in 1689 and his "General Chart" of compass variations in 1701, both important tools for navigation. This latter chart of terrestrial magnetism was designed to enable navigators to chart the variation between true north and magnetic north (to which compass needles point), and thus calculate longitude accurately. However, because compass variations are not constant, Halley had not solved the problem – although, in the absence of anything better, the value of his approach ensured that his chart was reprinted in 1745.

In Britain, although Parliament had established a Board of Longitude in 1714 and offered a substantial reward for the discovery of a method for determining longitude at sea, with the French following suit in 1715, the problem was proving intractable.

◁◁ In this Italian engraving Napoleon Bonaparte is shown with a map in his hand while negotiating peace with the vanquished Austrians who are forced to accept the existence of the new republics established by the French in Italy, as well as making other territorial concessions, in early 1801.

⋏ This scene from William Hogarth's *A Rake's Progress* (1735) shows a lunatic attempting to unravel the problem of longitude on the wall of a madhouse.

A more effective route of exploration appeared to be the expeditions that set off in 1735 to test the sphericity of the Earth. One was sent to Arctic Lapland, the other to the equator at Quito, and they demonstrated that the globe was distended at the equator, thus bringing a major European scientific controversy to a close. Descartes had thought (and the French wanted to believe) that the Earth was a perfect sphere, whereas Newton had argued that it was an oblate spheroid. On the result of these complementary expeditions depended the debate between Cartesian and Newtonian physics. Only European civilization had the capacity to carry out such investigations at this time.

European knowledge of the Pacific greatly increased from the 1760s, but there had also been important developments over the previous 70 years. The English buccaneer William Dampier sailed along parts of the coast of Australia and New Guinea in 1699–1700 and spread knowledge of it by publishing his *Voyage to New Holland*. In 1728, Vitus Bering, a Dane in Russian service, navigated the strait separating Asia from America that now bears his name, although he failed to sight Alaska due to the fog. In 1738–9, Martin Spanberg and William Walton, both also in Russian service, sailed from Kamchatka down the Kurile Islands to Japan. Spanberg produced the first map of the Kuriles.

The voyages of Louis Antoine de Bougainville (1729–1811), James Cook (1728–79), Jean-François Galoup La Pérouse (1741–88), and others from the 1760s transformed knowledge of the Pacific. They in turn benefited from the solving of the longitude problem by mechanical means. In 1761–2, clockmaker John Harrison devised a chronometer, the timekeeping of which was so accurate that, on a return journey from Jamaica, the ship carrying it found her distance run erred by only 18 miles. There were also improvements in the methods for finding latitude more precisely. Navigators were therefore able to calculate their positions far more accurately. Harrison's chronometer was used by Captain James Cook on his second and third voyages to the Pacific.

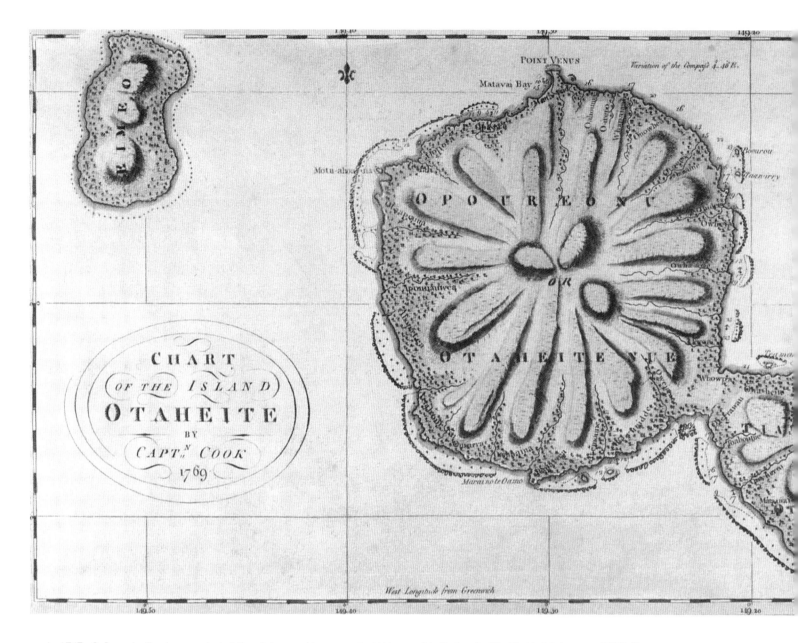

The island of Tahiti, described by Bougainville and Cook, was presented initially as an earthly paradise. It was initially named New Cythera, after the fabled realm of Aphrodite. Cook was sent to the newly discovered Tahiti in 1769 to observe the transit of Venus across the face of the Sun, which Edmund Halley had suggested would enable the calculation of the distance from the Sun to the Earth. It was after this that Cook went on to circumnavigate New Zealand.

In 1767–9, Bougainville circumnavigated the globe, reaching the New Hebrides in 1768, thus proving that they were not part of Terra Australis, as the Spaniard Quiros had thought in 1608. However, the outliers of the Great Barrier Reef prevented Bougainville from seeing the east coast of Australia. On his first voyage, Cook had conducted the first circumnavigation and charting of New Zealand. He also charted the east coast of Australia where, in 1770, at Botany Bay, he landed. As the first European to do so on the east coast, he claimed the territory for George III of Great Britain. Then, having run aground on the Great Barrier Reef, Cook sailed through the Torres Strait, showing that New Guinea and Australia were separate islands, before reaching the Dutch base of Batavia in Java.

On his second voyage, in 1772–5, Cook's repeated efforts to find the southern continent, efforts which included the first passage of the Antarctic Circle, failed. He had sailed to 71° 10' South, farther than any known voyage hitherto, when he encountered the ice outlier of Antarctica and reported that it was

not a hidden world of balmy fertility. On his third voyage (1776–9), Cook "discovered" Christmas Island and Hawaii, while, in 1778, he sailed to a new farthest north – 70°44' North, at Icy Cape, Alaska – and showed that pack ice blocked any possible northwest passage. By fixing the longitude of the Pacific coast of North America, Cook also showed that the continent was wider than had been hitherto believed, an important advance in its mapping.

In 1787, La Pérouse explored the northwestern Pacific, following the coast of Korea, Sakhalin, Hokkaido, and Kamchatka. By sailing through the Gulf of Tartary, waters uncharted by Cook, Lapérouse established that Sakhalin was an island off the coast of Asia.

Myth of the Northwest Passage

These and other voyages provided much information about what existed and what was fictional. Cook himself discredited the belief in Terra Australis. The voyages of Spanish explorers in 1775–92 – for example, Bruno de Hezeta and Alejandro Malaspina –

surveyed the Pacific coast of North America and showed that two features seen on earlier maps, a navigable Northwest Passage and a river giving access to an inland sea, did not exist.

These voyages led to better maps, although, in turn, errors were inserted. For example, in mapping New Zealand, Cook incorrectly had Stewart Island as part of the mainland. Nevertheless, European maps of the world became more accurate, as charts were printed, information compared, and maps checked. Atlases came to reflect this growing knowledge, and, in 1823–6, Admiral Adam John von Krusentern, who was in Russian service, published an *Atlas de l'Ocean Pacifique*.

The mapping of coastal waters was not restricted to the Pacific. Having conquered New France (the French-ruled parts of modern Canada) from France in 1757–60, the British surveyed Canadian Atlantic waters. The most prominent surveyor, the Swiss-born Joseph Frédéric Wallet des Barres, was ordered by the Admiralty to survey the coasts of Nova Scotia and Cape Breton Island, and in 1777 the first edition of an atlas of his navigational charts, the *Atlantic Neptune*, was published for sale. This was an attempt to provide a systematic charting of North American waters, and ultimately comprised 115 charts and maps.

There was also a need for mapping coastal waters in Europe. John Green wrote in 1717:

'Tis observable, that not only the sea coasts, in two several maps of the same parts commonly differ strangely from each other, but also rarely ever any agree in that respect with the sea charts which happens for want of consulting the Waggoners, either through their little concern for exactness, or imagining a map is to be drawn only by a map, and a chart from a chart.

This caused problems at a number of levels, not least for naval blockades. These problems were accentuated by difficulties in establishing location at sea. Thus, in 1708, when a French squadron carrying the so-called "James VIII and III", the Jacobite Pretender to the crowns of Scotland and England, succeeded in avoiding the British blockading squadron of Dunkirk in the mist, reaching Scottish waters before its pursuers, the initial landfall was made not at the mouth of the Firth of Forth, but, as a result of error, 100 miles further north.

As a result of the difficulties of mounting blockades, the British navy made major efforts to produce accurate charts of the waters off France and Spain. More problems were encountered in mounting operations far from home waters. When, in 1791, the British planned war with Russia in the Ochakov Crisis, they discovered that they had no charts for the Black Sea and had to turn to the Dutch. Indeed, the lack of knowledge left the British unclear whether the fortress of Ochakov, the crucial issue in the negotiations, really controlled the entrance to the River Dnieper, as was claimed. Ochakov is, in fact, on the northern shore of the Dneprovskiy Liman, a nearly landlocked section of the Black Sea into which the estuaries of both the Bug and the Dnieper open.

Ochakov is situated at the narrow strait which forms the seaward entrance of this section or bay, but the British lacked adequate maps and coastal charts to show this.

Travellers' tales

Mapping also illustrated travel on land. Exploration in the interior of Africa brought considerable information, although much remained obscure. The French Jesuit linguist Claude Sincara mapped Egypt in 1717 as a result of a visit to gather material about antiquities in the course of which he travelled to Aswan and identified the location of Thebes. The tour of Ethiopia by James Bruce's (1730–94) in 1768–73 increased knowledge about eastern Africa, while, in 1795–7, Mungo Park (1771–1806) explored the valley of the River Gambia and reached the River Niger at Segu, showing that it flowed eastwards. Journeys such as these, described in books such as Bruce's *Travels* (1790), Park's *Travels in the Interior Districts of Africa* (1799), and William Browne's *Travels in Africa, Egypt, and Syria* (1800), provided new information for mapmakers. Park's writings were used by James Rennell, better known as a mapper of India, to produce a detailed map of Park's journey. The map included indications of where latitudes were taken, and its use of a graticule and scale indicated the degree of precision that was sought.

In 1762, a team of Scandinavian and German experts took part in the first scientific expedition to the Arabian peninsula. Sailing down the Red Sea, this mission visited Yemen in 1763–4, recording its flora and fauna, and studying its peoples. Carsten Niebuhr (1733–1815), a German-born surveyor who worked in Denmark and was the sole surviving member of the expedition, published a *Description of Arabia* and *Travels through Arabia* (1772, 1774), accounts that included several detailed maps.

Based on information from missionaries, the Jesuit Samuel Fritz was able to compile a map of the Amazon, published in 1707. As with many maps, there was an agenda. Based at the Spanish centre of Quito, Fritz had extended his mission to the east. He hoped to spread Spanish authority in the same direction because he opposed the consequences of Portuguese slave expeditions against the native people of Amazonia. As a result, his map showed the headwaters of the Amazon's tributaries close to Spanish centres such as Quito and Lima, downplayed the obstacle of the Andes, and created the Amazon as an axis comparable to the equator and one that was properly open to Spain. This was enhanced by the omission of the Portuguese centres in Brazil.

Into the Amazon

At the same time, it is important, in making such implicit criticism, to be wary of neglecting the realities of physical and political geography of the period. There were in fact few links between the Amazon and the rest of Brazil. Overland routes were not possible, while coastal trade was affected by prevailing winds and currents, such that there was little trade between the Amazonian centre of Belém do Pará and Brazil. Instead, both traded directly with Lisbon. Similarly, control over Maranhão (Brazil north of the Amazon) had long been in dispute: France and Portugal had only reached agreement in the early 1700s.

Jesuit mappers were prominent elsewhere. In 1749, Joseph Quiroga produced a map of the Jesuit missions in Paraguay. This was of importance in spreading information about a disputed region about which little was known. In 1800, the German explorer Alexander von Humboldt (1769–1859), as part of his exploration of South America, travelled between the Orinoco and the Amazon river systems, producing accurate maps of what he saw.

In North America, where Jesuit explorers were also prevalent, travel in the interior – for example, west of the Mississippi – was rapidly incorporated into maps. Spanish surveys of the northern frontier of Mexico in the 1720s and 1760s led to more accurate mapping, while the successful Spanish effort in the mid-1770s to discover an overland route from Mexico to California, and thus avoid delay from headwinds, also led to better maps. This process was stepped up after the United States became independent in 1776. The Red River expedition of 1806 provided valuable knowledge, including a map of the river, which was to help subsequent exploration. Surveying led to an accumulation of new information, as well as to the checking, confirmation, or correction of what was already known: the two combined to improve the quality of maps.

There were still major limitations in the maps available. Louis Charles Desnos's map *L'Asie* (Paris, 1789) included all of Asia, but the mapping of Tibet was necessarily very vague. The *Carte de L'Inde* (1752) of Jean Baptiste Bourguignon d'Anville (1697–1782) labelled most of east-central India as a "large extent of country of which there is little accurate knowledge".

The public hunger for maps

Errors in maps nevertheless reflected a drive to map what was known to be there. Strong public interest in maps encouraged their publication. Wars in Europe were followed with the help of maps, such as *A True and Exact Map of the Seat of War in Brabant and Flanders with the Enemies Lines in their Just Dimensions* (London, 1705), a detailed map on which the moves of John Churchill, first Duke of Marlborough, and his French opponents could be charted. Similar maps appeared for particular battles, enabling readers to understand the general context, as well as the course of the battle. Thus the battle of Falkirk in 1746, a major clash in the Jacobite rising that had started in 1745, was rapidly commemorated in a map showing the general area. It included a plan of Falkirk and of the subsequent battle at Culloden, to which was devoted a separately published plan. Naval battles were also commemorated with maps, although, as a static presentation of a more complex and fluid set of events, they generally had only limited value, as for example with the maps of the Anglo-Bourbon battles of Malaga (1704) and Toulon (1744).

Knowledge of the world outside Europe grew and became more readily available. Maps of the West Indies and North America came to play a greater role in atlases published in the first half of the 18th century – for example, those published in London by Herman Moll (active 1678–1732), Senex and Emmanuel Bowen (active 1714–67) – and this markedly gathered pace with the Seven Years' War (1756–63) and the War of American Independence (1775–83). A *Universal Geographical Dictionary; or, Grand Gazetteer* (London, 1759) was, the title-page proclaimed, "Illustrated by a general Map of the World, particular ones of the different Quarters, and of the Seat of War in Germany". At the end of the Seven Years' War with France, the *Universal Magazine* of March 1763 provided a map of the extent of territory Britain now controlled in North America. Meanwhile, readers of the *London Magazine* who wished to follow the course of the war of 1760–1 between the Cherokees and British and colonial forces could turn to "A New Map of the Cherokee Nation… engraved from an Indian draught by Thomas Kitchin" in early 1760. Interest in North America encouraged the publication of maps. Thomas Jeffreys published a number of atlases, including *A General Topography of North America and the West Indies* (1768) and *The American Atlas, or a Geographical Description of the Whole Continent of America* (1776). A plan of the successful American and French siege of the British position at Yorktown in 1781 was printed at Philadelphia in 1782.

Atlases spread news of exploration, making it appear a process of discovery, and consciously emphasized the novelty of the knowledge they conveyed. Thus Antonio Zatta's *Atlante novissimo* (*New Atlas*) (Venice, 1779–85) prided itself on its account of recent explorations and provided the first appearance in an Italian atlas of the new islands explored by Cook.

Maps appeared in books and magazines, and were referred to in correspondence. Lady Elisabeth Hastings wrote to her half-brother, Theophilus, ninth Earl of Huntingdon, who was travelling in France in the early 1720s, "You oblige me much in letting me know the tour you take, for by that means I can have the pleasure of travelling with you by the map". Such interest fed the demand for maps.

Increased use of maps contributed to a greater degree of geographical knowledge. Thus, in his 1730 play *Rape upon Rape, or The Coffee-House Politician*, Henry Fielding was able to satirize the fears of the Londoner Politic, who is so concerned about reports of international developments that he neglects threats to his daughter's virtue, knowing that the audience would share the joke:

> Give us leave only to show you how it is possible for the Grand Signior to find an ingress into Europe. Suppose, Sir, this spot I stand on to be Turkey – then here is Hungary – very well – here is France, and here is England – granted – then we will suppose he had possession of Hungary – what then remains but to conquer France, before we find him at our own coast (II, xi).

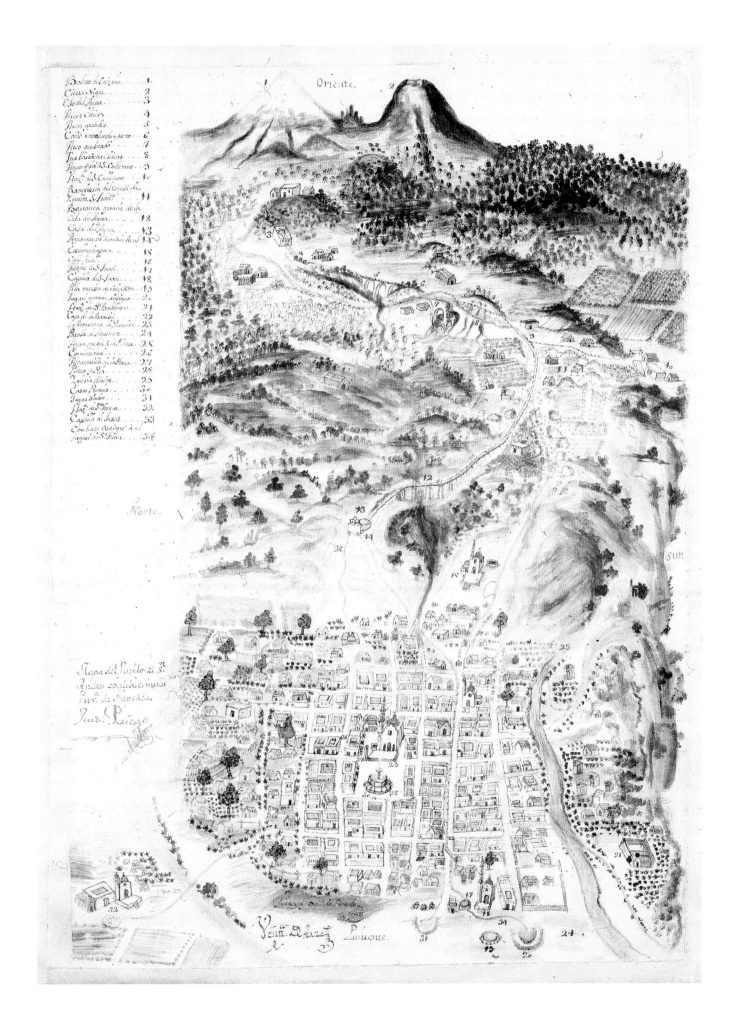

Errors and Omissions

So geographers, in Afric-maps,
With savage-pictures fill their gaps;
And o'er unhabitable downs
Place elephants for want of towns.

On Poetry (1733), Jonathan Swift

There were many errors in maps. This reflected the tension between admitting a lack of information, by leaving the map blank, and including interesting information based on the latest reports, which also added to a sense of completion and could ensure that a map appeared as both an improvement on earlier ones and better than rivals.

Swift's poetic criticism was certainly borne out by the mapping of North America. The "map of the long river" in the *Nouveaux Voyages de Mr le Baron de La Hontan dans L'Amérique Septentrionale* (1703) depicted a long river flowing west from the Mississippi to the Rockies at 46° North. This was incorporated into other maps, such as that of Canada by Guillaume de L'Isle (1703), and encouraged the widespread but erroneous view that there was a large body of water in the North American interior, similar to the Great Lakes, but further west. La Hontan depicted lakes, as well as a river flowing west from the mountains in the interior.

A large inland sea in the northwest of North America, possibly connected to the Pacific, was widely believed to exist, and it appeared in maps such as those of Joseph-Nicolas de L'Isle in 1752 (a "Mer ou Baye de l'Ouest"), Didier Robert de Vaugondy in 1765 (a "Mer l'Ouest") and Jean Covens and Corneille Mortier in about 1780 (a "Mer de l'Ouest"). As explorers moving west failed to find this sea, so it was assumed that it was yet further to the west. There were also different accounts of the relationship between the inland sea and two often supposed fixtures, the River of the West and the ice-free Northwest Passage. Although less inaccurate, the Lapie map of the region in 1821 included supposed straits and lakes based on misleading accounts about earlier explorations.

Errors were depicted elsewhere in the world. The fictitious "Mountains of the Moon" remained on maps of Africa, including James Rennell's of 1799, and this helped to account for the inaccurate and longstanding belief that the River Niger was linked with the Nile. In Australia, where the British settled from 1788, the interior was believed to contain great inland lakes or seas, and major rivers similar to those depicted in other continents. These waterways provided not only a goal for exploration and commercial exploitation, but also a subject for mapping, as in the 1827 map of the "Coasts of Australia and the supposed entrance of the Great River" drawn for the publication *Friend of Australia*. This river, the "Desired Blessing", was shown as flowing from a lake in the centre of the continent to the northwest coast. Explorers searched for these waters.

Another fictitious major lake, of Chamay, was long shown in the north of Burma – for example, in Guillaume de L'Isle's *Atlas Nouveau* (1726) – again as the source of major rivers. This was another instance of the contrast between knowledge of coastal regions and the far less satisfactory position for inland regions. It also reflected a sense that major rivers should have a dramatic source.

➤ The "great inland sea" as drawn for *Friends of Australia*, 1827. This map was calculated to encourage British colonization, and the inland sea, as well as the western mountain ranges, which summon up a river-making topography were purely imaginary. The geometric representation of surveyors' observation points on the eastern part of the continent were evidently designed to confer an air of scientific veracity on these more spurious features in the west.

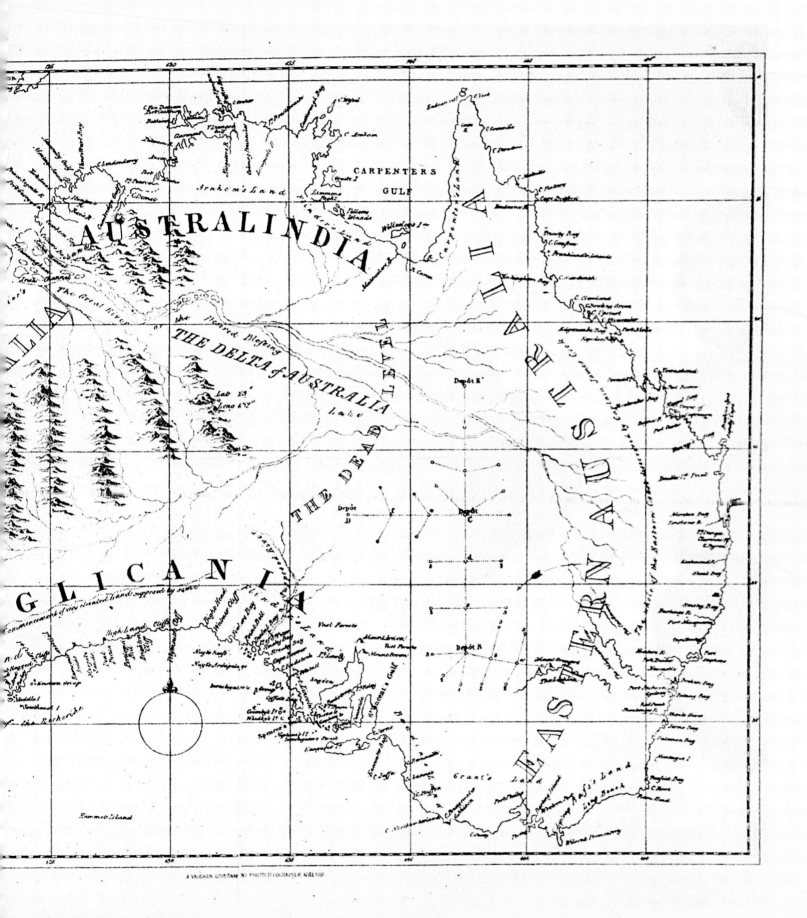

Fielding also drew attention to maps in the mind: "Map me no maps, sir, my head is a map, a map of the whole world", (II, v).

The value of as a polemical tool did not go unnoticed. In 1718, the engraver and mathematician Reeve Williams published a pamphlet in defence of British foreign policy, specifically British intervention in Mediterranean politics. The inclusion of a map added to the interest of this *Letter from a Merchant to a Member of Parliament, Relating to the Danger Great Britain is in of Losing her Trade, by the Great Increase of the Naval Power of Spain with a Chart of the Mediterranean Sea Annexed.* The *Worcester Post-Man* reported that a notable book was delivered to the Members of Parliament, with a chart annexed of the Mediterranean Sea, whereby it:

> "demonstrately appears of what importance it is to the trade of Great Britain, that Sicily and Sardinia shall be in the hands of a faithful ally, and if possible not one formidable by sea. That these two islands lie like two nets spread to intercept not only the Italian but Turkey and Levant trade".

Thus, the map was designed to support British backing for the territorial situation decided by the Peace of Utrecht of 1713, which had left Sardinia to the Emperor Charles VI, ruler of Austria, and Sicily to Victor Amadeus II, the ruler of Savoy-Piedmont. It was not necessary to have the map in order to understand the text, but the map helped both to clarify its arguments and to lend them weight. It thus became part of a process of validation that, in part, reflected the credibility that the apparently scientific character of maps conferred.

In European society, maps had moved on from being simply an aspect of a visual culture deriving its potency from iconography. This was natural in a society increasingly impressed by the idea that authority should take scientific form, as seen, for instance, in the major attempts in England to reconcile revealed religion to the insights gained by Newtonian science. It would be mistaken to ignore or underrate the limitations in 18th-century science, but it did represent an infinitely extendable attempt to understand natural forces and to encode them in laws that did not rest for their authority on a culturally specific priesthood or foundation myth.

Defining territories

Maps were also used by European powers, companies, and individuals to assert, define and exploit their transoceanic interests. They were particularly important for the mapping of frontiers. As maps played a role in locating and representing territorial disagreements between the imperial powers, this encouraged the mapping of areas where there was not as yet any European presence. For example, maps were employed in Anglo-French differences in the 1680s over the frontier between New France (Canada) and the territories of the (English) Hudson's Bay Company. The latter had been granted trading privileges in the

➤ The closing Pacific. This map of the North Pacific (1731) indicates knowledge of the Russian coast, but shows just how far that of North America is still limited north of lower California.

lands drained by rivers flowing into Hudson's Bay by Charles II, but there had been no idea about the extent of the area. As the company expanded the scope of its activities, it required more maps, although it was not until 1778 that it hired its first surveyor/map-maker.

Differing maps of what was a poorly mapped region – trans-Appalachia – also played a role in dramatizing the frontier disputes in North America between Britain and France that led to conflict in 1754 and the declaration of war two years later. In 1752, the French Ministry of the Marine, which was responsible

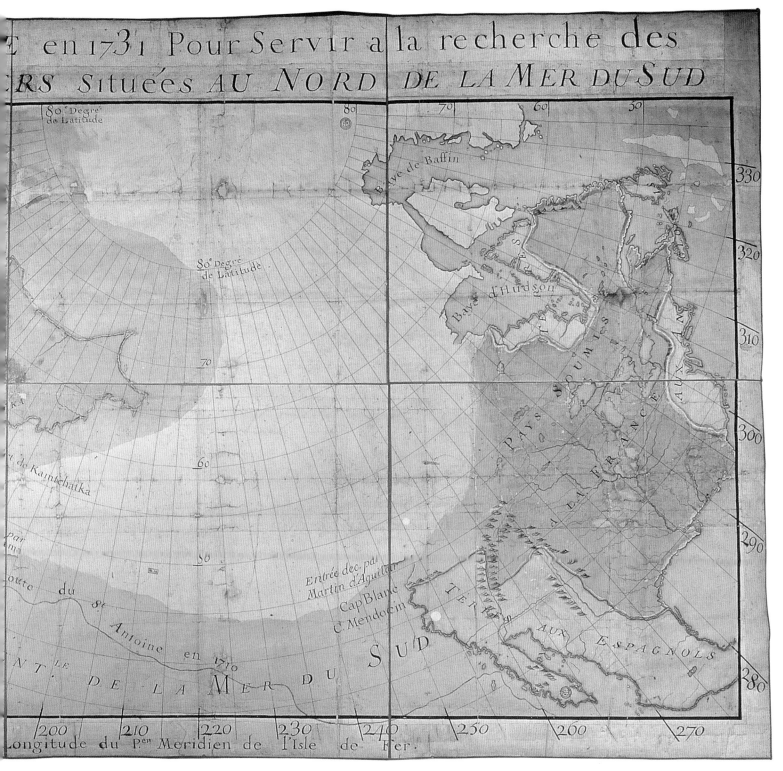

en 1731 Pour Servir a la recherche des
RS Situées AU NORD DE LA MER DU SUD

Pressure for authenticity

for the colonies, produced a set of seven large maps of Canada. In contrast, John Mitchell's *Map of the British and French Dominions in North America* (1755) was a bold statement of British views, with the depiction of the extensive territorial claims to the west of colonies such as North and South Carolina ensuring that America was divided in accordance with original charters and other British documents. That year, the Dutch foreign minister told the French envoy in The Hague, who showed him a French map by d'Anville, "if the positions are as this map shows, the French claims are correct, but the English have maps that support them".

The crisis in North America increased public demand for relevant maps, just as the capture of Louisbourg from France in 1745 during the previous conflict had led to the publication of broadsheet maps in Britain. New maps of North America were announced in the issues of the *Daily Advertiser* (a London advertising paper) of 3 August, 5 September, and 10 September 1755. The capture of Québec in 1759 led to the production for sale of more maps in Britain. Pressure was exerted on the British diplomats to map clearly the eventual territorial settlement at the

PAR

MAR

St. Marys

POTOWMARCK RIVER

Falmouth

Pt Tobacco

Somerset

Tappahanck

Raphannock River

BAY

Lewis

Fairfield

Mockjack Bay

Rosewel

Buppenhall

Corps l'Huissard

Legion de Lauzun

YORK Cty

Postes de Mr de Choisy

JAMES Cty

Toes Point

WILLAMSBURG

Glocester

Digges

Corps du Marquis de Simon

Redoute

Fort

Redoute

YORK TOWN

Volontaires de la Fayette

Corps du Cte de Rochambeau

Parc d'Artillerie

Corps d'Armee du General Washington

Burwell

Bray

Halfway House

Burwell

YORK COUNTY

Hog I.

JAMES

Rascow

ELIZABETH Cty

Seldon

Back Bay

Long Island

Egg I.

RIVER

Hampton

Warrasqueak

I OF WIGHT Cty

Jack Pt

Graney I

Sowels Pt

Fort George

Comfort Pt

Willowbys Pt

CHESAPEAK

Cape C

Armee Navale de France aux Ordres du Cte DE GRASSE avant la Victoire remportee sur l'Admiral GRAVES faisant le Blocus de la Baye de Chesapeak

Cape Henry

Smithfield

Lamberts Pt

NORFOLK Cty

PRINCESS ANN Cty

Norfolk

Lieues Marines d'une lie

Map of the siege of Yorktown and of the second battle of the Virginia Capes. The failure of a fleet of 19 ships of the line under Admiral Thomas Graves decisively to defeat 21 French ships on 5 September 1781 prevented the British relieving Cornwallis's encircled army at Yorktown. Cornwallis surrendered on 19 October 1781.

end of the conflict. In the *London Evening Post* of 23 September 1762, "Nestor Ironside" urged,

> "Let our negotiators take great care that the bounds of our dominions in all parts of the world, with which the new treaty, whenever it is made, shall meddle, be plainly and fully pointed at; and sure it would not be amiss, if authentic charts or maps were thereunto annexed, with the boundaries fairly depicted. The late peace of Aix la Chapelle [1748] proved indefinite for want of this precaution."

Indeed, in 1762, a map was joined to the instructions of the British negotiator, John, fourth Duke of Bedford, in order to help him negotiate the Mississippi boundary of the new British possessions.

Maps were also used for the frontiers between colonies ruled by the same power. Thus, a survey of 1728 which established the boundary between Virginia and North Carolina greatly increased knowledge of the back country of the two provinces. *The History of the Dividing Line betwixt Virginia and North Carolina* by William Byrd (1652–1704), one of the Virginia commissioners, is a vivid account of the difficulties of making the survey in terrain such as the Great Dismal Swamp. The attempt to fit this into the European knowledge grid involved the use of the same equipment, such as theodolites and levels, but the effort was far greater.

It proved difficult, however, to settle territorial differences between provinces. Despite tentative agreements between Pennsylvania and Maryland in 1732 and 1739, neither resulted in a permanent solution. In 1763, David Rittenhouse made the first survey of the Delaware Curve, which would not be defined satisfactorily until 1892, and the remainder of the Pennsylvania Maryland boundary was settled by Charles Mason and Jeremiah Dixon in 1764–7. The boundary line between Connecticut and Massachusetts was a serious issue in 1735–54. Violent disputes between Connecticut and Pennsylvania, beginning in 1769, were only settled by Congress's acceptance of the Pennsylvania claim in 1782. The Pennsylvania General Assembly ordered the survey of the northern line in 1785.

Territory as well as frontiers was mapped. This was directly linked to the attempt to profit from conquests and also served to assert control. The large-scale map of the Danish Caribbean island of St Croix (1754), the first large map of the Danish islands in the region, was a valuable tool for land speculators there.

Having conquered Île St Jean (Prince Edward Island) from France in 1758, and expelled the population, the British government surveyed the island and subdivided it into 67 lots which were given away by lottery in 1767. Eight years later, a map of the island, with its counties, parishes, lots, and coastal harbours, and with an inset map showing the island's position, was published. A supplementary map, showing new settlements and roads, followed in 1798.

Napoleon's invasion of Egypt in 1798 led to the first accurate map of the country. The French army carried out the trigonometric survey of the Nile valley and the Mediterranean coasts of Sinai and Palestine, all of which were areas in which it operated.

The resulting map, on 47 sheets, was, at least in part, designed as part of a geographical enquiry "to gather all the information necessary for making known the modern condition of Egypt", as well as to help military planning. These objectives clashed, and, in 1808, Napoleon declared the map a state secret. It was not published until 1818.

In addition, the French occupation led to a map of Cairo produced by Jomard. In turn, the British intervention in Egypt in 1801 that led to the defeat and surrender of the French forces increased British geographical knowledge of Egypt and of coastal waters, not least because this intervention included the dispatch of a force via the Red Sea route. Amphibious operations in the eastern Mediterranean depended on the charting of coastal waters.

Beyond the frontier

The southeast of the modern United States, an area of European expansion and imperial competition in the 18th century, naturally attracted cartographic attention. It also meant combining the geographical distinctions, the zones, that European cartographers had mapped individually around the world. Inland of coastline and coastal waters were the lands settled by Europeans – for example around Charleston – frontier zones where European power and influence successively diminished, and areas beyond the frontier of European influence.

In addition, mapmaking depended on activities in both the colonies and metropolitan centres. From the colonies, explorers and surveyors provided information, but mapping was still largely carried out in metropolitan centres: the process of accumulating information was separate to that of producing a map. In part, this reflected the nature of entrepreneurship, especially the central role of map publishers, but, in part, it was because information was interpreted by a process of comparison with already existing maps and with other sources of new information. The panoptic vision of large areas of the world enjoyed by modern satellites and suggested by past maps was denied surveyors of the day and other purveyors of information. Both were very much tied to the Earth's surface and, sometimes, had only a limited grasp of the exact location of what they were recording.

The contrast between the accumulation of information and map production was particularly apparent in the case of publishers who essentially used earlier maps. In the 18th century, the authority of existing maps, was challenged by the extent to which new information was frequently and rapidly made available to the European public.

The extent to which new information influenced maps was shown with the mapping by Guillaume de L'Isle (1675–1726), one of the leading cartographers of the period, who rapidly exploited

information provided by French explorers. De L'Isle's maps also served a political purpose. Those of North and Central America (1703) and of North America (1718) showed the British as restricted to the east of the Appalachians, whereas, in contrast, Thomas Nairn's map of 1711, which was to serve as the basis for several English maps, showed South Carolina extending to the Mississippi.

The differing claims of the two powers were finally settled by war, but, aside from competing maps of the entire region, there was the less glamorous and more painstaking tasks of charting and surveying. Thus, successive surveys of the Carolina coast led to improved maps, especially the coverage of the coast in Edward Moseley's detailed map of 1733.

Cartographic knowledge of the settled zone also increased with the surveys both of individual land grants and of towns. Thus, Claude Joseph Sauthier, whom the governor had brought to Carolina in 1767 as a surveyor, surveyed the towns of the province in 1768–70 and made plans of them. In the interior, knowledge increased with military activity and trade. Thus, in 1764, a coloured manuscript *Map of the Southern Indian District* was forwarded to the Board of Trade as part of a detailed report by John Stuart, the Superintendent for Indian Affairs in the Southern District.

Exploitation and initiative

Mapping was also important to the local progress of European control and exploitation of territory. It was crucial to the allocation of land, and thus to the way in which terrain was understood and organized for the benefit of Europeans. In addition, towns, including sometimes native areas, were laid out on European-imposed grid plans – although European knowledge of the native quarter was always more limited than that of the European quarter.

Furthermore, there are suggestions that the influence of non-Europeans on settlement patterns has been underrated. This can be seen in discussion of Pondicherry, the leading French base in India. A French settlement was established in 1674, although the grid system of streets was not designed by the French from the outset, but was implemented between 1725 and 1754. This account of European initiative has been countered with the argument that the grid system in Pondicherry represented an extension of earlier local patterns of town layout, and that a relative lack of knowledge of their role in urban morphology reflects a process of Eurocentric selection.

Even so, it is clear that in Pondicherry the development of the grid was controlled by the French. For example, the establishment of two main streets, rue de Madras and rue de Valdaour – now Gandhi and Nehru streets – involved evicting people and rebuilding several houses, mostly Indian owned. The process of control took many forms. In the Indian areas, brick and tile constructions, not the traditional straw and clay, were imposed.

⋏ This map of Canada, published in 1764, included the Indian routes west from Lake Superior which were explored by Pierre Gaultier de Varennes et de la Vérendrye in the 1730s and early 1740s. The Western Sea is shown too close to Hudson Bay.

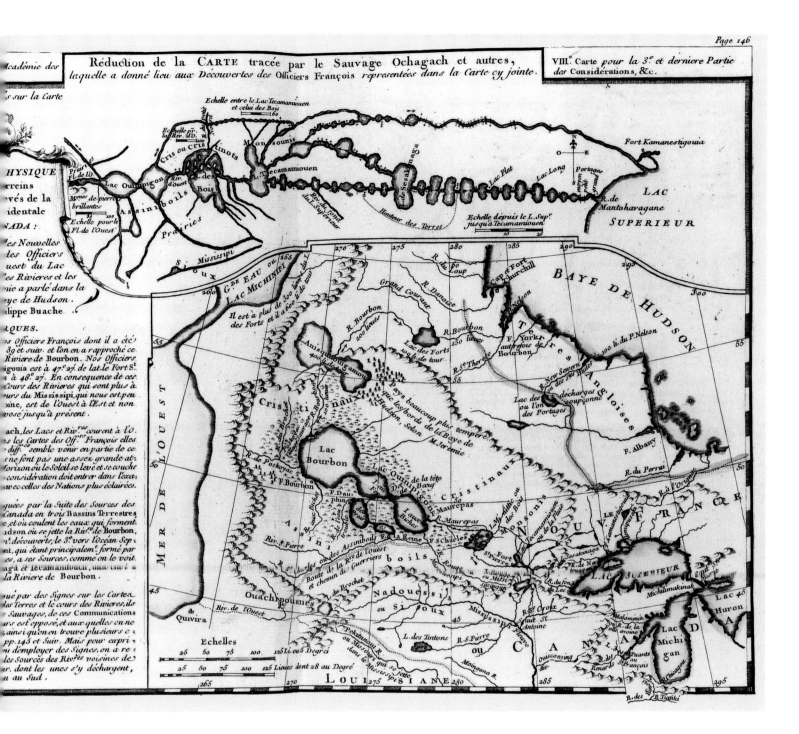

European methods were also important in China. In 1708–17, the Jesuit Jean-Baptiste Régis supervised the first maps of the Chinese empire to be based on astronomical observation and triangulation. In 1759–60, two Portuguese Jesuits surveyed Chinese conquests in Zungaria (Xiankiang) and Turkestan for the government. The first detailed Chinese map to cover northwest China was probably the *Shisan pai ditu* (c. 1770), produced by the Jesuits.

Fixing the boundaries of Europe

Within Europe, the habit of referring to maps increased during the 18th century. The use of triangulation helped in the accurate location of most places. The development of standard means of measuring distances made it easier for mapmakers to understand, assess, and reconcile the work of their predecessors. Maps were increasingly created for general reference, as well as for particular purposes – military, estate, or otherwise.

Maps also became more predictable, as mapping conventions developed. Even at the end of the 17th century, there was no standard alignment of maps, but in the following century the convention of placing north at the top was well established. However, this was less the case with estate mapping. The British Library has a map of 1777 showing mines, mills, and roads on and adjacent to an estate owned by the Duke of Medina-Sidonia near Jimena de la Frontera in Spain; this map is oriented with south-southeast at the top.

The British in India

After its territorial gains in the mid-18th century, the British East India Company was in dire need of at least reasonably accurate surveys of the Indian continent so that it could estimate the potential revenue from its acquisitions and defend them from attack.

One man above all aided the East India Company in its endeavour: James Rennell (1742–1830), who would become Surveyor General in Bengal between 1767–77, and earn the sobriquet "the Father of Indian Geography". Rennell served in the navy off India from 1760, including on an expedition to the Philippines on which he drew charts of harbours.

At the end of the Seven Years' War in 1763, Rennell transferred to the East India Company. He first charted the Palk Strait and Pamban Channel, between India and Sri Lanka, then transferred to land. In response to instructions from Robert, Lord Clive, Governor of Bengal, "to set about forming a general Map of Bengal with all expedition", he began to survey Bengal in 1765, measuring distances and directions along the major roads in order to produce "route surveys" of the entire Presidency of Bengal. This was accompanied by measure of the latitude and longitude of major points. Rennell last took the field as a surveyor in 1771, although some parts of Bengal were only surveyed in 1776.

Rennell produced a large number of maps which were to be the basis of his *Bengal Atlas* (1780), while his general map of Bengal and Bihar, sent to Britain in 1774, was based on no fewer than 500 original surveys. Rennell had been badly injured when he was ambushed on the frontier of Bhutan in 1766. Having returned to London and become a commercial cartographer, he went on to map the entire country in Hindoostan (1782), followed in 1788 by *A New Map of Hindoostan*.

This reflected both public demand and the growing amount of available information, although there were gaps in coverage, especially for west and central India. Rennell published a revised map of India in 1793. The cartouche of his map showed Britannia receiving the sacred scriptures of India from a Brahman, a depiction of a new triumphant deity, or, at least, destiny.

A An aquatint view of Pondicherry, the main French base in India, where they gradually developed a grid system of streets. A British siege of the city failed in 1718, but that of 1760–1 succeeded, in large part because of a powerful blockading fleet. The fortifications were then demolished. Pondicherry was captured again by the British in 1778 and in 1793.

➤ James Rennell's map of Hindoostan (1782). British cartography in South Asia reflected British imperial expansion. In contrast to the detail of Bengal and Carnatic, there was far less information for distant areas such as Burma and the Himalayas.

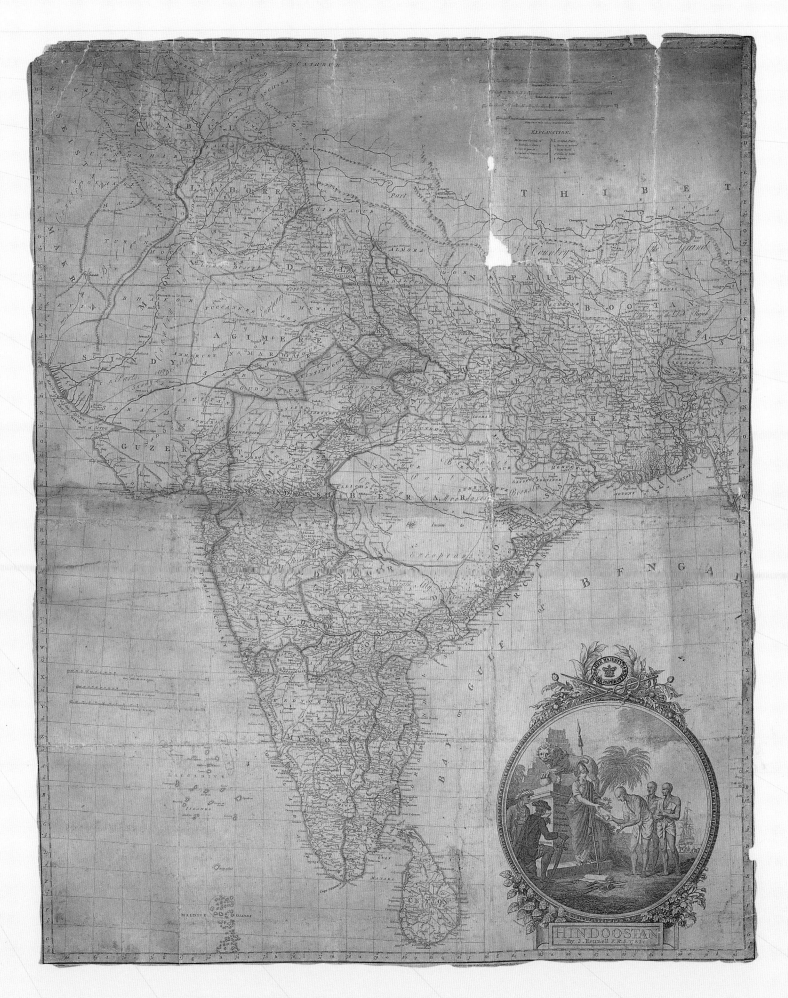

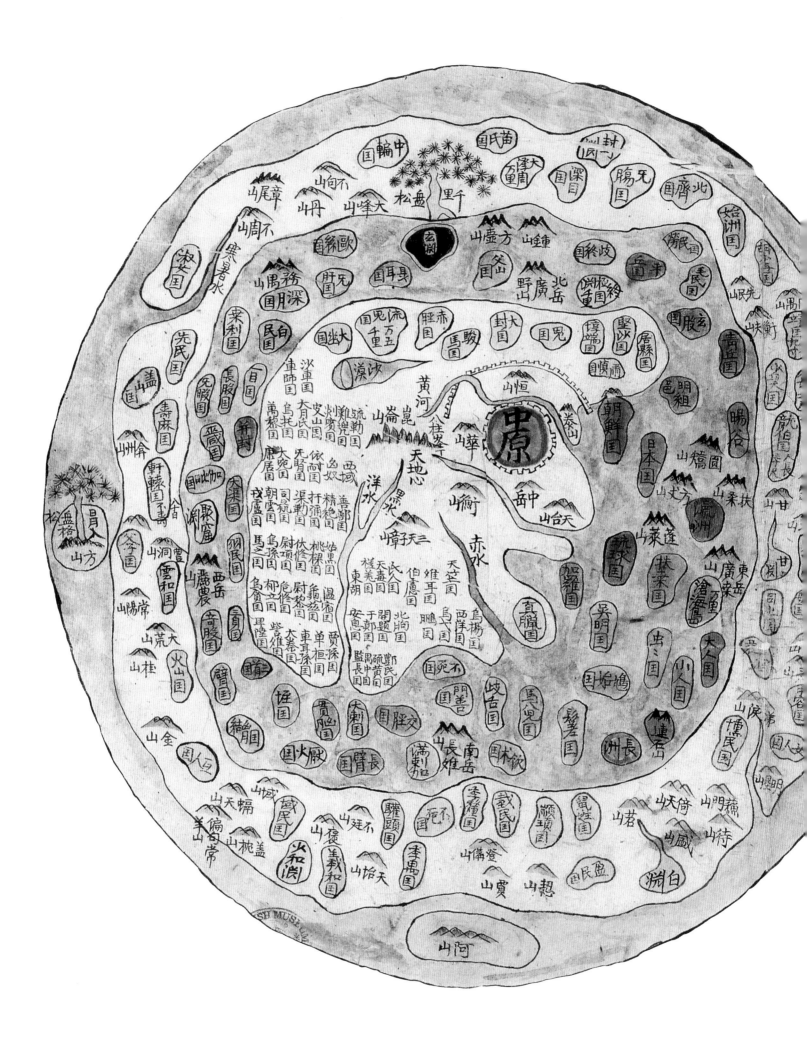

A traditional Korean map of the world, or ch'onhado, from a hand-drawn atlas of c 1750. China is at the heart of the central continent, with the Korean peninsula to the upper right. It is thought that the three lobes of the central landmass (from left to right) are Africa, India, and southern China. Most of the surrounding islands are fictitious.

Across Europe, improvements in cartography led to increasing awareness of cartographic idiosyncrasies and change and criticism of the efforts of predecessors, as in *The Construction of Maps and Globes* (1717), which has been attributed to the Irish-born geographer John Green. Travellers were better served by maps, not least those that showed routes on which posting (horse-hiring) services were available. In 1724 appeared the first edition of *Nouveau Voyage de France. Avec un Itineraire, et des Cartes faites exprès, qui marquent exactement les routes qu'il faut suivre pour voyager dans toutes les Provinces de ce Royaume. Ouvrage également utile aux François et aux Etrangers* by Jean-Aymar Piganiol de la Force (1673–1753). With 15 folding maps, this was one of the best French road books.

Mapping was also seen as a necessary complement to land registers, and thus as the basis of reformed land taxes. The Swedish Pomeranian Survey Commission of 1692–1709 was designed to provide the basis for a new tax system. Detailed land surveys of Piedmont and Savoy, establishing the ownership and value of land, were completed in 1711 and 1738, respectively, while such mapping was also carried out in Lombardy in the late 1710s.

Building on 17th-century military mapping, particularly by France and Sweden, large-scale military surveys became more important. The Austrians, who ruled Sicily between 1720 and 1735, used army engineers to prepare the first detailed map of the island. French military engineers of the period, such as Pierre Bourcet (1700–1780), tackled the problems of mapping mountainous regions, creating a clearer idea of what the alpine region looked like.

Between 1743 and his death in 1780, Bourcet produced maps of France's Alpine frontier. He mapped Corsica, which France had acquired in 1768. The mapping of the island was another expression of the assertion of French control, which also included road-building. Bourcet's work on the Alps was continued by Le Michaud d'Arcon (1733–1800), who also mapped France's frontier on the Alps and in the Jura.

Following the suppression of the 1745 Jacobite rebellion, there was a military survey of Scotland which served as the basis for more accurate maps. William Roy (1726–1790) of the Royal Engineers, who was responsible for this survey, also sought to improve the mapping of terrain. His investigations with Sir George Shuckburgh (1751–1804), a gentleman-scientist, were published as *Observations made in Savoy to ascertain the Height of Mountains by the Barometer* (1777).

Frederick's great lies

Having conquered Silesia in 1740-1, Frederick the Great of Prussia had it mapped. In 1753, he was obliged to assure the Polish government that his mapping of Silesia was not intended to regulate the Silesia–Poland frontier in his favour, one of his many deceits. Frederick's Austrian opponents also sought to map their territories as part of a general process of understanding and using resources, and also for military ends. A major military survey of Bohemia was begun in the 1760s, Lower Austria was surveyed from 1773, and a vast survey of Hungary was completed in 1786.

Maps were increasingly referred to by diplomats and politicians in crises and in times of war. Increased precision in the mapping of frontiers furthered their use. In 1712, during the negotiations over ending the War of the Spanish Succession, Jean-Baptiste Colbert, (1665–1746) the French foreign minister, urged his British counterpart to look at a map in order to see the strategic threat posed by the Alpine demands of Victor Amadeus II of Savoy-Piedmont. A map that formed part of an Anglo-Dutch treaty of 1718 delineated the frontier between the United Provinces and the Austrian Netherlands. This owed much to the publication in 1711 of the large-scale Eugene Henri Fricx (*active* 1706–40) map of the Low Countries.

In 1718, the frontier was fixed literally on a map, signed and sealed by plenipotentiaries as an annex to that treaty. This practice became established by the end of the century, helping to ensure the settlement of long-standing disputes. In 1715, Victor Amadeus II of Savoy-Piedmont complained about the nature of his alpine frontier with France, claiming that the intendant of Dauphiné was falsely defining both the extent of the valley of Barcelonnette and the alpine watershed. However, it was not until the Treaty of Turin of 1760 that an agreement was obtained. The treaty incorporated eight maps that delimited the watershed frontier. The frontier between Austria and Venice, over which there had been disputes for more than two centuries, was not settled until 1752.

The limitations of 18th-century cartography were illustrated during the crisis in 1762 when Peter III of Russia threatened war with Denmark in furtherance of the territorial claims of his Holstein-Gottorp dynasty. Walter Titley (1700–68), the British envoy in Copenhagen, attempted to secure a map that would throw light on the "hereditary animosity and ancient grudge" that lay behind the dispute. On 2 March, he reported,

"A map of the Duchy of Holstein, wherein the Royal and Ducal possessions are distinctly marked, is, I believe, one of the *desiderata* of geography. I do not know what there is any such map extant; but if I should happen to meet with one, you may be sure to have it. In the mean time I can send you here, in a very few lines, a list of the territories properly belonging to the Duke [of Holstein-Gottorp]."

A week later, Titley obtained and sent back to England a map produced in about 1710 by John Homann (1664–1724), the Nuremberg cartographer who was made Imperial Geographer in 1716, one of the leading German cartographers of the day. This map, in turn, was based on one surveyed in 1638–48 by Johannes

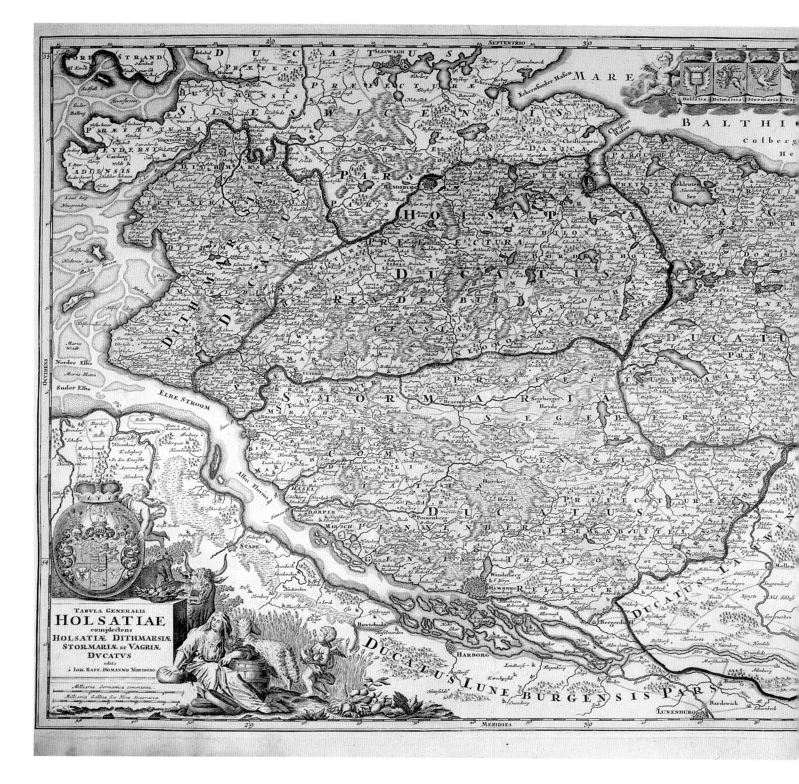

Mejer (1606–72), so that by the time Titley sent it the information was more than 110 years old. The map was not particularly accurate: some of the locations in Mejer's original map had been approximate and based on observation, rather than measurement. In 1763, a new large-scale survey, based on triangulation, was begun for administrative and taxation purposes, although it was not completed until 1806. With the map, Titley had written:

"Having found one of Homann's maps, wherein the several parts of the Duchy of Holstein were distinguished with colours, though not strongly nor exactly, I have spread a shade of deep burgundy upon all the possessions, which properly belong to the Duke; and the three ducal cities (which were very obscurely exhibited) I have marked with a small black cross, that may possibly catch your eye and help you when you look them out. These possessions lie in four different parcels, entirely separated from each other by the intervention of royal or collateral territory. I am not satisfied with this part; it is blind and indistinct and the river-courses seem not always

↗ A 1710 map of the Duchy of Holstein by John Homann, who was made Imperial Geographer in 1716. His colouring was based on the principles of Johannes Hübner – that the lands ruled by the same monarch or republic should be depicted in the same colour.

well traced; however it is right, as to the ducal dominions and may serve your purpose perhaps, till a better one can be met with.

Colouring the conquests

Homann's colouring was based on the principles of the Hamburg scholar and cartographer Johannes Hübner (1668–1731), who is claimed to be the originator of the idea that the lands ruled by the same monarch or republic should be depicted in the same colour. Geographical accuracy was not seen as crucial, however, while error was sustained by the continued use of old plates.

In Germany, in particular, single maps, as opposed to special atlases of base maps all showing the same area, were not a satisfactory way of showing princely territorial rights. It was usually beyond the ingenuity of even the most skilful cartographer to indicate on a single map areas of mixed jurisdictions, owing allegiance to different rulers for different aspects of their existence.

On 27 March 1762, Titley had sent another map home:

"You have herewith another map of Holstein, which is somewhat better, as being more distinct, than the first I sent you. The several territories are distinguished by colours. Green denotes the royal parts, the red the ducal. The yellow tracts belong to the Bishop and Chapter of Lubeck, and what little appears of the territory of Hanover is marked with a shade of blue. In the first map I had inadvertently put the famous baillage of Steinhorst under the same colour with ducal Holstein but in this it is restored to its proper sovereign, and I think with interest, for there are a few villages added under the blue colour which do not really belong to it. A very accurate chart of this Duchy, I believe is not to be had."

The problem of the interpretation of treaties made single maps even more inadequate, while, even in a major cartographic centre such as Hamburg, the British could encounter difficulties in obtaining maps of northern Europe in 1763.

Ministers and diplomats needed maps. In 1735, Lord Waldegrave (1684–1741), British envoy in Paris, obtained the maps of Italy and the Rhineland that Thomas, Duke of Newcastle (1693–1768), Secretary of State, sought in order to follow the conflict between France and Austria that was part of the War of the Polish Succession. In 1736, Sir Everard Fawkener (1684–1758), envoy in Constantinople, wrote to Claudius Rondeau, his counterpart in St Petersburg: "In one of your letters to His Excellency Mr Walpole I see you had sent him maps of the Crimea. If any such things are to be had, or any new maps that are thought to be exact of any part of her Czarish Majesty's dominions, especially towards the Euxin [Black] or Caspian Seas, or the routes now used from thence to Persia or China, I shall be very glad to have them".

In 1757, George Cressener (1700–81), Minister at Cologne, thanked the diplomat Onslow Burrish (d. 1758) for "the Map of

Bohemia" where Austria and Prussia were then in conflict: "it appears to be a very good one, and I hope I shall have frequent occasions of looking in it this summer". The bill of expenses of the King's Messenger Ralph Heslop for journeys to and from Paris in 1782 included additional expenses on the road to Paris for "a very large case of maps" needed for the negotiations for the settlement of the War of American Independence.

The French foreign office had created a geographic section in 1772 and, in 1780, acquired the collection of about 10,000 maps of the famous geographer Jean-Baptiste d'Anville (1697–1782). Sir James Harris, the Earl of Malmesbury (1746–1820), British envoy at The Hague, recorded of the Cabinet meeting he attended in London as the Dutch crisis approached its height in 1787 that the third Duke of Richmond, Master-General of the Ordnance, "talked of military operations – called for a map of Germany – traced the marches from Cassel and Hanover, to Holland, and also from Givet to Maastricht". Thus, the possibilities of French- and British-subsidized German intervention were outlined by the use of a map. The following day, William Pitt the Younger "sent for a map of Holland; made me show him the situation of the Provinces". In 1791, the British envoy in Vienna, Sir Robert Murray Keith (1730–1795), promised to obtain for the Foreign Secretary a copy of the map that defined the newly agreed Austro-Turkish frontier:

"The Imperialists had only three copies of the map of the frontiers of the two Empires (which is so often mentioned in the recent Convention); these they have given to the Turks and to the Prussian Minister. But they have engaged to deliver to each of the mediating ministers, on our return to Vienna, a correct map of that kind with all the limits carefully marked out according to this last adjustment. I shall think it my duty to send that map to your Lordship, as soon as it shall be put into my hands."

Napoleon redraws Europe

The French Revolution, which began in 1789 and led, from 1792, to a series of wars that continued until the final defeat of Napoleon in 1815, lent renewed energy to mapping. Conflicts were followed and planned on maps. George III used one to follow the Prussian invasion of France in 1792. In 1800, George Canning (1776–1827) wrote to his successor as under-secretary of state in the Foreign Office about Napoleon's latest successes, "What do you think of the Italian news? and what consolation does Pitt point out after looking over the map in the corner of his room by the door?" Pitt responded to the news of Napoleon's victory over the Austrians and Russians at Austerlitz in 1805, "Roll up that map; it will not be wanted these ten years". French military geographers, ingénieurs-géographes, accompanied the advancing armies and produced large numbers of maps of the areas in which they operated: from Portugal to Russia.

Frontiers within and outside France were radically redrawn and so had to be recorded. Within France, provinces were replaced by *départements*, and this led to the redrawing of maps. Previous governmental boundaries within France were now redundant.

The debate over how best to reorganize France had reflected a tension between utopianism and practicality. The former had led plans for a geometric system, such as that proposed in 1780 by Robert de Hassdn for using squares based on lines of latitude and longitude, as if France were a newly claimed colony. This idea influenced proposals made in 1789, but others sought areas of equal population size. Eventually, it was decided to allow variation. *Départements* were to be between 302 and 342 square leagues. Existing provincial boundaries, such as those of Normandy and Provence, frequently provided the context within which new *départements* were created, although elsewhere political interests played a major role in the allocation of territory.

Radicals and revolutionaries

This geographical reorganization was denounced by the Irish statesman and philosopher Edmund Burke (1729–97), in his *Reflections on the Revolution in France* (1790), the founding book of modern conservatism, and, although he exaggerated the degree of change entailed by the scheme, Burke correctly captured the potentially radical nature of surveying and mapping:

> "…in a new and merely theoretic system, it is expected that every contrivance shall appear, on the face of it, to answer its end; especially where the projectors are no way embarrassed with an endeavour to accommodate the new building to an old one … Nothing more than an accurate land surveyor, with his chain, sight, and theodolite, is requisite for such a plan as this … this new pavement of square within square … When these state surveyors came to take a view of their work of measurement, they soon found, that in politics, the most fallacious of all things was geometrical demonstration."

At the same time, the disruption of revolution made surveying difficult, as was shown when two French astronomers, Jean-Baptiste-Joseph Delambre (1749–1822) and Pierre-François-André Mechain (1744–1804), tried, from 1792, to measure the arc of the Paris meridian between Dunkirk and Barcelona in order to determine the precise length of the new measure of distance: the metre. It had been decided that this was to be one ten-millionth of the distance from the equator to the North Pole. The astronomers were to measure a portion and then extrapolate the full distance, but, thanks in part to the turmoil and conflict of these years, this task proved difficult. In any case, it was based on a flawed premise, because the length of meridians varies, as the Earth is not a perfect sphere. The Paris meridian had already been measured in 1712 and 1740, but it was hoped in the 1790s that advances in instrumentation would enable more accurate measurement, and this was part of the propaganda build-up for the metric system.

More mundanely, outside France, French victories led to extensive territorial changes, including the creation of new states,

such as the kingdoms of Italy and Westphalia, and the Grand Duchies of Berg, Warsaw, and Würzburg. In addition, states such as Bavaria, Württemberg, and Baden changed their boundaries on a number of occasions between 1792 and 1815. The legitimacy of such states depended in part on their mapping, which helped to assert their identity.

The wars also stimulated mapping by France's enemies, not least in Britain by the Board of Ordnance, as concern developed about a possible French invasion. Military needs were to be one of the major causes behind developments in mapping over the following two centuries.

The habit of referring to maps continued to increased during the 18th century. Land surveyors were numerous, and estate maps were produced in large numbers. They showed the location and size of fields and often marked features such as paths and woodland. Landowners could thus give a sense of place to reports from distant estates: in 1739–42, Wadham College, Oxford, had five maps made of its Essex estates. Such maps were also a display of property.

Landowners also used maps to help in the enclosure of open, common land and its division into plots. Enclosures required a detailed land survey. Information was crucial to the process, both to its economic value and as part of the legal procedure. To arrange their valuation and to replan the area, it was necessary to establish who owned lands. This involved determining what land would form the new plots, as well as the routes of roads and watercourses. The role of the surveyors could be seen in new, straight-edged fields and straight roads. This reflected the role of cartography as an aid to organization and control.

As a result, there could be a hostile response to surveying. Indeed, hostility to the enclosure of the former Malvern Chase in 1776 led local people to prevent the surveyor, John Andrews (*active* 1766–1809), from marking out the enclosure boundaries. He had produced a topographical map of Kent in 1769. A Dutch equivalent to enclosure maps were those of reclamation of marshland produced by polder authorities.

There were also important new initiatives in the production of printed county maps in the mid-18th century. Hitherto, the Elizabethan maps had been reprinted with scant alteration due to the absence of new field work. In 1695, Robert Morden (*active* 1669–1705) based his county maps on the earlier work. Now, new surveys of entire counties were undertaken and maps produced on detailed scales: one or more inches to the mile.

The first of the county maps – that of Cornwall by Joel Gascoyne – appeared in 1699. The following year, he produced proposals for a subscription survey and mapping of Devon. This was directed at the gentry who were told that the map would show "gentlemen's seats", that 'every gentleman who subscribeth, shall have his name engraven under his seat", and that, "upon payment, gentry could have their coats of arms engraved on the border". In the event, there was inadequate support.

➤ One of the many maps by Jean-Baptiste d'Anville held by the French Foreign Office in Paris. This colour engraving of 1763 is a map of the western part of the Roman empire. D'Anville was remarkable for his rigorously scientific approach to cartography, and if he was uncertain of something it was excluded. His maps were among the first to leave blank spaces, a revolutionary concept at the time.

This was a method of mapmaking open to fraud, and that itself was indicative of the growth of interest in cartography, as criminals always exploit opportunities. In its issue of 25 February 1727, *Mist's Weekly Journal*, a leading London newspaper, carried a report from Beccles in Suffolk:

"One Harman is committed to gaol for imposing on several gentlemen by styling himself the York Herald, and pretending to take a survey, and make a map of this and other counties, and also drawing out their coats of arms, by which means he got from them several sums of money."

An inch to the mile

By 1750, only eight counties had been mapped at one inch to a mile or larger. From 1759, the work was in part encouraged by prizes awarded by the Royal Society of Arts, one of the major "betterment" bodies of the period. The society had been prompted by a letter of 1755 from William Borlase, a Cornish clergyman. He had complained: "Our maps of England and its counties are extremely defective … and the headlands of all our shores are at this time disputed". Borlase had suggested that the society provide a reward for the best plan, measurement, and actual survey of a city or district:

"It may move the attention of the public towards geography and, in time, perhaps, include the administration to take this matter into their hands (as I am informed it does in some foreign countries) and employ proper persons every year from actual surveys to make accurate maps …, till the whole island is regularly surveyed."

In 1759, the Royal Society of Arts stipulated, as part of the competition, a trigonometrical survey, the accurate measurement of road distances, and a scale of one inch to a mile. The first to win the award was a 12-sheet map of Devon completed by Benjamin Donn (1729–98) in 1765. This showed roads and settlements, but, as was normal in the period, terrain was only partly covered: as yet systematic contouring had not been developed.

The prizes awarded were of value, but local demand was more important. By 1775, nearly half of the English counties had been surveyed at one inch to a mile or larger. Essex, for example, was surveyed by John Chapman in 1772–4 and the resulting maps published in 1777.

The range of material shown is indicated by the key of the map of Lancashire produced in 1786 by William Yates. Yates's map included: ecclesiastical information (churches with spires, churches with towers, chapels, rectories, vicarages, parochial chapels, and curacies); guides to settlement ("Borough towns which send Members to Parliament", "Market Towns which are not Boroughs", "Parishes which are not Market Towns", "townships" — all distinguished by type face, and "Market Towns and Villages in their true Form" — marking the area of

▷ France, following the division of the country into *départements*. In 1799, the number was fixed at 83, including Paris and Corsica. As the French Revolutionary Wars brought conquests, so the number rose. Within France, the allocation of territory to *départements* reflected in part historic divisions, especially provincial boundaries, but representation in the National Assembly, and the political strength of *départements* also played a role.

settlement, gentlemen's seats, and farm houses); communications (turnpike roads and mile stones with toll bars, cross roads, rivers with water mills, canals with locks, and bridges); as well as coal pits and county and hundred (voting constituency) boundaries.

The need for new road maps

The extensive road-building of the 18th century ensured that new maps were necessary for travellers in Britain. By 1750, a sizeable network of new turnpikes, radiating from London, had been

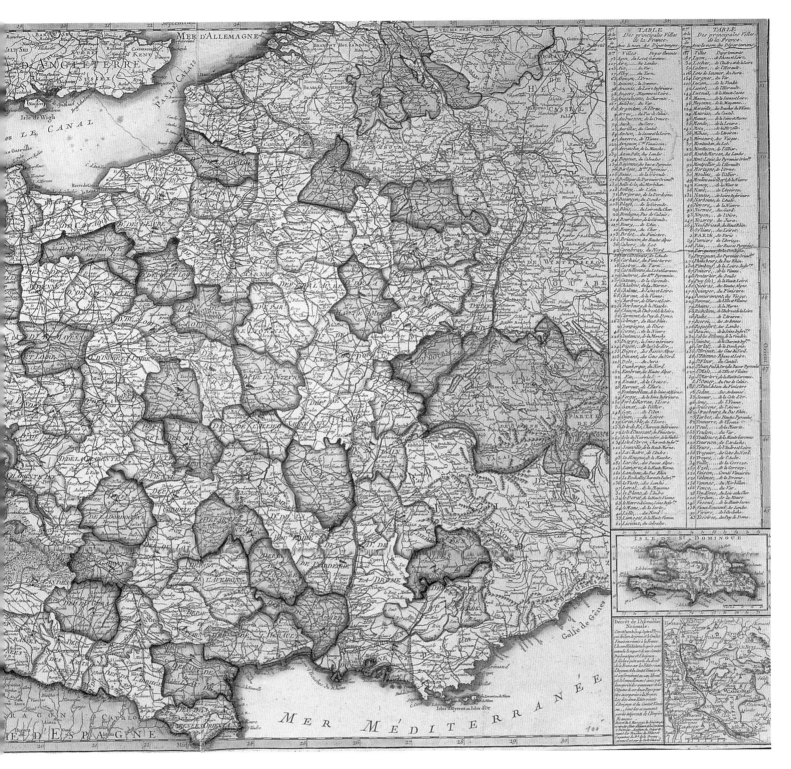

created, and by 1770 there were 15,000 miles of turnpikes in England. New routes, both roads and canals, were recorded in the maps of the period. Thus, the map of Staffordshire surveyed by Yates from 1769–75 – and which, engraved and published by Chapman in 1775, won an award from the Royal Society of Arts – showed canals as well as turnpike routes such as the Dudley turnpike of 1760.

In contrast, earlier county maps had not tried to provide a comprehensive (or often any) account of roads. Thus, Saxton, in the 1570s, did not show roads, although bridges were depicted.

During the latter part of the 18th century, the display of roads at the national level also increased. Road maps included *An Actual Survey of the Great Post-Roads between London and Edinburgh with the Country of Three Miles on each side* (1776) by Mostyn Armstrong (active 1769–91). Roads were shown on the map of England and Wales produced by Aaron Arrowsmith in 1816, and of the British Isles made by Cary in 1818.

The market for maps was good. For example, King George II's royal engraver of maps, Emanuel Bowen (active 1714–67), cooperated with Thomas Kitchin (1718–84) in engraving maps for

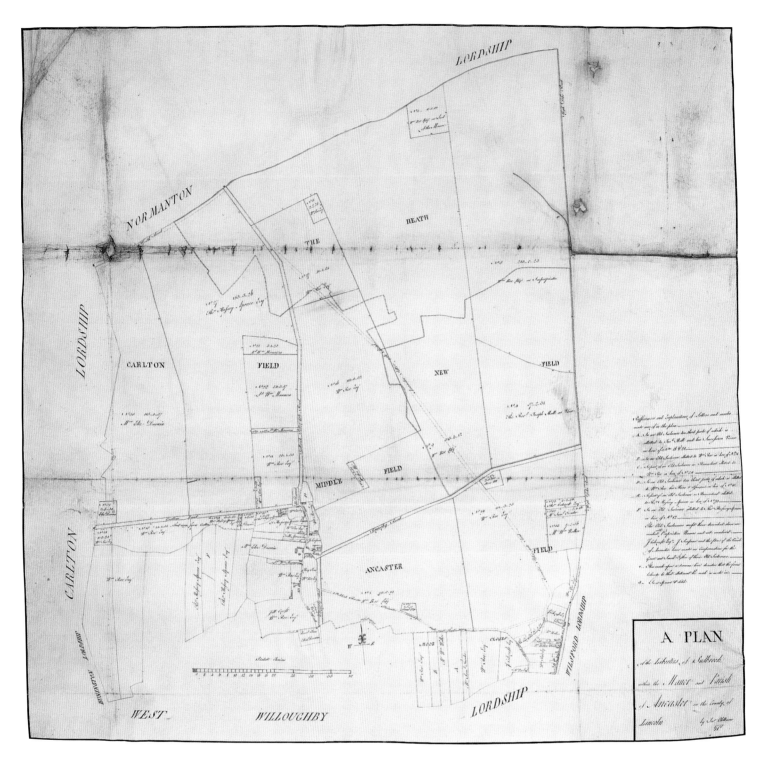

the *Large English Atlas*. The 45 maps were sold as a complete volume from 1760, the seventh edition appearing in 1787.

Entrepreneurs sought to take advantage of this demand. For example, John Cary, a map seller, also produced terrestrial and celestial globes, astronomical books, road books and maps, canal plans, geological maps, and, in 1798, he issued a new edition of Ogilby's *Britannia*.

There was also demand for town maps, such as James Corbridge's map of Newcastle (1723), a work that offered both precision and an attractive image. Corbridge illustrated the map with pictograms of the major buildings, for example, the leading churches. Isaac Taylor (1730–1807) followed the same policy in his map of Wolverhampton (1750). London was served by the *New and Accurate Survey of the Cities of London and Westminster* (1748) of John Rocque (c.1704–62).

Similar markets were also catered for elsewhere. In the newly independent United States, the first road atlas, *A Survey of the Roads of the United States of America*, by Christopher Colles (1738–1816) was published in New York in 1789. Colles used the device of strip maps employed by Ogilby. As a road atlas, Colles'

⋏ **Extract from the enclosure map for Ancaster, Lincolnshire, 1770, as a result of the Enclosure Acts (which were numerous during the 18th century. The control of the landscape was shown in the rectilinearity of the new plots. Older enclosures were more responsive to local topography.**

work provided a guide for those keen to travel, circumventing the problem posed by the dominance of coastal routes in early American transport.

The use of maps also extended to include landscape design, both to project plans for parkland surrounding country houses and to organize forests for hunting. The royal forests around Paris were mapped for the latter end, while British landscape designers prepared maps to show patrons how they might enhance the settings for their fine homes. This bridged the divide between architectural plans and the widespread use of maps for established estate purposes.

At a different level, society was well attuned to maps; they were used for jigsaws and other puzzles, as on John Wallis's *Wallis's Tour through England and Wales: A Geographical Pastime* (1794).

The scale of subjugation

Shaken by the Jacobite rising in Scotland in 1745, the British government had William Roy carry out a survey of Scotland between 1747 and 1755 in order to produce a map – known as the Duke of Cumberland's map – at a scale of one inch to 1,000 yards (1:36,000) that would, it was hoped, enable the army to respond better to further rebellion. Six surveying parties were employed in a move that was to parallel the road- and fortress-building of the same years.

Fortresses anchored the government position, and maps provided guidance in military planning, offering the prospect of a strategic, Scotland-wide response to any future uprising. Commerce rapidly followed. By 1776, George Taylor and Andrew Skinner could publish a *Survey and Maps of the Roads of North Britain or Scotland*, depicting roads for travellers in a strip-map format.

The Ordnance Survey was an instance of the same process: of defence encouraging a mapmaking that was soon directed to peaceful goals, at the larger scale. The French Revolutionary and Napoleonic Wars (1793–1815) led to a degree of modernization of the British state, including the introduction of income tax and a national census, as well as parliamentary union with Ireland. The Board of Ordnance, a government department, was given responsibility for mapping in order to help cope with a possible French invasion, which, indeed, was planned. This process predated the wars, although it was greatly encouraged by it.

The Trigonometrical, later called Ordnance Survey – the basis of the detailed maps of Britain to this day – began in 1791, although it continued triangulation work first begun in 1784 in order to link the observatories of London and Paris. The chain of triangles was completed in 1788. Three years later, the Corps of Royal Military Surveyors and Draughtsmen was founded, and by 1795 they had completed a double chain of triangles from London to Land's End.

A one inch to the mile map of Kent was published in 1801. Thereafter, the surveyors moved to the southwest of England, another potential invasion area which was covered by about 1810. There was a considerable emphasis on depicting "strong ground": terrain that could play a role in operations. This reflected the importance of relief and slopes, not only to help or impede advances but also for determining the sightlines of cannon.

Military purposes also drove forward much naval charting. James Cook charted the St Lawrence as part of the successful British attack on Québec in 1759. Among the working maps collected by Field Marshal Jeffrey Amherst (1717–97), there was "A Plan of the Island of Cape Britain [*sic* for Breton] reduced from the large survey" made according to the orders of the Board of Trade by Samuel Holland. Holland (1728?–1801) was surveyor-general of Quebec and the Northern District from 1764, and his task was to survey the coast and to produce charts for the use of the fleet. They were published in the *Atlantic Neptune*.

The Amherst collection also included a map of the "Wilderness Road" towards Ohio surveyed by Captain Thomas Bullitt, who, in 1773, had led a group of officers down the Ohio River and surveyed the present site of Louisville, before returning along the Wilderness Road. Two years later, a map of the Mississippi was published in London. It was based on an earlier journey by Lieutenant John Ross and on French sources.

Alexander Dalrymple (1737–1808), who had been appointed official hydrographer to the East India Company in 1779, in 1795 also became Hydrographer to the Admiralty. The Order in Council instructed Dalrymple:

> "to take charge of such plans and charts as are now or may hereafter be deposited in this office belonging to the Public, and to be charged with the duty of selecting and compiling all the existing information as may appear to be requisite for the purpose of improving the Navigation, and for the guidance and direction of the Commanders of Your Majesty's ships."

More generally, cartography was a crucial aspect of the ability to synthesize, disseminate, utilize, and reproduce information that was central to British hegemony. For example, the movement of ships could be planned and predicted, facilitating not only trade, but also amphibious operations. Maps served to record and replicate information about areas in which Britain had an interest and to organize, indeed centre, this world on themes of British concern and power.

Thus, European knowledge was now directed to different goals. Whereas, in the 1490s, it had been employed to divide the newly glimpsed globe between Portugal and Spain in a papally sanctioned world order, now British interests were served. Yet, aside from particular states, there was a more general process of Europeanization. A powerful (and lasting) instance was provided by the grouping together of regions, most prominently as continents, in response to European ideas. Thus, for example, the South Atlantic world of the west coast of Africa, Brazil, the Guianas, and the West Indies were subordinated to a European model in which Africa and the New World were separate.

Of course, just as European perceptions of other areas and peoples were heavily influenced by earlier views, not least the classical legacy, so, as they came into contact with new peoples, they were also influenced by interlocutors. Thus, at the local level, pre-existing antagonistic relations between native peoples, and the resulting perceptions, could greatly affect the European newcomers.

At the same time, whatever the manner in which a native population saw the space in which it lived, this was subordinated to European assumptions and cartography. Thus, in accordance with a long-established cartographic tradition that included Islamic mappers, the world of Islam was divided between Africa, Europe, and Asia, although this ignored persistent political, cultural, and economic links, especially in the lands that bordered the eastern Mediterranean and also, although less strongly, those around the Red Sea.

In the late 18th century, the improved understanding of longitude provided more accurate maps. Given a common reference, therefore, the reports and observations of explorers and navigators could be more accurately assimilated into the existing knowledge grid, a situation that had been very different to the position 300 years earlier.

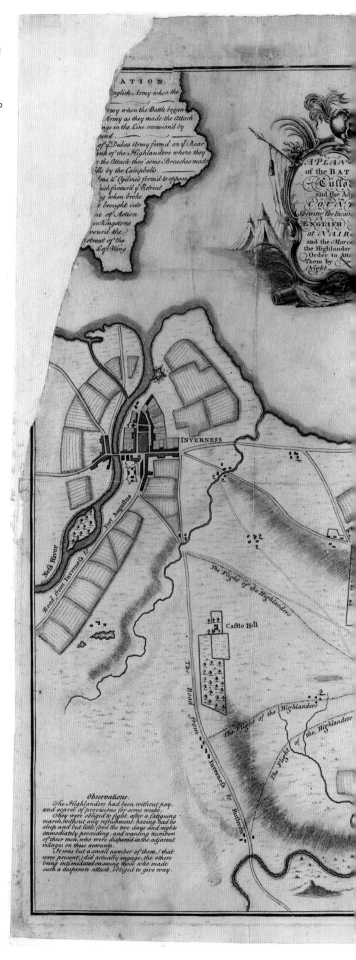

➤ A plan of the Battle of Culloden, 1746. Such works reflected public interest in the battle and the absence of existing maps with which people could follow the course of the campaign. The map helped on location, although it could not clarify many of the details. The terrain, for example, was partly waterlogged, and it was difficult to see what was happening amid the smoke of the guns. The outnumbered Jacobites were thinned by the artillery and infantry of the Duke of Cumberland's army as they advanced, and the clansmen who did reach the royal troops were driven back at bayonet point.

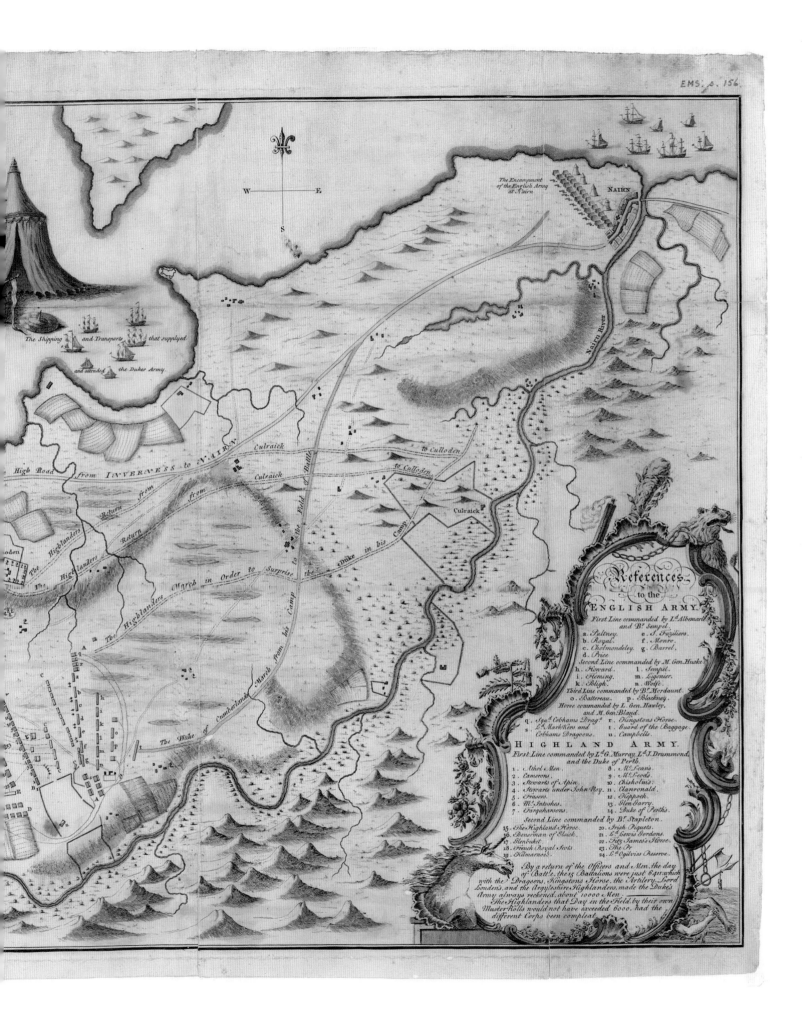

The Encampment of the English Army at Nairn

NAIRN

Nairn River

The Shipping and Transports that supplyed and attended the Dukes Army.

High Road from INVERNESS to NAIRN

Culraick

Culraick

to Culloden

to Culloden

Culraick

The Highlanders March in Order to Surprise the Field of Battle

Return from

Return

The Highlanders

The Highlanders

The Duke of Cumberlands March from his Camp.

The Duke in his Camp.

References to the
ENGLISH ARMY.

First Line commanded by Ld. Albemarle and Bt. Sempel.
  a. Pultney.   e. S. Fuziliers.
  b. Royal.   f. Monro.
  c. Cholmondeley. g. Barrel.
  d. Price
Second Line commanded by M. Gen. Huske.
  h. Howard.   l. Sempel.
  i. Fleming.   m. Ligonier.
  k. Bligh.   n. Wolfe.
Third Line commanded by Bt. Mordaunt.
  o. Battereau.   p. Blackney.
Horse commanded by L. Gen. Hawley.
and M. Gen. Bland.
  q. Sqd. Cobhams Drago. r. Kingstons Horse.
  s. Ld. MarkKers and   t. Guard of the Baggage.
    Cobhams Dragoons. u. Campbells.

HIGHLAND ARMY.
First Line commanded by Ld. G. Murray, Ld. J. Drummond,
and the Duke of Perth.
  1. Athol Men.   8. M. Leans.
  2. Camerons.   9. M. Leods.
  3. Stewarts of Apin. 10. Chisholms.
  4. Stewarts under John Roy. 11. Clanronald.
  5. Frasers.   12. Kippoch.
  6. M. Intoshes.   13. Glen Garry.
  7. Farquharsons.   14. Duke of Perths.
    Second Line commanded by Bt. Stapleton.
  15. The Highland Horse. 20. Irish Piquets.
  16. Benerman of Elsick. 21. Ld. Lewis Gordons.
  17. Glenbuket.   22. Fitz James Horse.
  18. French Royal Scots. 23. The Pr
  19. Kilmarnock.   24. Ld. Ogilvies Reserve.

By a return of the Officers and Men, the day
of Battle, the 15 Battalions were just 6411 which
with the Dragoons, Kingstons Horse, the Artillery, Lord
Loudens, and the Argyleshire Highlanders, made the Dukes
Army always reckond, about 10000 Men.
The Highlanders that Day in the Field, by their own
Muster Rolls would not have exceeded 6000, had the
different Corps been compleat.

EMS: p. 156

RENVOIS POUR QUELQUES ÉTATS
de la Confédération Germanique.

1 au Roi de Prusse	10 aux Princes d'Anhalt	
2 aux Princes de Nassau	11 aux Pᶜᵉˢ de Schwartzbourg	
3 au Roi de Bavière	12 aux Pᶜᵉˢ Hohenzollern	
4 au Roi de Hanovre	13 aux Pᶜᵉ de Reuss	
5 à l'Electeur de Hesse Cassel	14 aux Pᶜᵉ de Lipp	
6 au Gᵈ Duc de Hesse Darmstadt	15 au Pᶜᵉ de Lichtenstein	
7 au Duc de Brunswick	16 au Pᶜᵉ de Waldeck	

Lieues communes de France de 25 au degré

Lieues de 20 au degré

Milles de 60 au degré

Milles de 15 au degré

Commerce and Empire

Although, during the 19th century, maps and atlases increasingly came to approximate to their modern printed forms, at the beginning of the period at least, they were still concerned with conveying information of a different kind. For example, the *Genealogical, Chronological, Historical and Geographical Atlas* (London, 1801) of "Le Sage" (pseudonym of the Marquis de la Caussade) made much use of "genealogical and chronological maps" – in other words, genealogical tables and time-charts. The "geographical" aspect was of secondary importance, and, instead "Le Sage", who had fled the French Revolution, presented all his "maps" as devices to fix the relative location of different types of information.

"Le Sage" returned to Paris in 1802, and that year's edition of his atlas was officially adopted by the Ministry of the Interior for use in French schools and by the Foreign Ministry for the use of overseas legations. It was one of the most successful atlases of the age, with numerous editions produced in Paris, as well as American editions in Philadelphia and St Petersburg (Florida), and German and Italian translations.

The use of the word "atlas" to describe a book that tried to locate and present information through the use of tables was also seen in *Atlas éthnographique du globe ou classification des peuples anciens et modernes d'après leurs langues* (Paris, 1826) by Adrien Balbi (1782–1848). But such atlases were not to dominate; instead, geographical precision increasingly became the keynote of 19th-century cartography.

Technological advances greatly affected the development of mapping in the 19th century. Mechanized papermaking became commercially viable in the 1800s, leading to the steam-powered production of plentiful quantities of inexpensive paper. The steam-powered printing press developed in the same period.

Lithography made a major impact from the 1820s and contributed to an increase in the quantity and range of maps produced, not least the development of thematic mapping. In lithographic transfers, the design for an engraved plate was transferred to a litho stone on which alterations could be made, for example, the redrawing of boundaries, without affecting the original plate.

Alterations might be made on the stones between different printings of the map. From the late 1850s, plates were being engraved which seem never to have been printed from directly – they were used solely as a source of lithographic transfers. A much finer line and neater lettering could easily be achieved, and lithography was less expensive than copperplate engraved maps.

Entrepreneurs experimented with a variety of production techniques. For example, in the United States, cerography, or wax-engraving, was developed in the 1830s, a technique used by Sidney Morse (1794–1871) in 1842 to produce his *Cerographic Atlas of the United States*. This was an inexpensive way to produce relatively detailed maps, not least because printer's type was employed for lettering; cost was important as publishers sought to expand their market.

Cerographic maps were to play a major role in 19th- and early 20th-century American cartography, distinguishing it from that of Europe, where such maps were regarded as inferior, both aesthetically and in terms of precision, to lithography.

Colour makes its mark

Colour printing came to play a more prominent role in mapping and was seen as both a commercial opportunity and a challenge. Multicolour printing from more than one plate had become possible with the advent of engraving, although it was never common. Colour became more important in the 19th century when it was used to enhance the aesthetic quality of maps. Map-colouring ceased to be a manual process and was transformed by the development of colour printing. The Edinburgh map publisher John Bartholomew and Son introduced what was termed "contour layer colouring" in a commercial series of maps that were put on show at the Paris Exhibition of 1878.

The use of colour enhanced the appeal of maps. It also increased the density and complexity of information that could be conveyed, and thus made the use of maps as an explanatory device easier. There was now more information in the average map that had to be assimilated, not least through a process of separating out the components, then integrating them in a comprehensible form. In this lay much of their interest. Furthermore, distribution maps – for example, of populations, rainfall, and disease – played an increasing role in scientific investigation and exposition, whether with the science of mankind or with biological and physical sciences.

Bartholomew, founded in Edinburgh in the 1820s, was one of the specialized map publishers established to exploit the commercial opportunities of maps in a professional way. Other specialized publishers included Justus Perthes (founded 1785) in Gotha, W and AK Johnston (founded 1826) in Edinburgh, and both the Arrowsmith family concern (c. 1770–1873) and George Philip and Son (founded 1834) in London. In America, a number of publishers sprang up, including EH Butler in Philadelphia and Colton in New York. Once established, they needed not only to produce maps, but also to define new markets to supply.

The triangulation begun by the Trigonometrical, later Ordnance Survey was virtually completed by 1824, after which work started on a six-inch map of Ireland comprising 1875 large sheets. Completed in 1846, this was designed to help improve the

◄◄ This *Physical and Political Map of Europe* was created by A Lorain, Geographer Attaché at the Dépot Général de la Guerre in Paris, in 1835.

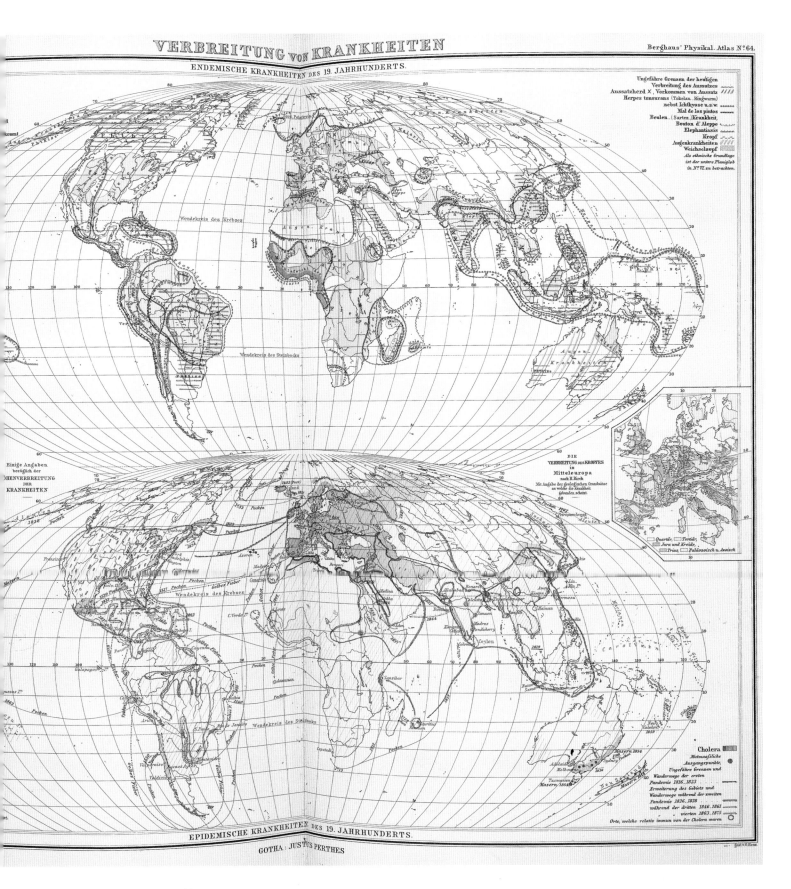

ENDEMISCHE KRANKHEITEN DES 19. JAHRHUNDERTS.

Berghaus' Physikal. Atlas No. 64.

DIE
VERBREITUNG DES KROPFES
in
Mitteleuropa
nach H. Birch

EPIDEMISCHE KRANKHEITEN DES 19. JAHRHUNDERTS.

GOTHA: JUSTUS PERTHES

⋏ A map showing the distribution of disease
around the world from Heinrich Berghaus's
Physikalischer Atlas (1886). It was originally published
in 1845–8 by the Gotha firm of Justus Perthes. The
growth of knowledge about distant areas aided the
production and distribution of maps which, in turn,
testified to the interest in thematic information.

information on which the land tax was assessed. The first 90 sheets of England and Wales at one inch to the mile, covering up to a line from Preston to Hull, were published between 1805 and 1844.

This so-called "Old Series" began with four sheets for Essex, published in 1805, although from 1811 to 1816 the War Office banned the sale of maps to the public. Thereafter, their sale helped to cover the costs of the survey. The one-inch map of Kent based on the Ordnance Survey was published privately by William Faden (1750–1836) in 1801, but was really another county map. Thereafter, the survey decided to publish its own maps, not stopping at county borders. A national numbered series began with Essex, while Kent was reissued in the new format in 1819.

The process of mapping took longer than had been anticipated because, in 1820, it was discovered by a naval survey ship that the Ordnance Survey had given an inaccurate direction for the island of Lundy. As a result of this and other errors, most of the 1820s and early 1830s were spent in resurveying. It was necessary to make new theodolite observations. Many of the problems with the original survey were due to the haste with which it had been carried out as a result of the method of paying surveyors by the square mile. This method of payment was changed from 1834.

The Battle of the Scales

Coverage of England and Wales by the Ordnance Survey was not completed until 1874, although sheets for all bar the Isle of Man had been published by the end of 1869. There was also mapping at other scales and, in what was known as the "Battle of the Scales", debate raged over what scale to use. Surveying on a scale of six-inches to the mile began in 1841, but a 25-inches (actually 25.54 inches) to the mile survey, authorized in 1854, became the standard, apart from in mountainous and waste areas where the six-inch scale was retained. In other areas, the maps at six-inches and one-inch to the mile were prepared by reduction from the 25-inch plans. In addition, large-scale town plans were prepared at a five-feet to the mile scale from 1843, altered to 10-feet to the mile in 1850 and to 1:500 (close to 10 feet) from 1855.

In 1863, it was decided that the entire country was to be mapped at six and 25 inches to the mile, with the towns at 1:500. This, or to be exact, 25.54 inches to the mile, represented a scale of 1:2500, which had been recommended as an international standard by an International Statistical Conference that met in Brussels in 1853. It had based its conclusion on surveys already carried out in Europe, especially France.

Larger scale mapping was particularly useful for property and tax purposes, as well as for planning economic expansion, above all the building of railways. Thus Ordnance Survey maps could serve as a basic information tool, either used directly or amended for other purposes. Surveys of Ireland and Scotland began in 1825

and 1837, respectively. Similarly, in France, military engineers played a major role in mapping.

The provision of public maps produced in a uniform fashion lessened the need for individual maps covering specific parts of the country. Thus the tradition of county mapping in England, which had continued into the 19th century, with maps such as John Cary's *New Map of Lancashire* (1806) and the county maps produced by the brothers Christopher and John Greenwood from 1817–34, gradually went into decline.

Within Britain, there was steadily more mapping, much of which was functional. The reorganization of farmland and common land through enclosure continued to require the production of maps. Population growth and wartime pressures on food supplies ensured much enclosure from 1793–1815, including nearly one-third of Bedfordshire, Cambridgeshire, and Huntingdonshire. Aside from specific acts, General Enclosure Acts were passed in 1801, 1836, and 1845.

⋏ This compass and theodolite by Troughton & Sons, c 1870, has a detachable arc and compass that can be replaced by sight vanes. Theodolites are the most useful of surveying instruments because they can measure the horizontal angle between two points and their angle of elevation at the same time. The basic theodolite comprised the following elements: a horizontal circle divided up into degrees; a compass; a vertical semicircular arc divided into degrees; and a telescope with a bubble level.

In addition, the 1836 Tithe Commutation Act led to the mapping and valuation of titheable land, with field-by-field tithe surveys that displayed field boundaries, roads, woods, and buildings. Although it had originally been proposed that the survey should be conducted in a uniform fashion across England and Wales, this was not acceptable to Parliament, and, as a result, the maps varied in detail, scale, and acceptability to the commission that oversaw the implementation of the plan.

The resulting variety stemmed from crucial factors when considering mapping projects: costs and objectives; in short, the "fit-for-purpose" nature of mapping and maps. Many parishes were unable or unwilling to meet the cost of the large-scale survey deemed appropriate by the commission and felt that their maps were acceptable. Indeed, only 1458 out of the 11,785 maps that were produced were rated as "first-class".

Individual public bodies also commissioned maps. For example, the British Library holds two pages from a dismembered manuscript atlas of detailed plans of English and Welsh ports drawn up in about 1810. The atlas formed one of a series that ran until the middle of the century. These maps were probably used as a means for controlling smuggling, a process that required detailed local knowledge. The surviving plan of Poole harbour shows the area for which the port authority was responsible, emphasizing the nature of the coastline and its defences, and the location of the Salt Office. The library also has a manuscript plan of Valetta, the port of Malta, to show naval property transactions in the 1830s as a record of naval ownership.

Empire-building

Imperial powers vigorously mapped the territories into which they expanded. This helped both during the initial conquest and in the maintenance of power. As a result, the military played a major role in mapping, although other agents of the imperial state were also expected to help.

In India, army officers played a leading role. William Lambton (1753–1823), for example, began the triangulation of India in 1800. This ensured a more accurate base for maps than those by James Rennell. Lambton became superintendent of the Great Trigonometric Survey of India, which was established in 1817. His successor, Captain George Everest (1790–1866), who became superintendent in 1823 and surveyor general in 1830, and after whom Mount Everest is named, employed a grid covering the entire subcontinent. Lambton had laid down the "Great Arc", the central north–south axis for the grid, which he surveyed along the 78th meridian. The survey was largely completed in 1890.

Based on the survey, the *Indian Atlas* of J and C Walker was commissioned by the East India Company in 1823. Produced at a scale of four miles to one inch, this topographic map series offered an impressive range of detail, although it was not finished until 1907. Whereas the Indian cartographic tradition focused on routes, the British concentrated on area and emphasized fixed scales in a way that the Indians did not. At a different scale, detailed revenue surveys from 1822 led to large-scale cadastral maps for most of India. The building of more than 20,000 miles of railway by the British was also accompanied by much mapping.

India was not the sole region actively mapped by the British. Elsewhere, new colonies were swiftly mapped by the British and other imperial powers. John Barrow (1764–1848), private secretary to Lord Macartney (1737–1806), governor of Cape Colony – which the British had conquered from the Dutch in 1795 – was instructed by the governor to gather topographic knowledge so that he could draw up a map, which he did in 1801. In Australia, once a way had been found across the Blue Mountains in 1813, Governor Lachlan Macquarie (1762–1824) commissioned the surveying and building of a road to the Bathurst Plains to the west of Sydney.

An active process of land grants helped encourage expansion, and the government sought to control this by organizing surveys, under John Oxley and Thomas Mitchell (*active* 1820s and '30s). These served as the basis for an expansion of government structures; 19 counties were declared in New South Wales in 1826.

Maori opposition

Because mapping was associated with imperial control, it was often unwelcome. In New Zealand, the Maoris often resisted cadastral surveying, and violent clashes occurred in 1843, 1863, and the 1870s. A triangulation survey of the country began in 1875, again with Maori opposition.

In Canada, problems in defining the frontier with the United States were accentuated by a lack of accurate maps. The Treaty of Paris of 1783 had stipulated a line due west from the Lake of the Woods to the Mississippi, but the latter is in fact south of the lake. The eventual boundary chosen in 1818 was from "the north-western point of the Lake of the Woods, along the forty-ninth parallel of latitude". It was not, however, known whether the northwestern point of the lake was on the parallel. As a result, with the example of past disputes before them, the negotiators agreed that, if not, a line should be drawn north or south to intersect with the parallel. This led to the Northwest Angle, an isolated spur of American territory.

Once agreed, the frontier had to be surveyed. However, the frontier had not been agreed west of the Rockies. Joint occupancy was the solution until the Oregon Boundary Treaty of 1846, but residual tension was memorably expressed in geographical terms. James Polk (1795–1849) campaigned for the presidency in 1844 on the platform "54° 40' or fight", but, in the event, he was willing to settle without the inclusion of British Columbia and Vancouver Island. Manifest Destiny could only provide so much.

Maps played a crucial role in determining the Maine–Canada border. Competing claims were recorded by maps, which helped to clarify both the differences and the eventual reconciliation reached in the Webster-Ashburton agreement of 1842.

Within Canada, the Admiralty and the Hudson's Bay Company played the major role in filling in the map, as they searched for the Northwest Passage. They also sought information that would be of economic value, especially the attempt to discover links between the Mackenzie Valley and the Pacific watershed, finally achieved in 1851.

Exploration was encouraged by John Barrow, now the leading civil servant in the Admiralty. In 1817, he published a map to illustrate his theory of an open sea between the Davis and Bering straits, an indicator of the extent to which cartography did not necessarily improve in accuracy with time. Earlier maps had shown the northern end of Baffin Bay as closed, but Barrow preferred to doubt Baffin's maps, not least because he thought icebergs were driven south in Davis Strait by an ocean current. A series of expeditions, begun in 1818, brought new information that was rapidly incorporated into maps. The disappearance of the ice-trapped Arctic expedition in 1847 led by Sir John Franklin (1786–1847) spurred a hunt for survivors during which a vast amount of geographical information was gathered. There were, in fact, no survivors, and only some skeletons were found in 1856 of those who had died while trekking overland from the stricken ships.

Elsewhere in Canada, the Hudson's Bay Company had been responsible for the mapping of the interior of Labrador from the 1810s to the 1830s. In the late 1850s, there was a new surge in the mapping of the Canadian Plains and southern Rockies, undertaken by the Canadian expedition of 1857–8 and its British counterpart of 1857–60.

To the heart of Africa

Another formidable task, the mapping of the interior of Africa, was begun by explorers. Their exploits enthralled newspaper readers and the public in general, who demanded maps in order to follow the explorers' routes. Thus, in 1857, John Arrowsmith (1790–1873) published a *Map of South Africa showing the Routes of the Reverend Dr Livingstone between the years 1849 and 1856*. Livingstone's route was coloured red, while rivers and outlines of lakes delineated with dotted lines were, as a note on the map stated, "from Oral information generally".

Not all areas, however, were opened to imperial cartography. The Chinese rulers of Tibet closed the country to foreigners in 1792, and, although Europeans reached Lhasa in 1811 and 1846, it remained largely unknown until 1865, when the British sent the first of a series of Indians – trained as surveyors, but disguised as pilgrims or traders – to the region. They were provided with concealed instruments, as well as strings of prayer beads containing eight fewer than the usual 108 beads in order to help establish distances. The first of these pundits reached Lhasa in 1866, and their information led to the mapping of the major routes, although not of surrounding regions.

Maps helped imperial powers perceive local interests and threats. Thus, the British followed Russian advances in Central Asia

on maps and saw them as a threat to the "Northwest Frontier" of British India – although, in doing so, they unduly minimized the problems the Russians faced with the terrain and the native population. In December 1838, the Duke of Wellington wrote to the London bookseller John Hatchard (1769–1849), requesting a copy of "Arrowsmith's map of Central Asia".

From sea to shining sea

The British empire was the biggest, but the most lasting was that created by the United States where mapping was linked to exploration, classification, and the creation of new communication routes, giving a shape to the territories over which America had acquired sovereignty. Exploration and mapping enjoyed considerable government backing. In 1803, Thomas Jefferson (1743–1826) persuaded Congress to finance an expedition up the Missouri River. This was entrusted to Meriwether Lewis (1774–1809), Jefferson's private secretary and an army captain, and to his former commanding officer, William Clark (1770–1838). Their Corps of Discovery reached the Pacific in November 1805, before returning to St Louis in September 1806 with a great deal of information, including route maps.

This expedition whetted American interest in expanding to the Pacific. In 1806, the self-serving General James Wilkinson (1757–1825), governor of the Louisiana Territory, sent Lieutenant Zebulon Pike (1779–1813) from St Louis to find the source of the Red River, which was seen as the southern boundary of the territory. Pike was given secret orders to chart the route to Santa Fé, which Wilkinson hoped to seize from the Spaniards for his own ends. Pike reached the Rockies, but was captured by the Spaniards, although that gave him an opportunity to report on New Spain and Texas when he returned. In 1819, an expedition under Major Stephen Long (1784–1864) that crossed the Great Plains to the Rockies included two topographers.

The institutional framework and cohesion for this purposeful exploration was provided by the army's Corps of Topographical Engineers, which was created in 1838 when the Topographical Bureau expanded and organized as a fully-fledged staff corps under the control of the army. This corps, which was supplemented by the Coast Survey, played a major role in the exploration and mapping of the West, and also provided maps for the Mexican-American War of 1846–8. Military surveyors used native maps and geographical information, but only to the extent that they were concerned with locating, understanding, and utilizing the lands they surveyed in the context of an expanding state.

Army engineers also played a major role in the exploration and mapping of routes for a transcontinental railway and for other railway routes, such as the survey in 1853 by Lieutenant Amiel Whipple (1817–1863) of a possible southern route from Fort Smith through Arizona into southern California. The Pacific Railroad Survey Act of 1853 ensured political and financial backing, and the pace was quickened by competition between the

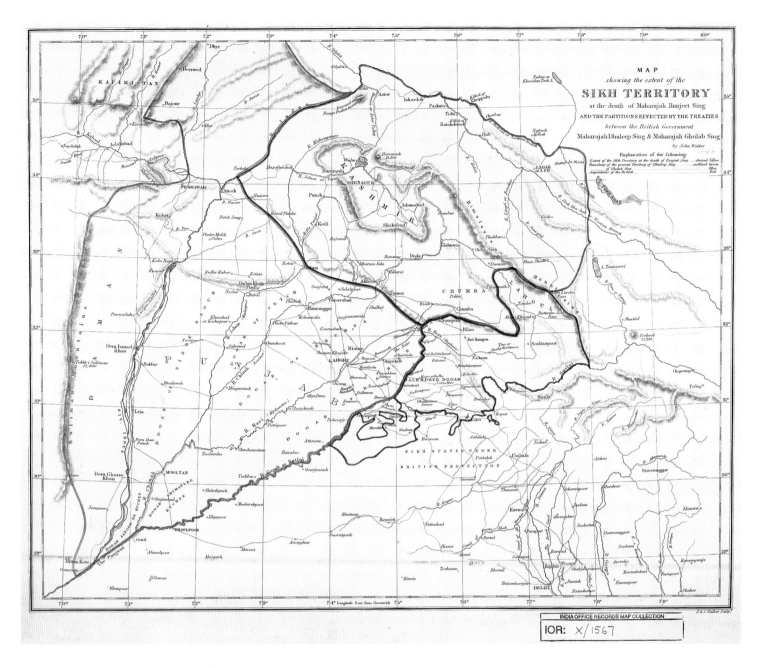

At the top-right of the map:

MAP
showing the extent of the
SIKH TERRITORY
at the death of Maharajah Runjeet Sing
AND THE PARTITIONS EFFECTED BY THE TREATIES
between the British Government
Maharajah Dhuleep Sing & Maharajah Gholab Sing
by John Walker

Explanation of the Colouring:

INDIA OFFICE RECORDS MAP COLLECTION
IOR: X/1567

⌃ The extent of Sikh territories at the death of their leader Ranjit Singh in 1839 and of the subsequent territorial divisions down to the end of the first Anglo-Sikh War (1845–6) is shown in this map by John Walker (1787–1873). Walker was also responsible for the *Atlas of India*, (1825–68). The two Anglo-Sikh wars greatly increased British cartographic knowledge of the Punjab.

sponsors of particular routes. The resulting surveys were published as Senate executive documents.

There were casualties in the struggle for information. Captain William H Warner, a US Topographical Engineer was killed by Pit River Natives in northeastern California in 1849. Lieutenant John Gunnison (*b.* 1812), who set off in June 1853 from Fort Leavenworth to find a route between the 38th and 39th parallels, was killed with seven of his men by Ute at Sevier Lake.

Force was also a powerful factor in the mapping of America. In 1849, James Simpson's (1818–1883) exploration of what was to be northwestern New Mexico and northeastern Arizona was undertaken as part of John Washington's punitive expedition against the Navajo. Simpson was able to explore the Canyon de Chelly only after Washington had defeated them. Simpson also advised on the route for a railway line from Texas to the Colorado River and then California.

In 1851, Captain Lorenzo Sitgreaves followed Simpson. He, too, was a member of an expedition to control the Navajo which sought information about the region, not least to open up a possible rail route. The expedition had several skirmishes, especially with Mohave and Yuma in the Colorado Valley. Although it failed to find an acceptable rail route, the expedition did add greatly to information about Arizona.

Military purposes encouraged further exploration in the region in 1858–9. Concern about the possibility of war with the Mormons in Utah led to efforts to find first a river route to the Great Basin via the Colorado River, then to explore the route from Santa Fé. In the first attempt, the prefabricated paddle steamer USS *Explorer* soon fell victim to the Colorado's rocky bed, but Lieutenant Joseph Ives (1829–1868) led the expedition up the Colorado and, via the Grand Canyon, to the Painted Desert, and thence to Fort Defiance.

From 1867, Clarence King (1842–1901), head of the Geological Exploration of the 40th Parallel, was responsible for surveys of the Rockies and the lands to the east that included the drawing of detailed maps, while Lieutenant George Wheeler (1842–1905) of the United States Geographical Surveys West of the 100th Meridian surveyed and mapped the southwest of the United States beyond that meridian from the same year.

In 1872, the Escalante, the last river of any size unknown to European Americans in what became the 48 states, was discovered in southern Utah, as were the Henry Mountains, the last unknown mountain range. There was still, however, much to survey and map. From 1869, Ferdinand Hayden (1829–1887), the survey director of the Interior Department's United States Geological Survey of the Territories, had surveyed much of the Rockies. As a result of his survey in 1871, he produced a map of the Yellowstone region that helped to persuade Congress to allocate more of it than they might otherwise have done as the country's first national park. In 1873–6, Hayden was responsible for a thorough survey of Colorado which eventually was pushed forward by eight parties working simultaneously.

Boundaries imposed on natives

Having bought Alaska from Russia in 1867, the Americans acquired a vast new territory to explore and map: the Russians had mapped only part of the interior, although in 1865–7 the Western Union Telegraph Survey had reconnoitred a telegraph route across Alaska. The Army, Navy, Coast Survey, and Revenue Marine competed in exploration, but it was in the 1890s that the Geological Survey was responsible for the mapping of much of the interior.

The role of army engineers was not restricted to the West. A Supreme Court decision that placed interstate commerce under the federal government led, in 1824, to the General Survey Act and to the assignment of the surveying of routes for canals and roads to the Corps of Engineers.

It is only recently that attempts have been made to map the United States – and, indeed, other areas that saw imperialist expansion – in terms other than those of this expansion. Thus, in 1981, Jack Forbes produced a striking *Atlas of Native History* (Davis, 1981), in which he employed the "names used by the native people themselves" and sought to "present real political conditions", ignoring "the claims of white governmental units" which, Forbes argued, had come to compose a "mythological map".

For Forbes's 1845 and 1861 maps, no "white" frontiers were shown west of the line of white settlement; instead, forts and isolated areas of settlement were depicted. Whereas the *New American Atlas* (Philadelphia, 1823) of Henry Tanner (1786–1858) took the Alabama–Georgia state line through the native territory between the two states, in Forbes's map *The United States Area as it really was in 1820*, there was no such line. Most of Florida was shown under native, not American, control. A similar effort still

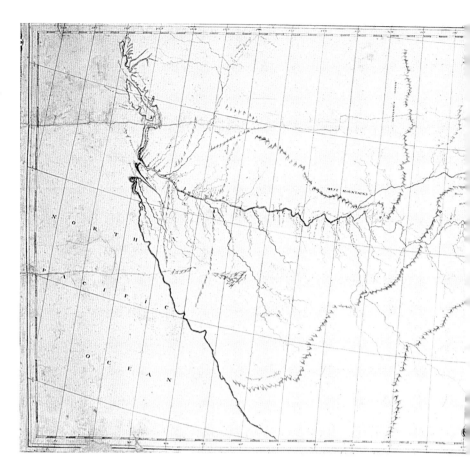

needs to be made to map Africa, not in terms of the European claims and agreements – such as that reached at the Congress of Berlin (1884–5) – which formed the basis of contemporary maps, but with reference to the situation on the ground now.

The use of maps to provide information that would help the exploitation of territory was not restricted to communication routes. A similar process was also involved in geological surveys, another aspect of the accumulation and depiction of knowledge in which mapping played a central role.

Accompanied by cross sections, these surveys offered a three-dimensional mapping that appeared to make sense of the surface of the Earth and enable it to be exploited for human purposes. Thus, John Wesley Powell (1834–1902), the influential director of the American Geological Survey until 1894, saw geological mapping as fundamental to scientific exploitation: the West was to be classified as mineral, coal, pasturage, timber, and irrigable lands, although he warned about the dangers of misusing arid regions. The survey had already mapped much of the West.

In New Zealand, geological surveys in 1859 were followed in 1864 by the search for coal and gold. In Canada, the Geological Survey founded in 1842 was particularly active in mapping from 1866, not only the land's geology, but also other aspects of its geography.

More generally, imperial powers enforced their own cartographic ideas on the peoples and regions that they had conquered. They were prone to draw straight lines on maps with

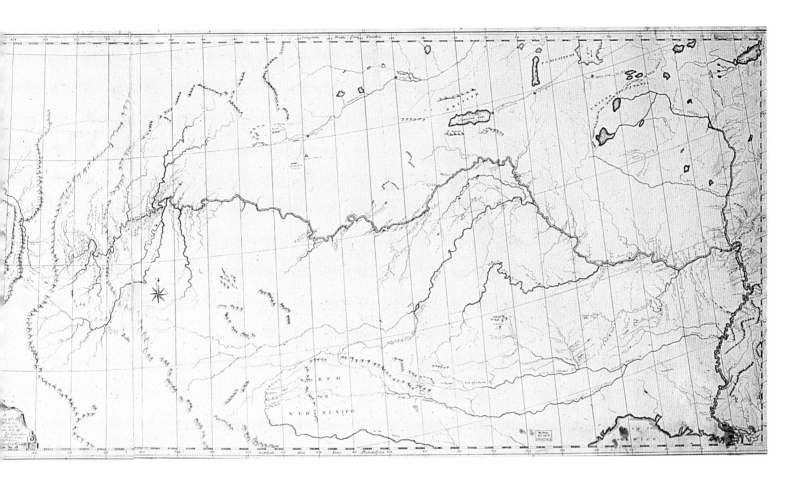

no regard for ethnic, linguistic, religious, economic, and political alignments and practices, let alone drainage patterns, landforms, and biological provinces. Even when there was interest in such issues, such as with the *Linguistic Survey of India* by Sir George Grierson's (1851–1941), the use of linear boundaries violated the more complex, zonal nature of differences between cultures.

In addition, military surveyors played an important role in mapping areas in which European forces campaigned. They also helped the process of European colonialization and drew attention to mineral deposits and possible trade routes. The maps that were produced for European governments and purchasers ignored or underrated native peoples and states, presenting Africa and other areas, such as Oceania, as open to appropriation.

This mapping helped to legitimize imperial expansion by making the world appear empty, or at least uncivilized, unless under European control. States, regions, natural features, and cities outside Europe were identified by European, not native, names. European atlases used the Mercator projection, rather than an equal-area projection, such as the one devised by the Scottish cleric James Gall in 1855. The Mercator projection exaggerated land masses in high latitudes, such as Canada and the British Isles, and minimized the Tropics.

Nineteenth-century imperialism is commonly seen as a solely European process, but this is misleading. The use of cartography as part of a process of power projection and imperial presentation and consolidation was not the sole preserve of European and American expansionists. For example, in Latin America, the independent states clashed with each other and also sought to extend their power within the areas to which they laid claim. In Argentina, this entailed the conquest of native tribes and the settlement of Patagonia, a southward expansion matched in Chile. The role of mapping in these and similar developments has not been adequately studied.

Plumbing the depths

In addition to mapping conquered territory, the imperial powers charted the oceans. This was especially true of Britain. Britain, indeed, had the greatest need of charts, not only because of the global commitments of British naval power, but also because of the limited range of earlier charts. In 1805, HMS *Victory*, Nelson's flagship, had to rely on a French chart that was 40 years old in order to navigate in the western Mediterranean.

Three years later, the Charting Committee of naval officers was appointed by the Admiralty to advise on how best to overcome the problem. The committee recommended the purchase of charts from commercial map publishers; the buying back of the copyright of charts made by naval officers and produced by the commercial sector (a process symptomatic of the close relationship between the state and commerce in British map publishing); and the provision of a set of charts for each naval station as rapidly as possible. There was also an effort to obtain information on the coastline from the Ordnance Survey. An atlas

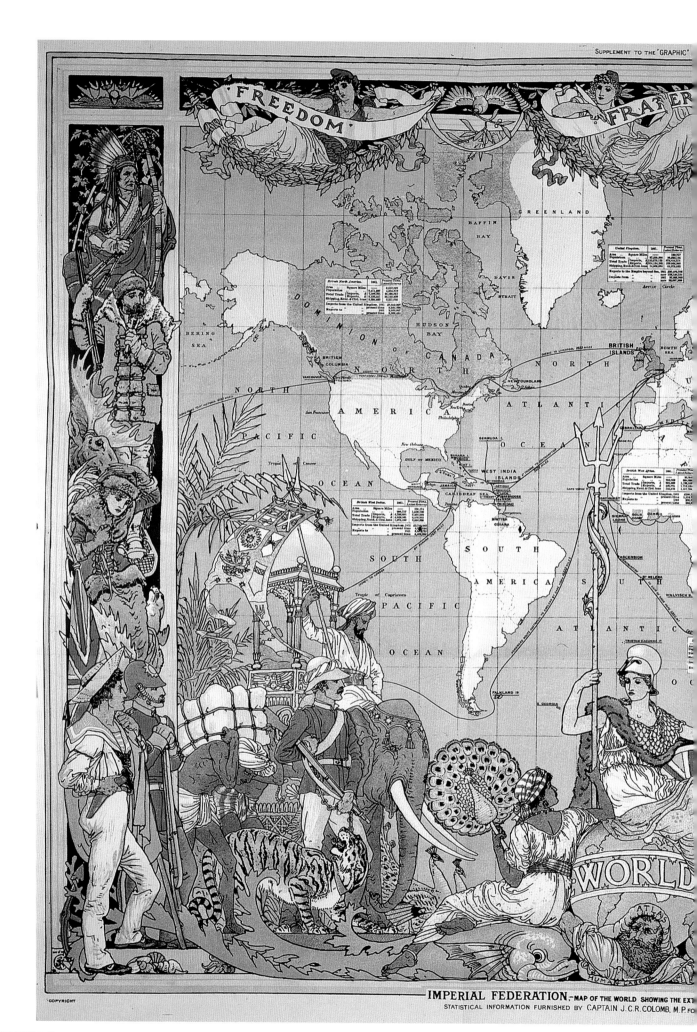

FREEDOM · FRATER

IMPERIAL FEDERATION.—MAP OF THE WORLD SHOWING THE EXT
STATISTICAL INFORMATION FURNISHED BY CAPTAIN J.C.R. COLOMB, M.P. FO

FEDERATION

MAP OF THE WORLD.
SHOWING THE EXTENT OF THE BRITISH TERRITORIES IN 1786.

E BRITISH EMPIRE IN 1886.
R.M.A. — BRITISH TERRITORIES COLOURED RED

MACLURE & Cº QUEEN VICTORIA STREET, LONDON

◁ Colour conventions also developed in mapping. The use of pink or red to denote the British empire began in the first half of the 19th century. Henry Teesdale's *New British Atlas* (1831), in its map of India, was one of the first recorded examples of the use of red to show British possessions. The 1841 edition of this atlas was the first to use the red convention for all British colonies. The colour red was probably chosen for its striking effect. It did not come into general usage until after 1850, with the development of colour printing, and was popularized by school wall maps and atlases. Foreign maps, however, continued to use other colours to depict the British empire.

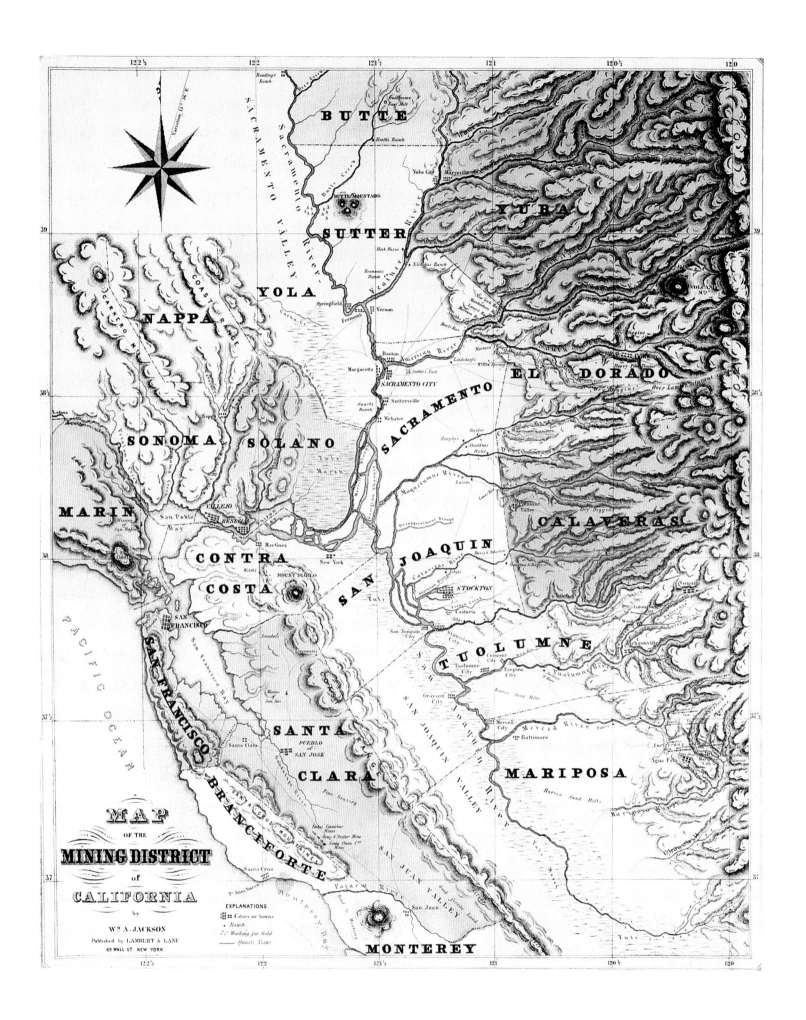

MAP
OF THE
MINING DISTRICT
OF
CALIFORNIA
by
Wᴹ A. JACKSON
Published by LAMBERT & LANE
69 WALL ST NEW YORK

EXPLANATIONS
⊞ Cities or Towns
• Ranch
⸪ Working for Gold
— Quartz Veins

of *Charts of the English Channel*, containing 31 charts for naval use, appeared in 1811.

The British charted coastal waters across the world. From 1821, the extensive range of charts produced by the Admiralty was offered publicly for sale, a policy designed to produce funds for more surveying, and, indeed, catalogues were published from 1825. Much of this was far-flung and not off coasts controlled by Britain. For example, a coastal survey of 1822–4 brought back much information about East Africa.

The Role of the Royal Navy

The careers of individual naval officers responsible for such surveys of coastlines and nearby waters reflected the range of British activity. Sir Francis Beaufort (1774–1857), whose father, the Reverend Daniel Beaufort (1739–1821) had published a map of Ireland in 1792, entered the navy in 1787, receiving 19 wounds in 1800 when he cut out a Spanish warship from under the guns of Fangerolle Castle. In 1807, he surveyed the entrance to the Plate estuary, a valuable aid to the warships in preparing for what was to be an unsuccessful attack on Buenos Aires.

In 1810–12, as a frigate captain, Beaufort was active in Turkish waters, seeking to suppress pirates and to survey the coast, only to be badly wounded in a clash. Beaufort subsequently produced charts based on his survey. In 1829, he became Hydrographer to the Navy, a post he held until 1855. Soon after his appointment, Beaufort plotted on a map of the world the coasts covered by surveys. Concerned by the large distances not tackled, he pressed on to fill the gaps. The results were shown in individual careers.

Edward Belcher (1799–1877) surveyed the coast of West Africa in the early 1830s, an area of growing concern as the British sought to suppress the slave trade. Later in the decade, he surveyed the west coast of South America, an aspect of what has been seen as the British "informal empire" in Latin America. As commander of the *Samarang* in 1842–7, Belcher surveyed the coasts of Borneo, the Philippines, and Taiwan.

Belcher's predecessor as commander of the *Sulphur*, Frederick Beechey (1796–1856), had surveyed the north coast of Africa, as well as the Pacific coast of South America. Both Beechey and Belcher published narratives of their surveying expeditions. In 1837–43, HMS *Beagle* surveyed Australian coastal waters, and in 1848 HMS *Acheron* began the first systematic survey of New Zealand waters, being succeeded in 1851–5 by HMS *Pandora*, which produced detailed harbour charts. The two ships covered nearly all the coast and sent 250 charts to the Hydrographic Office.

Some of these charts were used in war. The collection of the Royal United Services Institution (of London) includes a *Chart of the island of Chusan enlarged from a chart by Alexander Dalrymple* [Hydrographer of the Navy 1795–1808], *and corrected in many places by observations made during an expedition under Captain Sir H Le Fleming Senhouse on HMS* Blenheim *between 30th August and 4th September 1840.* It was used in Britain's First Opium War with

China, which led to the charting of the seas round Hong Kong in 1841 by HMS *Sulphur*, under the command of Belcher.

Beaufort also pressed forward the re-charting of the coasts and inshore waters of the British Isles, being responsible for what was to be known as the Grand Survey of the British Isles. This involved a critical examination of existing surveys, then the filling of any gaps, a process that also threw up errors in the Ordnance Survey, making revisions in those maps necessary also. This re-charting was completed in 1863 when the survey of the Isles of Scilly was finished.

Lakes were also mapped. In the United States Lieutenant Henry Wolsey Bayfield (1795–1845) carried out hydrographic surveys of Lake Huron between 1816 and 1825. Beechey's friend, Captain George Back (1795–1878), named a lake after him on his attempt in 1833–4 to find the missing John Ross expedition and to continue the survey of the Arctic. Back's information was incorporated into the map of the region published by Arrowsmith in 1835. Their successive maps of 1821, 1832, 1835, 1837, and 1852 reflected the rapid increase of knowledge. Back's companion, Richard King, recorded their method in 1834:

> "The survey of the river [Thlew-ee-choch or Back's River] was made by taking the bearings of every point with a pocket compass, the distances estimated by the time occupied in reaching them and a connected eye-sketch made of the whole. This mode of dead-reckoning is extremely simple and, when corrected by celestial observations, is sufficiently accurate for geographical purposes."

Into deeper waters

Later in the century, the laying of submarine telegraph cables encouraged the mapping of deep waters, as well as of shallower bodies of water, such as the Persian Gulf, where cables were laid. In 1848, a chart of the gulf was prepared, but the Anglo-Persian War of 1856–7 and the Indian Mutiny of 1857–9 led to a quest for more information, and, in 1857, a fresh survey was set in place. A general chart of the gulf completed in two sheets in 1860 comprised a new map of the islands and principal points round the gulf, including details of some of the coastline. The rest of the coastline was derived from old maps.

The chart, published by the Admiralty in 1864, was useful to the cable-layers, although new surveys were necessary before the cable could be submerged. The seabed was surveyed in 1862–3, but this was not the total of imperial mapping in the region. In 1863, Lieutenant Colonel Lewis Pelly (1825–1892), the acting resident in the gulf, travelled by land around the northern end of the Persian Gulf and produced a report for the British authorities in Bombay that was supported by a map indicating the boundaries of the territories, whether independent or not, around the gulf.

The charts available also served as crucial tools for explorers, enabling them to help locate their travels and thus to contribute

◁ William A Jackson made this *Map of the Mining District of California* in 1851. It shows the counties of California around the San Francisco Bay during the Gold Rush, which had started in 1849. Towns and gold camps are both shown.

to the incremental quality of mapping. The Newberry Library in Chicago has a copy of the Hydrographic Office's *Chart of the South Polar Sea* (1841) that was used by John Davis to chart the expedition of Sir James Clark Ross (1800–1862) to Antarctic waters in 1841. Davis annotated the chart with the course and daily locations of the two ships on the expedition and added, as an insert on the chart, a manuscript map of part of the Ross Sea coast that the expedition discovered.

Sharing the spoils

The British were not the sole charters of waters. In 1802–3, Nicolas-Thomas Baudin (1754–1803), the commander of a French scientific expedition, explored much of the Australian coast, and the French explorer Dumont d'Urville (1790–1842) explored waters off the North Island of New Zealand in 1827.

The Russians, too, were active. They explored the coast of Alaska and made unsuccessful attempts to discover a Northwest Passage from the west in 1815–18 and 1820–1. Knowledge of the Arctic Ocean north of Siberia was expanded in 1820–4 by Baron Ferdinand von Wrangel (1796–1870). Further west, the New Siberian Islands had been "discovered" by the hunters Ivan Lyakhov and Ivan Sannikov between 1770 and 1806.

As so often with exploration, however, the subsequent systematic exploration and mapping was of equal importance, as it fitted these discoveries into the matrices of European knowledge. Matvey Gedenshtrom did just this for the New

Siberian Islands in 1809–10, and the survey was completed by P Pshenitsin in 1811. In 1820–4, Pyotr Anzhu, a naval officer, expanded and improved their surveys – part of the process by which knowledge was upgraded and verified.

The Americans played a role, particularly in New World and Pacific waters. In 1838, Lieutenant Charles Wilkes (1798–1877) was placed in charge of the Depot of Charts and Instruments, and given command of a six-ship expedition to explore the Pacific. This led to the first human sightings of the Antarctic continent.

Wilkes also explored the Pacific coastline of North America as a means of asserting American interests. In 1854–5, an American naval expedition, the North Pacific Surveying Expedition, greatly expanded hydrographic knowledge of Japanese waters. In 1855, the *Water Witch*, a lightly armed American naval steamer which had ascended the Paraná river on a mapping expedition, was fired on by Paraguayan forces leading, in 1858, to the dispatch of an American squadron which produced an apology, an indemnity, and permission for the mapping expedition to proceed.

Cartography and nationalism

Maps served the cause of developing states in a number of ways. They helped to familiarize people with the shape of countries and how boundaries might change with conquest and acquisition. Thus, maps of France produced after the Franco-Prussian War of 1870–1, marked in black the lands ceded to Prussia. The map of Maine in the

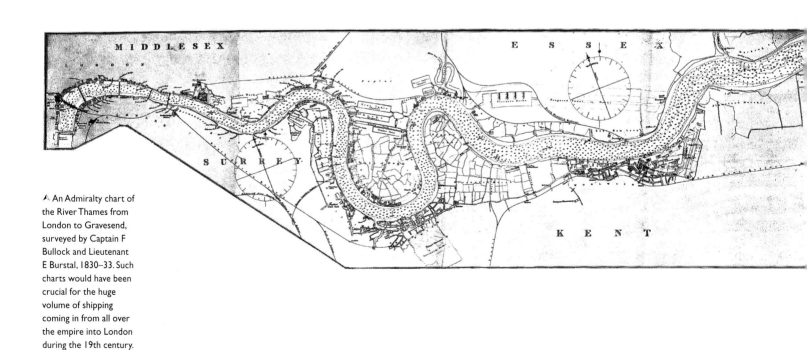

⚲ An Admiralty chart of the River Thames from London to Gravesend, surveyed by Captain F Bullock and Lieutenant E Burstal, 1830–33. Such charts would have been crucial for the huge volume of shipping coming in from all over the empire into London during the 19th century.

Cerographic Atlas of the United States (1842) depicted the American interpretation of the contested frontier with Canada.

Politics affected mapping as countries such as Poland that lacked independence, asserted their cartographic identity. In Bulgaria, under Ottoman control from the close of the 14th century until 1878, the first map with a Bulgarian text – *Karta na segashnaya Bolgariya, Trakiya, Makedoniya i na prilezhashtite zemi* (*A Map of Present Day Bulgaria, Thrace, Macedonia and the Enclosing Lands*) by Alexander Hadzirousset – was not published until 1843. The first Bulgarian atlas was printed in Vienna in 1865. The publication of an atlas of Finland by the Finnish Geographical Society in 1899 marked a declaration of hostility towards Russian rule.

The 19th century was not only an age of nationalism but one which also saw the development of national education systems. The establishment of mass schooling organized on a national basis led to a major demand for educational material and, in particular, works of reference. Furthermore, the growth of geography at university level and in the public consciousness expanded the demand for atlases and maps.

Publishers responded and produced material affordable to every pocket. This was related to a general increase in book-reading and the growth of a literary culture that helped to shape the readership for maps in general. Readers were greedy for information, and their hunger was served by both maps and globes. Used in particular to teach geography, the production of globes also expanded.

Tour de France

Literary nationalism, books celebrating and uniting all that was known about one's homeland, found a ready readership, and publishers were keen to feed the demand. In France, the old 16th-century idea of a *Tour de France* by rulers, workers, and others, which served to unite national territory – and, significantly, Paris with southern France – in the public imagination, was a constant theme in publications. These included didactic works for children. Constant Taillard's *Les Jeunes Voyageurs* (Paris, 1821) offered "Letters on France, presenting a general map of France, particular maps of the departments, agricultural products, curious natural phenomena, the names of famous men, etc". Other works in similar vein followed, including Amable *Tastu's Voyage en France* (Paris, 1846); G Bruno's *Le Tour de la France par deux enfants* (Paris, 1877); Constant Améro's *Le Tour de France d'un petit parisien* (Paris, 1885); and Gaston Bonnefont's *Le Voyage en zigzags de deux jeunes français en France* (Paris, 1889). The France thus depicted was the best country, complete unto itself, centred on Paris.

Governments, and individuals eager to press home calls for action, were also eager for information. There was a great interest in statistics and the mapping of the resulting information. Thus, the *Statistical Atlas of the United States Based on the Results of the Ninth Census* (New York, 1874) was followed by a work produced by two members of the staff of the Tenth Census, *Scribner's Statistical Atlas of the United States, Showing by Graphic Methods their Present Condition and their Political, Social, and Industrial*

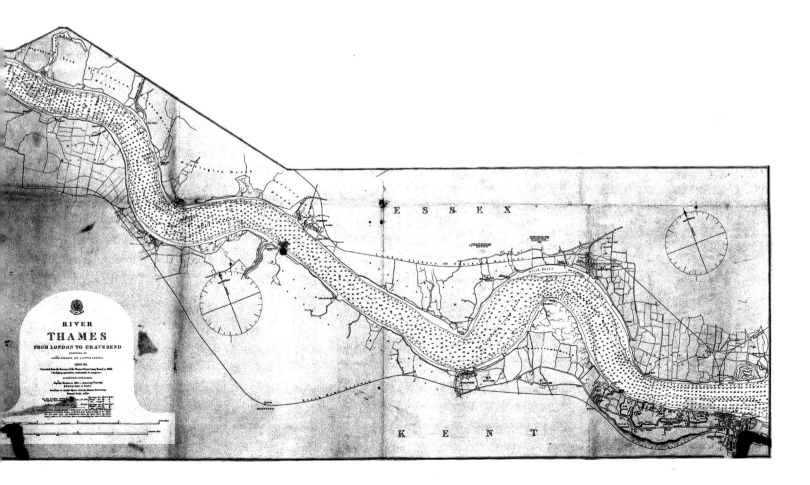

Picking the prime meridian

A View of the Observatory in Greenwich Park, belonging to the Kings Professor of Astronomy

Unlike lines of latitude, which were always standardized from the equator, fixed midway between the poles, the prime meridian, the starting point for measuring longitude, could be anywhere of a mapmaker's choosing. Even though John Harrison's chronometer solved the problem of calculating longitude at sea in the mid-18th century, it took more than another 100 years before a single prime meridian was accepted as the international standard.

Until the establishment of the Greenwich meridian – the British prime meridian – as the international prime meridian, the different maritime countries had their own meridians. For the Dutch, it passed through Amsterdam, for the Spaniards, Tenerife, for the Portuguese, Cape St Vincent, and so on. Several American cartographers constructed their maps with zero longitude passing through Washington or other American cities, and the notion of an American meridian was seen as a crucial aspect of national self-definition.

In 1850, Congress decreed that the Naval Observatory in Washington should be the official prime meridian for the United States, an act not repealed until 1912. The French did not abandon the Paris meridian until 1911. In 1880, at least 14 different prime meridians were still regularly in use. However, an international conference of 1884 chose the British line, the Greenwich meridian, as the zero meridian for time-keeping and for the determination of longitude. This was an aspect of the systematization of knowledge and the globalization of regulations in a period that saw international trade grow to hitherto unprecedented heights.

The choice of the British prime meridian as the international standard reflected the fact that Britain had the world's largest and most far-flung empire and was the world's most important trader. The choice affected mapping by clarifying the standard. It was a critical step in the development of international rather than simply national standards.

The choice of meridians was linked to the development of national standard times. For example, New Zealand Mean Time, introduced in 1868, was based on the meridian of 172° 30' E, with the meridian being Greenwich. This time was transmitted round the colony daily by telegraph from the government observatory in Wellington. Thus the establishment of Greenwich as the prime meridian allowed people around the world to share standardized timekeeping as well as a standardized mapmaking system.

⋏ This unattributed engraving of *c.* 1750 shows Greenwich Royal Observatory "belonging to the King's Professor of Astronomy" where the international meridian was finally settled. Founded in 1675, it was a centre for the study of astronomy and navigation, subjects closely connected with mapmaking.

➤ A map of Oxfordshire using Greenwich as the prime meridian (see top right hand corner). Engraved by Thomas Jeffrys in 1768, the map is decorated with the arms of Oxford University and the city.

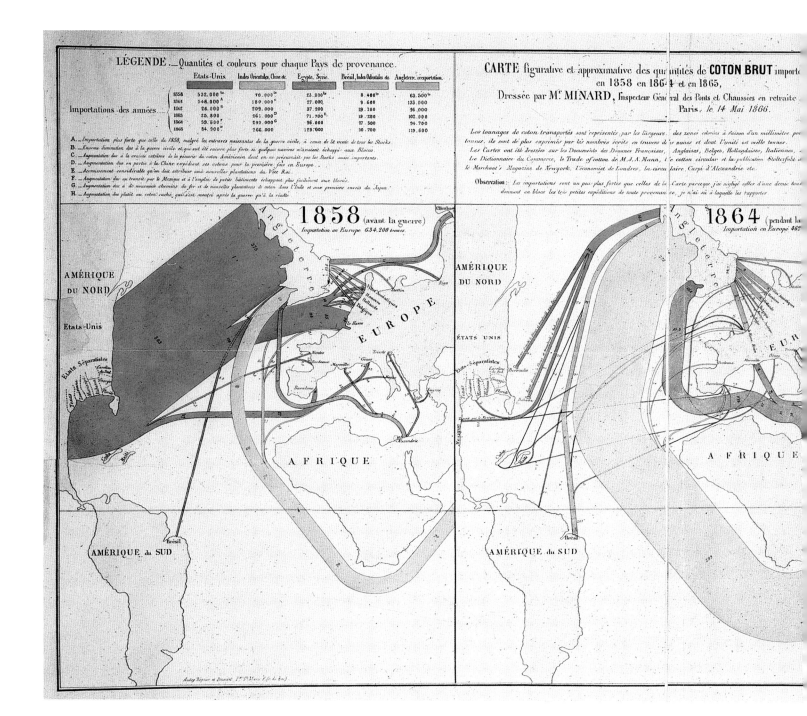

Development (New York, 1883). Statistical series collected by governments, such as censuses, were designed to be complete and were based on the systematic collection of information.

Such mapping was linked to government planning and to discussion over public policy. Much of the initiative was still taken by individuals, most famously with physician John Snow (1813–58) whose map of deaths from cholera was published in his *On the Mode of Communication of Cholera* (1855). Snow was convinced that the distribution of water was linked to the incidence of the disease, and his research led to the closure of the public water pump in London's Broad Street, after which the number of new cases of cholera fell.

In 1889, Charles Booth (1840–1916) produced his *Descriptive Map of London Poverty*, while Henry Mayhew (1812–87) mapped

London crime. Both highlighted menace. Booth showed the "Lowest class. Vicious, semi-criminal" often living close to the wealthy. Booth, a leading Victorian social reformer, highlighted the prevalence of poverty in his *Life and Labour of the People of London* (1889–1903). His maps classified and coloured streets in terms of the general condition of the inhabitants, who were in turn categorized in seven bands from lowest grade to wealthy.

A very different form of cartographic argument was offered in 1884 when the American map publisher Rand McNally produced a map for the Democratic Party showing the wide tranches of the United States that had been given to railway corporations, with a pointed accompanying text including the statement: "We believe that the public lands ought ... to be kept as homesteads for actual settlement".

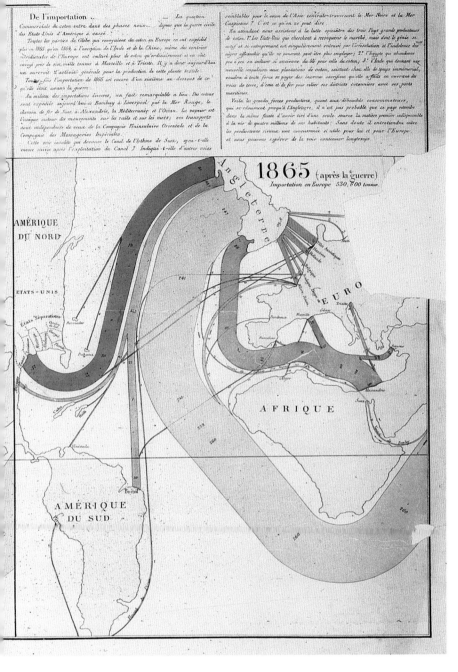

improvements, there were major extensions of road networks, and they served a growing number of users. This was true both of countries such as Britain and France that already had widespread road networks in 1800 and of those where networks were largely created after that date, as in most of the United States.

In Britain, alongside extensive new road-building, there was a marked increase in the construction of bridges which made road transport quicker. Furthermore, the major growth in coach services from the late 18th century, prior to the advent of the railways, meant that travellers demanded more detailed road maps, some of which showed coaching routes. Distances were more accurate as the result of the publication in 1798 of *New Itinerary* by John Cary (1754–1835), which was based on a perambulation of more than 9000 miles of road.

Aside from maps for travellers, there were also maps linked to road construction. These served legal as well as engineering and entrepreneurial goals. From 1773, any two justices of the peace could require a map to be produced for any projected diversion or closure of a highway. In the event of there being no objection, the order and the map that went with it were confirmed by the quarter sessions.

The production of such maps became more common in the early 19th century and was part of the processes of evaluation and authentication. Precision was sought in the maps, and, in 1807, the minimum scale was increased to four inches to the mile. Eventually, Ordnance Survey maps were used as base maps, reflecting the general process by which these maps became the authoritative series. Thus, Ordnance Survey material was the basis for *The Survey Atlas of England and Wales* (published by JG Bartholomew, Edinburgh, 1903).

Railway expansion also spurred on the demand for maps as new routes were planned. For example, in Canada, the potential routes for a railway between Halifax and the St Lawrence River, surveyed in 1864–5, were shown on a map, which helped to clarify the decision to choose a route as far from American territory as possible. This was followed by the survey of possible routes west to the Pacific. In the event, Sandford Fleming (1827–1915) proposed a route across the Rockies through the Yellowhead Pass, but this was rejected in favour of the Kicking Horse Pass, and it was necessary to survey anew.

The choice of routes was frequently designed to serve political purposes that related both to geopolitical issues – such as the vulnerability of Canada to American attack – and to idealized views of the nation. Thus, in France, the early railways served economic ends, being built, as in England, to move coal over short distances.

There were ideas for creating a more integrated rail network based on more grandiose economic needs, for example, linking Boulogne to the textile and steel industries of Champagne and thence to the Saône-Rhône axis, crossing, in Champagne, with an axis between Alsace and the lower Seine. However, a more

∧ An 1866 map of the raw cotton trade before, during, and after (1858, 1864, 1865) the American Civil War. Imports from North America are in blue; South America, light blue; India, tan; Egypt, brown; re-exports, red. The Union blockade on Confederate ports hit the Lancastrian spinning industry, which then increased exports from India and Egypt. The end of the war led to a revival in imports from North America.

Roads quicken the pace

The rapid expansion of towns and the opening up of new communication routes ensured that people wanted new maps. The canal boom in Britain in the late 18th century was followed by canal building elsewhere. Works such as the Erie Canal (1825) in the United States and the Rideau Canal (1832) in Canada were seen as major achievements, crucial to economic progress.

The number and different types of maps increased in order to satisfy specific needs, including legislative compliance. For example, from 1794, proponents of canal schemes and surveyors were required to submit plans and sections with any private canal bill presented to Parliament.

Although roads tend to be overshadowed by railways in accounts of 19th-century transportation and transport political rationale came to prevail with a national plan, imposed in 1842, that led to a system radiating from Paris and linking it to all parts of the country, especially the frontier regions.

Transverse links that did not focus on Paris were not part of the mental map of the Second Empire, but the need to consider constituencies under the Third Republic produced the Freycinet plan in 1879, which led to the building of what were termed "lines of local interest", a clear sign of the hierarchy of political space.

In Britain, plans had to be drawn up for any proposed railway and deposited with both Parliament and the local justice of the peace. During the "mania" or railway-building boom of 1844–5, more than 1000 plans were submitted.

The variety of reasons for railway mapping can be clearly seen in the Britain of the period. The Railway Clearing House created in 1842 established standard rates and apportioned through revenues. This required a calculation of the total mileage run over the tracks of one company by the trains of another. Meanwhile, the Distances Section of the House's Mileage Department was responsible for plans, which were published in book form from 1867 by an employee, John Airey, who also produced sheet maps of particularly busy areas.

Railroads and railway guides

There was much mapping of the new railway systems. This was produced both by individual companies keen to encourage passengers to use their routes and by commercial publishers, such as Rand McNally and George Cram in the United States, eager to serve a new market for transport information. For example, Rand McNally's *New Railway Guide Map of the United States and Canada* was published to accompany the company's *Railway Guide* (1874). The two were carefully linked with a note on the map: "To find the population and general description of any railroad or river town on this map, or to find the corporation name of any line of railroad upon which towns are situated, see general index of railroad and river towns in Rand, McNally and Co's Railway Guide, pages 1 to 23."

The resulting range of maps included a variety of formats. Alongside small maps that could be used by individual travellers, for example pocket-maps, were large display maps of railway networks. These were given particular prominence in major stations; some, such as those at England's York Station, were even fired into the tiles. Railway timetables also often contained maps. In Britain, the first *Railway Timetable* by George Bradshaw (1801–1853) appeared in 1839.

Railway maps were matched by those for other transport systems, although in each case there were specific features that required consideration. Thus, whereas railway (like canal) maps generally covered a large distance, those for tramways, horse-pulled buses, and trolley-buses faced the difficulty of making their routes and junctions among the bustling city streets readily comprehensible.

As a sign of an accelereated and rapidly changing society, maps also increasingly came to show, alongside existing routes, those that were under construction or planned. This reflected confidence in the ability to locate with precision what was to be built and also an awareness of the importance and interest of showing what was being planned.

Railway maps were of particular value to tourists, whose needs were increasingly served by mapmakers. Guides now carried more maps than in the 18th century, and these maps laid out both regions as a whole and also particular sites within them.

◄ Part of the East End of London from Charles Booth's *Descriptive Map of London Poverty* (1899). Booth classified and coloured streets in terms of the general condition of the inhabitants who were categorized in seven bands from lowest grade (vicious, semi-criminal) to highest (upper classes, wealthy).

A very different cartography was produced by railway companies encouraging settlement or other economic purposes such as the movement of goods. For example, in the United States, railway companies produced maps to help attract settlers to the federal land grants they had received. This was one aspect of a more general interest in mapping property, both rural and urban. Thus, alongside estate mapping in the United States came county maps that marked the division of the land. In towns, business directories contained maps which reflected the rapidly changing layout that followed redevelopment and new

development. The inclusion of maps permitted more effective use of the directory and its listing of business premises.

Official statistical cartography developed in some countries, – for example, Prussia – but the influence of commercial concerns, such as transport companies, and of consumers had more impact. People became more accustomed to seeing maps in Bibles, newspapers, and magazines, and on stamps. Consumer products also featured maps, especially on tins, of biscuits, for example. During its coverage of the "Gill's Hill murder" near Elstree on 24 October 1823, the *Birmingham Chronicle* included in its 13

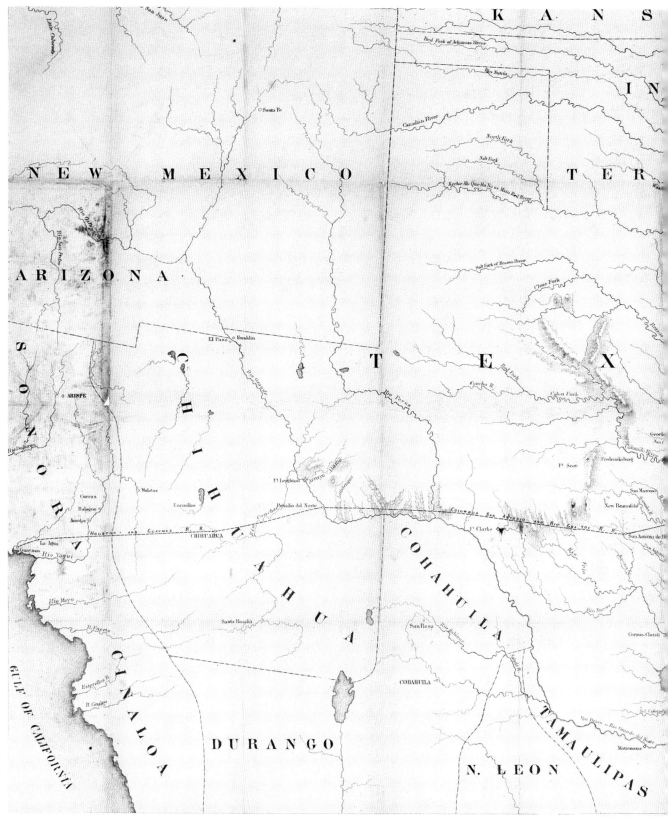

➤ This 1860 map by AM Gentry shows the lines of the Texas and New Orleans railroad, most of which ran along the Gulf coast and the Mississippi River.

November edition not only four sketches, but also a map. This depiction of the crime provided more information than the ballad that amused Sir Walter Scott:

> They cut his throat from ear to ear,
> His brains they battered in,
> His name was Mr William Weare,
> He dwelt in Lyon's Inn.

Nineteenth-century children grew up seeing maps displayed on school classroom walls, a splash of colour suggestive of new horizons brightening up spaces otherwise lacking in imaginative appeal. Like their newspaper-reading parents, children learned to read maps.

Maps and atlases were used as tools in the classroom, and in 1854, *Mitchell's Series of Dissected Maps* appeared. These were

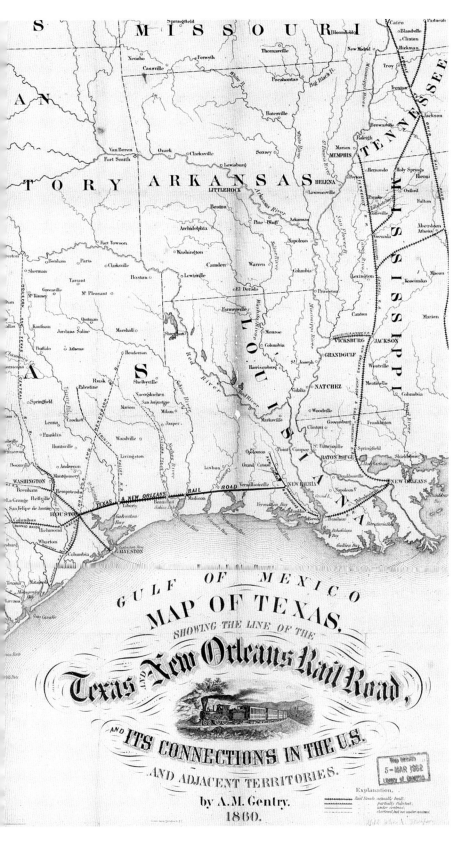

Maps came to play a more important role in fiction. In Arthur Conan Doyle's short story *The Disappearance of Lady Frances Carfax*, a devout missionary, Dr Schlessinger, claimed that he "was preparing a map of the Holy Land, with special reference to the Kingdom of the Midianites" but is exposed by Sherlock Holmes to be the villainous Australian Henry Peters.

The art of war

Wars and military planning led to the production of many maps, and the development of the military's ability to produce them. Warfare also encouraged public interest in maps of wars and battles; people craved information and accuracy. This was true of both Europe and the United States.

Alongside growing literacy, the public's interest in wars – near and far – increased; nationalism and imperialism combined to this end. Thus, whereas, a French newspaper reader in the 1790s did not expect to see any maps in his newspapers, despite his country's engagement in a bitter war, his descendants a century later wished, and indeed expected, to see maps recording France's imperial advance, whether in West and North Africa, Madagascar, or Indochina.

The presence of military correspondents – who sent back eyewitness sketches – coupled with recent advances in production technology which enabled these sketches to be rapidly redrawn, engraved, and printed, made it possible for newspapers to meet the demand for the frequent inclusion of maps. Thus, in this regard, the development of illustrated journalism helped to foster both demand and supply.

Public interest in war provided opportunities for publishers and led to some innovative cartography. For example, in 1855, Read and Co of London published a *Panoramic View of the Seat of War in the North of Europe*, a map that adopted an aerial perspective on Anglo-Russian hostilities in the Baltic during the Crimean War; it also provided a useful supplement to newspaper reports of operations in waters about which British readers knew little. The same technique was used for some maps of the American Civil War (1861–5), for example those produced by John Bachmann in 1862 such as his *Bird's-Eye View of Louisiana, Mississippi, Alabama and part of Florida*, which helped to explain the naval campaign that led to the Union admiral David Farragut's capture of New Orleans and Baton Rouge.

In that conflict, the scale of map production was vast: between 1 April 1861 and 30 April 1865, the daily press on the Union side printed no fewer than 2045 maps relating to the war. There had been few maps in American newspapers prior to 1861, but the war helped to establish them as a major feature of the press.

The public need for maps during the war was also served by the publication of large numbers of freestanding maps, especially in the North. These included theatre of war and battle maps, such as that of the Potomac area – for example *Bacon's New Army Map of the Seat of War in Virginia* (1862) – which enabled those "at

jigsaws of maps of the United States, and of the eastern, western, middle, and southern states. They were presented as being educational as well as amusing: "The object of these maps is to make the young people familiar with the locality of the different parts of their own country … They serve as an amusement for a leisure hour, and the frequent use of them cannot but indelibly impress on the mind the relative locality of each state".

◁ In 1898 Canada issued the world's very first Christmas stamp; 20 million stamps were issued. It depicted a world map with the countries that were dependencies of Great Britain in red.

home" to follow the movements of relatives and others. Thus, in 1862, while Union forces campaigned along the Mississippi, James Lloyd brought out his *Map of the Lower Mississippi River from St. Louis to the Gulf of Mexico* (New York).

In the Confederacy, conversely, there was a severe shortage of press operators, printers, wood-engravers, and printing materials, all of which combined to ensure that the appearance of maps in Southern newspapers was rare, although some, such as the *Charleston Mercury* and the *Augusta Constitutionalist*, did print a few.

Newspapers under fire

That newspaper publication of maps was not always welcome to the military was an early warning of a problem set to become more pressing. On 4 December 1861, the front page of the *New York Times* offered "The National Lines before Washington. A Map exhibiting the defences of the national capital, and positions of the several divisions of the Grand Union army". The accompanying text began:

"The interest which attaches to the military operations of the National army on the line of the Potomac, has induced us to present the readers of the *Times* with the above complete and impregnable lines on the Virginia side of the National Capital … The principal permanent fortifications, which the rebels, if they attempt them, will find to be an impassable barrier to their ambitious designs upon the Capital, have been enumerated by title and position in the General Orders of General McClellan, but are, for the first time, located and named upon the present map … Another novel and useful trait of our

present map is its geographical definition of the territory occupied by each of the eight divisions constituting the grand defensive army.

McClellan, who had no real feel for the populist dimension of American politics, fiercely demanded that the paper be punished for aiding the Confederates. The Secretary of War restricted himself to urging the editor to avoid such action in the future. The following spring, however, the War Department established a voluntary system to prevent journalists with McClellan's Army of the Potomac from publishing compromising maps.

When American armies operated abroad, the public also expected maps. John Disturnell (1801–77) had published a map of Mexico in 1846 which, as a result of the Mexican-American War of 1846–8, he found to be in such demand that he brought out several editions. Disturnell's map was also used to record the eventual territorial settlement reached under the Treaty of Guadalupe-Hidalgo of 1848.

War with Spain in 1898 led to the publication in the United States of two atlases, while the American National Geographic Society first included a map with their magazine in 1899: this was of the Philippines, which America had conquered from Spain the previous year.

Public interest also led to the production of maps of recent wars, in America and elsewhere. *Maps and Plans, Showing the Principal Movements, Battles and Sieges, in which the British Army was Engaged during the War from 1808 to 1814 in the Spanish Peninsula* (London, 1840) by James Wyld (1812–87) was followed by the excellent atlas that accompanied the *History of the War in France and Belgium in 1815* (London, 1844) by William Siborne

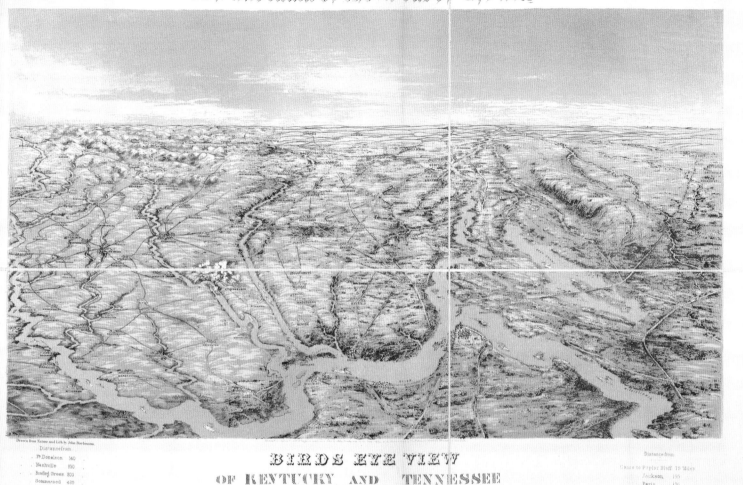

Drawn from Nature and Lith by John Bachmann.

Distance from
Ft.Donelson   340
Nashville   230
Bowling Green   200
Sommerset   430
Louisville   ...
Cincinnati   470

Distance from
Cairo to Poplar Bluff 75 Miles
Jackson   195
Paris   170
Memphis   265

BIRDS EYE VIEW
OF KENTUCKY AND TENNESSEE

SHOWING CAIRO AND PART OF THE SOUTHERN STATES.

John Bachmann, Publisher,
115 & 117 Nassau St. New York.

John Bachmann produced a series of bird's-eye views of spheres of conflict in the American Civil War. This map looks southward and depicts Kentucky and Tennessee, showing Cairo and part of the Southern States. Bachman listed the distances from Cairo to various places of import, such as Memphis, seen 265 miles further down the Mississippi river, and Nashville, 230 miles away to the east (centre left on the map).

Siborne (1797–1847). Following in the same footsteps, the United States saw the map of the Gettysburg battlefield by John Bachelder (1825–1894) published in his guidebook *Gettysburg: What to See and How to See It* (Boston, 1873) and *Battles of the American Revolution ... with Topographical Illustration* (1876) by Henry B Carrington (1824–1912).

Considerable effort was devoted to accuracy. Based on an extensive personal survey, Siborne had earlier produced a model of the battlefield of Waterloo that was publicly exhibited. Bachelder's map carried the endorsement of the Union commander at Gettysburg, Meade. Interest in geographical and cartographical aspects of war also led to the publication of *Die Elemente der Militär-Geographie von Europa* (Weimar, 1821) by Friedrich Wilhelm Benicken (1783–1829), a retired captain in the Prussian army, and to the *Atlas des plus mémorables batailles, combats et sièges* (Dessau, 1847) by the Freiherr von Kausler, a major general in the Württemberg army.

Maps were also much sought after by the military: Arthur Wellesley (1769–1852), first Duke of Wellington, who was a firm believer in the need to understand terrain – not least because he wanted to position his troops on reverse slopes in order to protect them from artillery fire – used a mobile lithographic printing press for maps in the Peninsula War (1808–13), an example of what became even more common; the military employing new technology. In 1809, Napoleon created an Imperial Corps of Surveyors with a staff of 90. Naval charting was also pushed forwards in these years as part of the conflict between Britain and France (1793–1802, 1803–14, 1815).

Throughout the century, defence needs led to mapping for new fortifications, such as for the mapping of Devonport and its environs in 1848 when faced with the prospect of a French invasion and, in the face of the same threat, of other sites on the south coast in the early 1860s. In 1841, a map of the fortifications in the Paris region was produced as part of the programme of fortification, as was a map of the fortified zone around Langres which appeared in 1869.

In 1855, during the Crimean War with Russia, the British War Office founded a Topographical Department. They needed to get

Maps of power

The age of nationalism led to the active use of maps as tools of political propaganda. They were an eye-catching and easily intelligible means by which to depict international relations – events that were happening thousands of miles away from home – and to advance a particular nation's aspirations on the world stage.

In 1924, the 21st edition of *The Howard Vincent Map of the British Empire* appeared. Proudly depicting a world much of which was coloured red, this map proclaimed Britain's triumph in the struggle of states. The text printed on the map provided a list of colonies and a declaration of the value of the empire:

> "The mutual inward and outward trade between the several possessions of the British people amounts annually to more than £600,000,000, and embraces every single article required for food, clothing, education, commerce, manufacture, or agriculture, and for all the pursuits, associations, and pleasures of every one of His Most Gracious Majesty's Loyal and Devoted Subjects in the United Kingdom and throughout the Empire. This great mercantile interchange is capable, moreover, of limitless expansion, by reason of the diversities of climate and geological conditions. Greater Britain that is the possessions of the British Peoples over the sea is one hundred and fifty-three times the size of Great Britain."

Most states lacked such confidence, and the maps shown here indicate the tensions of imperial competition. They also show, in the depiction of countries as people or animals, an attempt to make such competition more comprehensible and even humorous to the man in the street. The anthropomorphic device of attributing human personality to a state was not new, but it took on a greater lease of life during the 19th century as a result of interest in anthropology and ethnicity, and a new evolutionary attitude toward the success or failure of peoples.

Thus, the Japanese map pictured opposite shows China as threatened by the Russian octopus. This approach did not capture the respective strength of states. For example, Japan, which does not appear in the map as a threat, defeated China in 1894–5 and Russia a decade later. Similarly, the European map makes Russia appear stronger than was in fact the case.

Russia's tentacles

These maps captured the problem of how best to depict international relations. The depiction of Russia as an octopus was one that enabled the sense of insidious pressure and multiple threats to be presented, not least because it was possible to show the tendrils closing around Turkey and Persia.

The celebration of British interests in South Africa accorded with the propagandist tradition that also saw the use of visual images on stamps, tins, murals, and other devices.

Many European states were new, and it was necessary for them to stamp their visual image on the mind of their subjects, reminding them where they owed loyalty. This was also a time of imperial interests. Thus, as mapmakers at one level struggled to give precision to newly-gained territories, at another level they used a simpler cartography to produce images of power and threat.

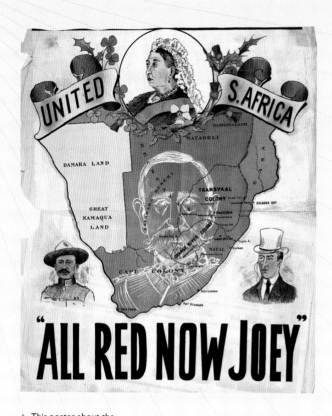

⋏ This poster about the Boer War dates from shortly after the capture of Pretoria on 5 June 1900. The central figure is Lord Roberts, the British military commander; on the left is Baden-Powell, founder of the Boy Scouts, who made his mark at the successful defence of Mafeking; and on the right is Joesph Chamberlain – the Joey of the title – Secretary of State for the Colonies 1895–1903. After the fall of Pretoria, the British considered the war over, hence the triumphant tone of this poster. But a guerilla war was to continue for another two years which, although eventually won by the British, took a huge toll on British forces and morale, and signalled the start of the slow decline of the British imperial ideal.

> The original French caption to this *New Map of Europe* by Paul Hadol (1835–75), created in c. 1870 read as follows: England, isolated, raving and almost forgetting Ireland which she holds on a lead. Spain is smoking, leaning on Portugal. France repels invasions from Prussia, who advances one hand on Holland, the other on Austria. Italy is saying to Bismarck, "Lift your feet up from there." Corsica and Sardinia … a real Parisian urchin who laughs at everything. Denmark, who has lost her legs in Holstein, is hoping to get them back. European Turkey is yawning and waking up. Asian Turkey inhales the smoke of her Turkish pipe. Sweden leaps like a panther. And Russia looks like a bogey-man who would like to refill the basket on his back.

> This map is taken from *A Humorous Diplomatic Atlas of Europe and Asia*, and is annotated in both Japanese and English. The caption at top left is dated March 1901 placing this within a month of the start of the Russo-Japanese War, which was opened by a surprise Japanese attack on Russian naval vessels at Port Arthur in China. Written in English by a Japanese, the caption explains that the map takes up the image of Russia as an avaricious black octopus from an English source. The author goes on to anticipate great Japanese victories over the Russians in China and Manchuria. Japan's eventual victory over Russia at the end of the war the following year marked the first time an Asian power had defeated a European power in modern times, and established Japan as a major force in world affairs.

NOUVELLE CARTE D'EUROPE DRESSÉE POUR 1870

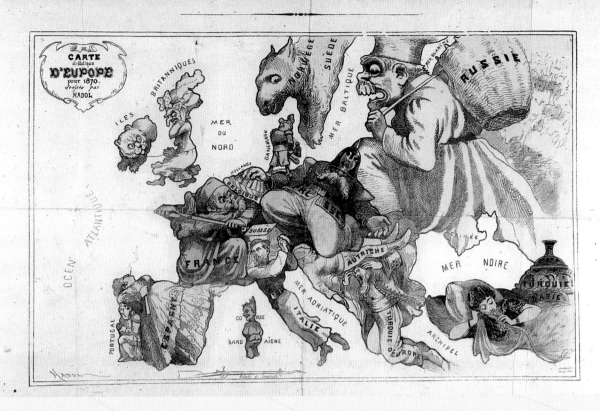

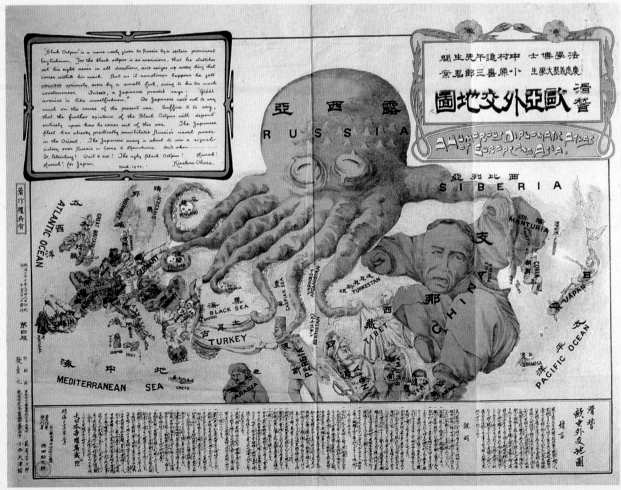

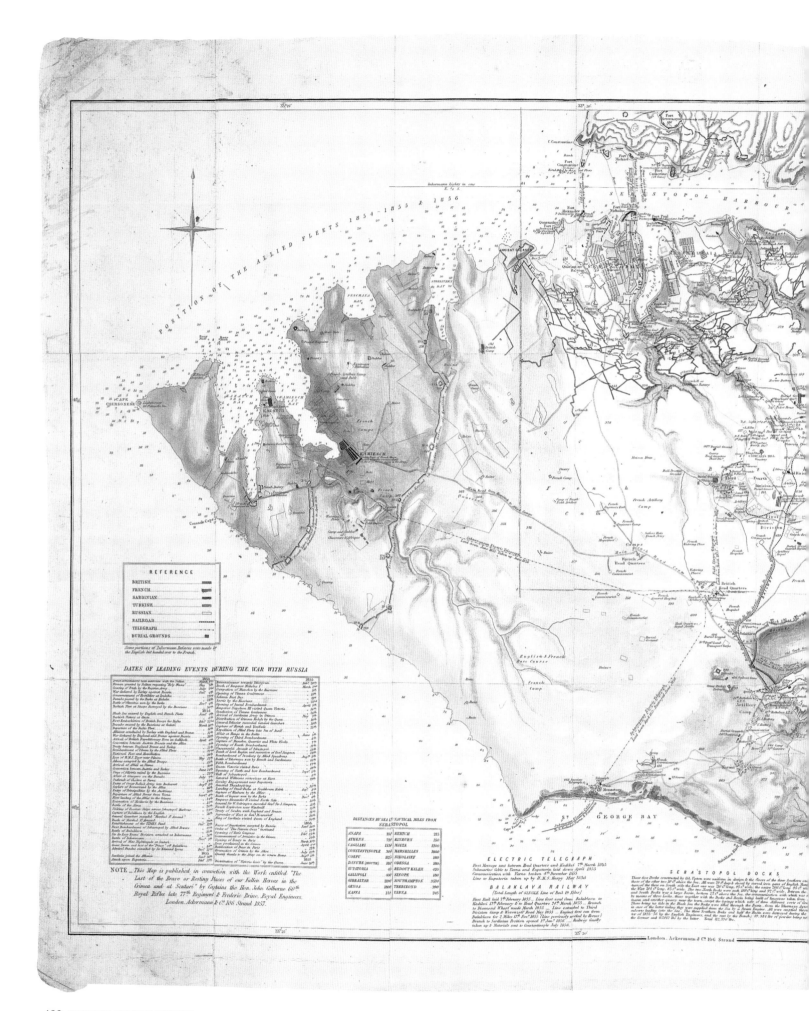

maps from wherever they could. In the absence of aerial, let alone satellite, surveillance, the acquisition of cartographic information about hostile territory was a particular problem.

A map of the harbour and area surrounding Sebastopol – the crucial British target in the Crimea – dated 1855, bears the note "Tracing of a drawing found on a Russian engineer officer and now in the possession of the French Depot de la Guerre just communicated by ... Marshal Vaillant Minister of War to Lieutenant Colonel Jervis". Jervis was director of the Topographical and Statistical Depot at the War Department, and France was then an ally. Another map, of 1887, at a time when the British were occupying Upper Burma, is endorsed "sketch map of the Tagaya district, Upper Burma by Moung San Done, Thungyip of Myaing". Also once in the collection of the Royal United Services Institution this map is now in the British Library.

The American Civil War

In the American Civil War (1861–5), field commanders on both sides used maps extensively, although at the outset they were hampered by a shortage of adequate maps. Commercial cartography could not adequately serve military purposes, and thus the armies turned to establishing their own map supplies.

By 1864, the Coast Survey and the Corps of Engineers were providing about 43,000 printed maps annually for the Union's army. In that year, the survey produced a uniform 10 mile to the inch base map of most of the Confederacy east of the Mississippi, a sure sign of the way in which Union forces were now pressing into their opponent's homeland. And in order to advance effectively, the Union forces needed maps – maps were central to understanding terrain and devising overall strategy, and, thus, to making tactical decisions.

Lithographic presses produced multiple copies of maps rapidly. This was crucial, given the scale of operations and the need to coordinate forces over considerable distances. These matters of scale and coordination had also become true of battles. Their scale was such that it was no longer sufficient to rely completely on the field of vision of an individual commander and his ability to send instructions during the course of the engagement. Instead, it was necessary to plan far more in advance. This was particularly

◁ Compiled from surveys carried out by the Royal Engineers during the Crimean War, this map of 1857 shows the allied army positions in relation to Sebastopol before the Battle of Balaklava (which is marked to the right centre of the map). British positions are shown in red, French in blue, Turkish in yellow and Russian in green.

important in preparing artillery positions, in mounting and responding to frontal attacks, and in coordinating attacks, as union army leader George B McClellan (1826–85) conspicuously failed to do at Antietam in 1862.

It was necessary to understand terrain in order to control it and also for specific reasons, including the interplay of rail links and field operations, and the best use of water sources. The Union forces had a particular need for maps as they were advancing into the Confederacy.

Planning the Campaign

More generally, in a military world in which planning, and personnel specifically for planning, came to play a greater role, maps became more important. They were the fundamental tool of the General Staff, and the first sheets of the Prussian General Staff map appeared in 1841. France re-established an Army Geographical Service in 1885. This looked forward towards the major use of maps in both world wars. Maps were important for a systematic process of effective and rapid decision-making, and for the implementation of strategic plans in terms of timed operational decisions and interrelated tactical actions.

The General Staff system owed its origins to Prussian war preparation, and mapping played a crucial role in its development. The Land Survey section of the Prussian General Staff was created in 1816. This section was responsible for producing maps, and it trained its officers in the necessary trigonometric, topographic, and cartographical skills. All officers in the staff were expected to work in the section for a number of years, and four of its six heads between 1820 and 1914 spent several years there: Helmuth von Moltke (1800–91), the most successful chief of the General Staff, spent his first three probationary years in the section. Its maps were important to the war gaming that was seen as crucial to a staff officer's education. Other states copied Prussian war-gaming methods after Prussia's spectacular victories over Austria (1866) and France (1870–1).

During the Franco-Prussian war, the French army had few maps of eastern France, but this changed as Prussian staff work was copied. The École Supérieure de la Guerre was founded in 1878 in order to provide France with a staff college. In the United States, the General Service and Staff College was created at Fort Leavenworth in 1902. The British also took care to organize their maps. In 1881, the War Office began to number their maps in sequence. Maps were used to study past campaigns, as when the American staff colleges followed Prussian campaigns, and also to plan operations, as with the German Schlieffen Plan.

The military's use of maps was matched by the public, most obviously in war gaming. At Oxford, the University Kriegspiel (War Games) Club played war games on Prussian maps of the campaigning zone on which Austria was defeated in 1866 and also on Ordnance Survey maps of parts of England. The club's president was Hereford George (1838–1910), a pioneer of military history and geography at the university, and the author of *Battles of English History* (London, 1895), *Napoleon's Invasion of Russia* (London, 1899), and *Relations of Geography and History* (Oxford, 1901). *Kriegspiel* had been introduced at the British Royal Military College in 1871.

Nevertheless, the problems posed for planning and operations were to be shown in World War I, particularly for the British and French attacking the German colonies in Africa. Thus, in German East Africa (Tanganyika), the Royal Navy knew in 1914 from signals' intercepts that the German cruiser *Königsberg* was at Salale, but Salale was not marked on the naval charts, and it took 11 days to identify it. A lack of adequate maps made it difficult to predict terrain or watercourses. Problems with maps also faced Ottoman operations in the Caucasus in 1914 and German planning for an Ottoman invasion of Egypt in 1915.

War waged by timetable

More generally, maps had to be carefully interpreted, crucially, for example, with the German invasion of Belgium and France in 1914. Maps had to be read in light of how swift the opposing forces were able to move, depending on terrain, and how difficult they would find it to mount an offensive. The French could readily use their rail system to move troops from east France to support Paris, whereas the Germans faced the problems of taking over the rail systems of conquered areas, including different gauges of track and the lack of a lateral system to match that of the French. The use of maps did not always ensure that commanders could locate their units as accurately as might be anticipated.

Aside from strategic planning, there was a developing interest in geopolitics. In 1904, in a paper given at a meeting in London, "The Geographical Pivot of History", which he published that year, Halford Mackinder (1861–1947), the leading British geopolitician, used a map to display Siberia as the pivot at the heart of Eurasia, claiming that Siberia was impregnable to attack by sea and threatened to overrun the whole of Eurasia. There were sceptics: Spencer Wilkinson, a journalist and military historian, criticized Mackinder for using a Mercator projection that exaggerated the size, and therefore the menace, of his pivot. Leo Amery (1873–1955), a journalist who was to be a leading politician, argued that geopolitics, and therefore maps, would be reconfigured by new technology in the shape of air power: "a great deal of this geographical distribution must lose its importance, and the successful powers will be those who have the greatest industrial base".

Thus, the pressure to produce precise cartographic images of territory became more acute during the 19th century. This was true for warfare, government, and other purposes requiring survey and spatial analysis. This pressure was spread by Western power, and, accordingly, in 1849, Lord Dalhousie (1812–60), governor-general of India, produced a memorandum about British negotiations over Sind in India:

> ➤ The battle of Antietam, 20 September 1862, ended the run of victories by the Confederates under Robert E Lee during the American Civil War. However, the larger Union army under George B McClellan failed to coordinate its attacks on the enemy left, right, and centre, and its breakthrough on the Confederate right came too late. This map was made by a Lieutenant Wiliam H Willcox, who served on Brigadier General Doubleday's staff. Doubleday commanded the !st Division of the I Corps of the Union forces and saw heavy action with his Division in the Cornfield and West Woods. His name is marked on the map near these sites, to the upper centre of the map.

MAP OF THE
Battlefield of Antietam,
Prepared by
LIEUT. WM. H. WILLCOX, TOP. OFF. & A.A.D.C.
ON
BRIG. GENL DOUBLEDAY'S STAFF.
FROM ACTUAL SURVEYS

UNION FORCES.   REBEL FORCES.

Scale of Miles.

"The want of a correct map of the Khyrpore territory was the principal cause of the delay which has taken place in settling these questions. We called for a map on the 24th October 1846 and on the 12th February last were furnished with a copy of one showing the positions of the districts and villages named in articles 2 and 6 of the draft treaty."

However, as modern warfare more clearly indicates, an understanding of place, while very useful at the strategic, operational, and tactical levels of war, was less helpful in enforcing will, the true goal of conflict. Indeed, by creating a deceptive sense that other peoples and lands were readily knowable, mapping was actively misleading.

This relates to a more general problem with mapping, the need to understand what is shown. For example, it is important to appreciate the issue of scale. This is not new. In a different context to Henry Fielding's satirical description of the people "Politic" in 1730, but nevertheless making the same point, the Tory politician Robert Gascoyne (1830–1903), third Marquess of Salisbury, then Secretary of State for India, declared in Parliament in 1877, as the "Eastern Question" reached its height:

"I cannot help thinking that in discussions of this kind, a great deal of misapprehension arises from the popular use of maps on a small scale. As with such maps you are able to put a thumb on India and a finger on Russia, some persons at once think that the political situation is alarming and that India must be looked to. If the noble Lord would use a larger map – say one on the scale of the Ordnance Map of England – he would find that the distance between Russia and British India is not to be measured by the finger and thumb, but by a rule."

No such map was available, but Salisbury was stressing that maps had to be understood if they were to be used effectively.

Dynamic information

In the 19th century, maps were increasingly able to play the role expected from them in Western culture: offering precision in location and comprehension in coverage. This also enabled their use for analysis and planning. While this function had been true of maps from the outset in terms of route-planning, now it was extended to a wide range of activities. Thanks to thematic mapping, cartography was becoming part of a dynamic information system.

All three words – "dynamic", "information", and "system" – are appropriate. "Dynamic" reflected the provision of new information and the awareness that this was a constant process. "Information" reflected the sense that this was the prime purpose of the map; in particular, the role of display was less prominent and maps lost many of the elaborate, decorative features of the past. And finally, "system" reflected the role of maps in conjunction with other sources of data.

◄ *Delineation of the Strata of England and Wales with part of Scotland* (1815) by William Smith, an engineer and geologist who began work on the map in 1805.

In particular, thematic mapping depended on accurate statistics. Data needed to be located, established, and its density displayed. For example, isolines – lines linking points of equal density – were mapped. They were used to show barometric pressure from 1827 and precipitation from 1839, and were to be the basis of the contour maps that came to offer an effective (and universally applicable) depiction of height and terrain, replacing earlier systems such as hachures.

Natural phenomena

Meteorological maps played a role, alongside hydrographic, geological, botanical, and zoological maps, in *Physikalischer Atlas* (two vols, Gotha, 1845–8) by Heinrich Berghaus (1797–1884). An English version, *The Physical Atlas: A Series of Maps and Notes Illustrating the Geographical Distribution of Natural Phenomena* (Edinburgh, 1848) by Alexander Keith Johnston (1844–1879), spread the idea. The atlas included ethnographic maps of Europe and North America. They reflected both increased interest in the mapping of zoological and biological distributions, and a concern with ethnicity that demonstrated the impact of nationalism. Other subjects mapped in England in the 1840s included literacy, crimes, bastardy, pauperism, improvident marriages, saving bank deposits, and "spiritual constitution".

Geological mapping was an important instance of the development of thematic mapping. The understanding of different strata provided the analytical tool, but it was maps that transformed popular understanding of the subject. The geologist William Smith (1769–1839) published his landmark *Delineation of the Strata of England and Wales with part of Scotland* (1815), which was followed by more detailed and sophisticated mapping. Official geological mapping developed in the 1830s, and by 1890 the geological mapping of England and Wales was complete. This was seen as a way to provide information on the location of minerals and building material.

Utilitarian ideals were central to 19th-century mapping. Knowledge was considered to be of immediate benefit, and the benefits that flowed from serving this need encouraged investment in surveying and mapping. The spread of Western models to other parts of the world, especially, through emulation by reform and renewal movements to China, Japan, and Turkey, ensured that the Western view of cartography became, at least at the levels of government, business, and education, the world view.

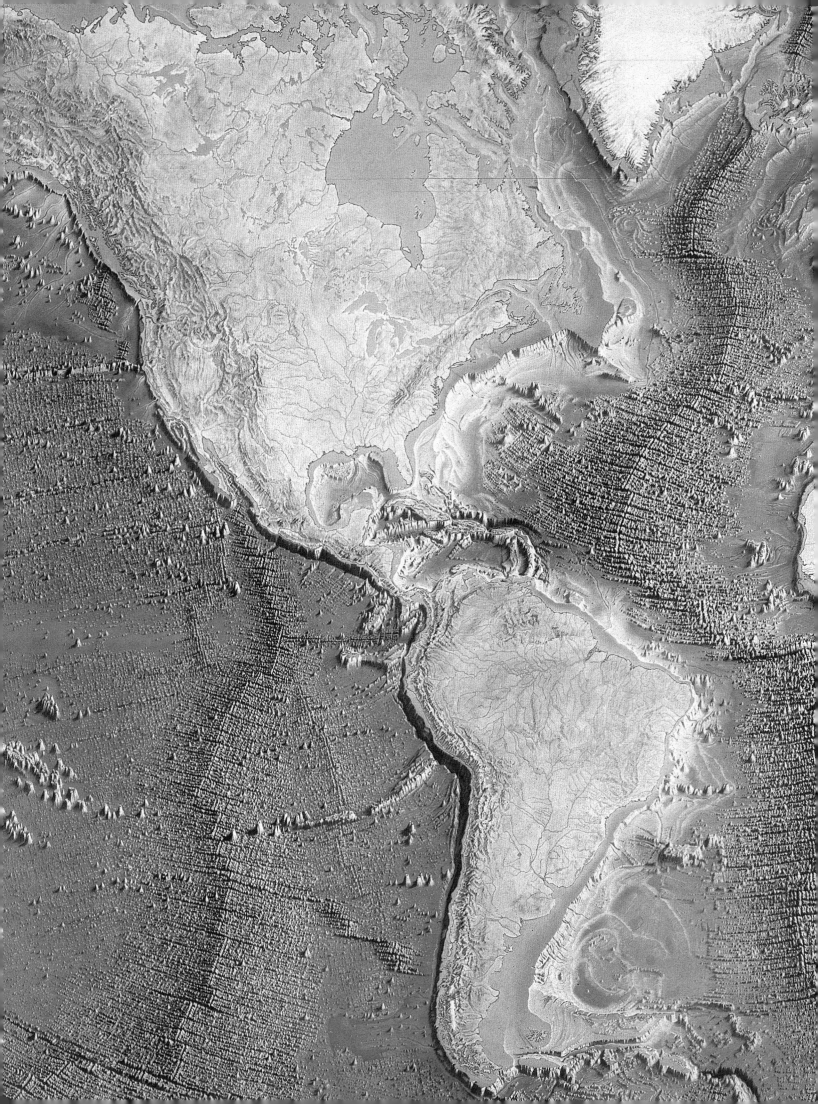

The Modern Age

Most of the maps ever produced have been made in the 20th century, and yet the history of mapping in this period has received the least attention. Why this is is open to question: perhaps we do not think of the recent past as history; perhaps we are unaware of the attractiveness and importance of recent maps; or it may be because we deem early mapping to have been the heroic age of cartography.

But the recent past and the here and now are, in fact, as readily deserving of this honour. The ability to map our world and other galaxies from the sky and from space has, literally, created a whole new dimension for cartography.

Maps have become a major part of the fabric of life. This reflects both the extent to which a far larger percentage of the world's population undertake long-distance travel and the extent to which economies depend on the movement of goods. Precision in location is essential, and it is provided by mapping.

These are signs not simply of a faster paced world, but also of one in which most people do not live close to where they grew-

up and most do not work on the land. Space and time – often understood in terms of journeys – have become important commodities that require accurate measurement and that need to be expressed visually.

The visualization of space is a major feature. In an age that relies increasingly on visual imagery rather than the printed word, we have become accustomed to reading plans and maps as part of daily life both at work and at leisure.

The fusion of plan and map was captured brilliantly in the 1931 map for the London Underground by Harry Beck (1903–74). This was inspired by electrical circuit diagrams, and depicted the various tube lines diagrammatically and as being straight.

Prior to Beck's innovative map, maps presented by London Underground were designed to be accurate in terms of distance and direction. The first such map, produced to show all the Underground lines, as opposed only to those of an individual company, was issued in 1908. This depicted the lines superimposed upon a central London street map – the same

◄◄ World Ocean Floor Panorama, 1977. This map showing tectonic plates and ocean trenches reflects the knowledge acquired by one of the most impressive aspects of 20th-century exploration, that of the ocean floors. Understanding tectonic-plate geology has helped to lead to a greater understanding of developments on land.

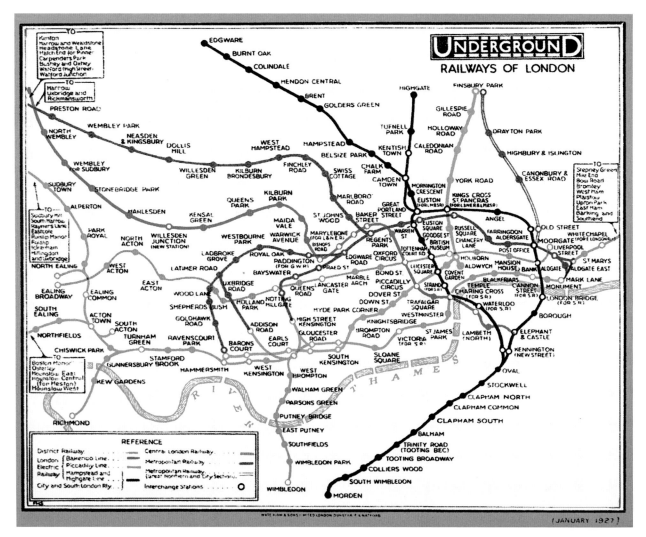

◄ The 1927 London Underground map designed by FH Stingemore, a pocket map that offered an accurate representation of the system. The map recorded the recent expansion of the network on to the suburbs, for example to Edgware in 1924. South of the Thames, the Northern Line reached Morden in 1926.

pattern used for maps of overground railways, such as Macaulay's Metropolitan Railway Map (1859).

By the 1920s, the street-map background had been dropped from the Underground map, but Beck's diagrammatic form was yet to be introduced. Using a topological structure and abandoning scale, Beck's map shrank the apparent distance between suburbia and the inner city, implying that peripheral destinations, such as Morden, were within easy travelling distance of central London.

The variety of ways in which maps can present locations and the distances, or space, between them is such that they can show either an accurate, literal representation or give a more distorted, diagrammatic account, of space. Whether they are of a tube system or a housing estate, a golf course or a school, maps are central to the way in which we seek every day to locate and understand the space around us.

The technology revolution

Changes in methods of cartographic production throughout the past century have been important in facilitating the spread of mapping. Maps can be generated faster and in greater quantity than ever before. Their central point can be changed readily,

different projections and perspectives can be adopted easily, and complex data sets can be mapped rapidly. The standard Western cartographic characteristics produced using coordinates have now been integrated with the computer processing and depiction of data to create a cartographic technology that appears to offer scientific precision and to be comprehensive.

The 20th century saw innovations in both design and reprographic techniques to which a number of factors contributed. The role of new materials, the information revolution, and experimentation and application in modern science and industry were important, as was the pressure for improvements in cartography, graphic analysis, modelling, and display that arose from military competition.

From the late 1920s, cartographers reverted to engraving; however, instead of metal plates, they used glass plates and, subsequently, transparent plastic sheets. In the late 1940s and early 1950s, there was a rapid spread in the use of transparent overlays of plastic material for scribing.

Maps were compiled using a multileveled system of overlays, with information registered on a typeset base map. Photomechanical laboratories then produced colour negatives from which to print plates. This complex procedure started with

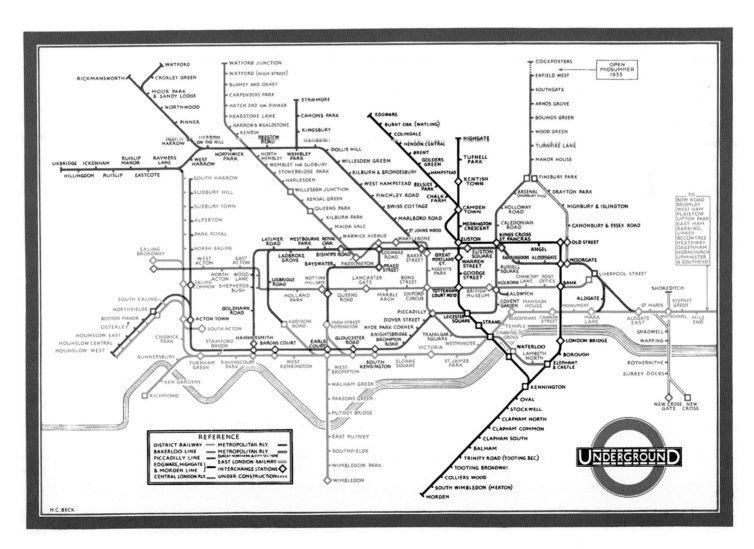

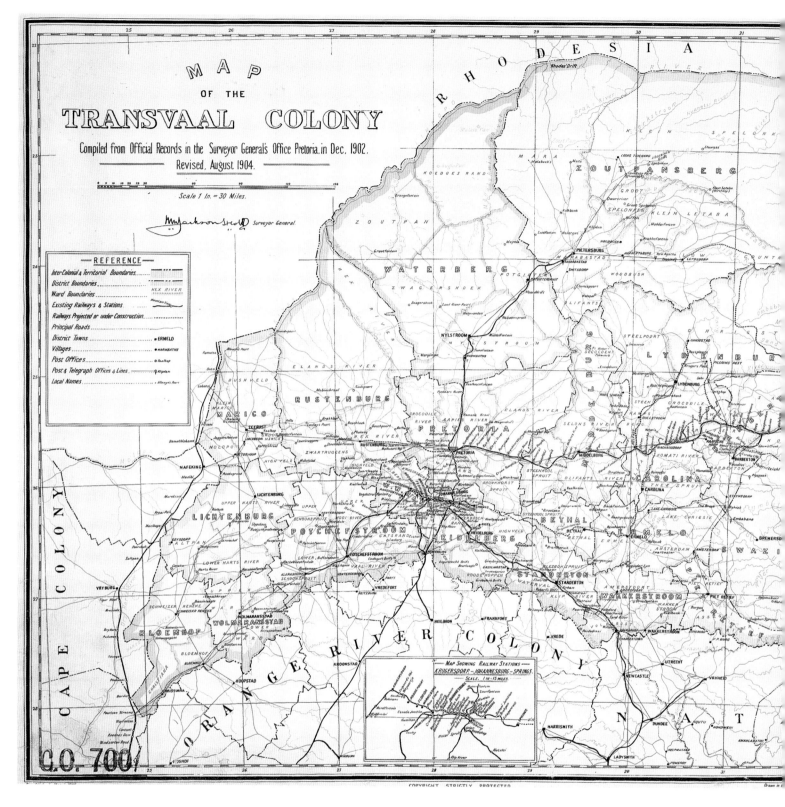

the preparation of the set of "peel coats" (photographically opaque films) on which the information for each colour on the map was "scribed" (cut) away. The reproduction house exposed each peel coat to make appropriately coloured printing films which were then combined for proofing. With one peel coat for each tint on a map – a single map might require 10 or 12 – this was not only expensive in terms of materials, but also meant that the effect of the combined colours could not be evaluated until

the proof was made. Any correction to lines or colour might involve changing several peel coats – unwanted lines were covered, new ones drawn on – and this created serious problems in matching up the original and the corrected versions.

A less complex method for more simple maps involved a coloured (painted or airbrushed) baseboard, with the line work either painted on or supplied as overlays, and with each piece of type stuck down by hand on a further overlay. Corrections were

⋏ Map of the Transvaal, which had been conquered by Britain in the Boer War of 1899–1902. Once they had conquered it, the British were keen to acquire accurate cartographic interpretation, then to map the area. This map

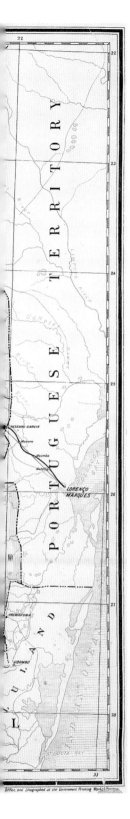

made to the coloured base by repainting it, a clumsy procedure which led to inferior quality and the risk that type might fall off during handling. The considerable disadvantages of both these printing methods resulted in strong pressure not to make changes.

From page to screen

Computer technology transformed the printing of maps, not least by giving greater flexibility. Computers can store the source material for maps in a single database and produce maps as a vertical scan made up of many minute dots which records symbols as dots, lines, or surfaces. This information can then be viewed on screen, corrected or changed, and the entire map printed out in one process.

Geographic base maps are stored as digital images. Manuscript and printed maps can be added to the computer database by digitization, using either an automatic scanner or a cursor that traces the lines on the map, with the position of the cursor being recorded by an electronic coordinate system.

The depiction of movement and change was a particular problem for the conventional atlas format. The cartographer Charles Paullin suggested as early as 1932 that "the ideal historical atlas might well be a collection of motion-picture maps, if these could be [reproduced] on the pages of a book without the paraphernalia of projector, reel and screen". But it was the computer and digitization that would transform mapping.

Computer mapping packages were developed both to produce atlases and to present maps on screen. Computers rapidly construct spatial information systems containing diverse, interrelated layers of data, in contrast to the inherent limitations of the static, two-dimensional paper map.

The first computer-aided maps to appear in a scientific journal were weather maps generated by the first ENIAC (Electrical Numerical Integrator Computer) numerical calculator in 1950. By the 1980s, powerful desktop computers had made popular access to a vast range of data commonplace, and the first prototype of an electronic atlas was developed in Canada in 1982.

The great increase in the power of personal computers, and the development of relevant software and hardware packages, enhanced the cartographic applicability of computers. By 1989, MundoCart/CD, the digital map of the world on CD-ROM, was commercially available and this made interaction with the data used to compile modern maps much easier.

GIS (geographical information systems) have also come to play a major role in cartography. GIS are automated, digital information systems concerned with data relating to locations stored on computers; they are a by-product of the computer programmes developed for use in the Cold War arms race. Information is converted into numbers and can then be mapped through an automated system.

With digitization, everything becomes a lot easier. You can make as many changes as you wish. Colours and typestyles can be

changed individually, or globally through a project, literally at the touch of a button; and line work can be modified as easily. If you want to update the map at any time, this can be done in a matter of moments, for the cost of the new film involved.

Design and cartographic processes can be integrated more easily. It is possible endlessly to modify bases in order to fit particular design requirements. The entire world coastline and drainage are available on databases; they can be outputted in different projections, choosing different sizes and centre points. This saves the time-consuming process of drawing coastlines for individual maps.

It also makes it easy, for example, to rescale a map by 10 per cent more or less while designing the spread on which it goes. And it is easy to design, use, and modify complex and pictorial symbols, and to achieve fades and blends which, before digitization, had been very clumsy or downright impossible processes. Therefore, it is much easier to design a map that not only looks good and is accurate in its own right, but also looks good when integrated with other elements such as timelines, photographs, text, artwork, and so on.

Eventually, many atlases will probably be generated and stored digitally, and presented differently for the particular requirements of individual users: an atlas will more clearly become a database.

Charting the unchartable

Technology, in the shape of aerial photography, dominates the account of how new information was obtained in the last century. However, in the early decades of the 20th century, this information was obtained by a process of filling in the gaps on the ground, as the exploratory drives that had been so prominent in the late 19th century were pushed to completion into seemingly innaccessible areas.

This was largely due to the continued exploration and mapping of inland regions, especially in central Africa and central Asia. Thus, there was exploration in the Himalayas and Tibet. In 1913, the source of the River Brahmaputra was traced to the Tsangpo in Tibet.

Tibet was extensively explored by Westerners in the early decades of the 20th century. So, also, was much of the interior of the African continent, as boundaries were clarified and colonial governments went about their business of collecting taxes, planning railways, and administering their territories. Exploration was accompanied, or followed, by better surveys, as mapping was seen as crucial both to government and to competition with other imperial powers.

This process was given a fresh burst of life as colonial territories were reallocated after World War I, again in 1935–6 as Italy conquered Abyssinia (Ethiopia), and after World War II. The rejuvenation of surveying can be seen with Britain, the leading colonial power in Africa. For example, in Swaziland in southern Africa, the British had initially relied on early sketch maps. The first

shows the importance of rail links. To the colonial mind, they helped to organize space, alongside the district boundaries that are clearly mapped. In contrast, terrain or population distribution appear of no particular importance.

Aerial Photography

Manned flight, which began in aircraft (as opposed to balloons) in 1903, was rapidly followed by the use of aerial mapping. Photography proved the key. Cameras, mounted first on balloons, then on aircraft, were able to record detail and to scrutinize the landscape from different heights and angles.

A flight over part of Italy by Wilbur Wright (1867–1912) in 1909 appears to have been the first on which photographs were taken. The range and speed of aeroplanes gave them a major advantage over balloons. Instruments for mechanically plotting from aerial photography were developed in 1908, while, during World War I, came the invention of cameras able to take photographs with constant overlap.

This type of photography produced a wealth of information that was used for many sorts of maps and also helped to change assumptions about mapping. As has often been the case with cartography, war provided one of the major drives behind new developments and greater efforts. It was a quick leap from using balloons and aircraft for reconnaissance and to spot the fall of shells, to providing accurate maps to assist artillery fire and operations on land, and to help air attacks. The intensity of reconnaissance photography was such that the Germans were able to produce a new image of the whole Western Front every two weeks, and thus rapidly to produce maps that responded to changes on the ground.

In the period between the wars (1918–39), there were further developments with aerial photography. In the 1930s, these included the introduction of colour film and of infrared film. Infrared images can present colours otherwise invisible to the eye, and infrared film can distinguish readily between camouflaged metal, which does not reflect strongly in the infrared colours, and the surrounding vegetation, which does.

During World War II, the use of aerial photography greatly expanded and improved, while, equally significantly, the analysis of the film by photo-interpreters became more expert and reliable. Photo reconnaissance was important for military planning, as with the German attack on the Soviet Union in 1941, which was preceded by long-range reconnaissance missions by high-flying Dornier Do-215 B2s and Heinkel He-111s, and the Allied invasion of Normandy in 1944. In addition, to help bombers, existing printed maps were acquired and supplemented by the products of photo reconnaissance and other surveillance activity. To guide their bombers to targets in Britain in 1940–1, the Germans used British Ordnance Survey maps enhanced with information from photo reconnaissance.

The aerial dimension also encouraged the use of particular perspectives and projections for maps. In the United States, the innovative cartographer Richard Edes Harrison (*active* 1930s to 1970s) introduced the perspective map to American journalism in 1935. His orthographic projections and aerial perspectives brought together the United States and distant regions, and were part of a worldwide extension of American geopolitical concern and military intervention. The role of aircraft, dramatically demonstrated to the Americans by the Japanese surprise attack on Pearl Harbor in 1941, led to a new sense of space which reflected both vulnerability and the awareness of new geopolitical relationships.

⋏ A US Navy flying boat captures this shot of a large convoy while on patrol in the North Atlantic, 15 November 1941. Such photographs illustrated clearly certain aspects of the convoy system, such as inter-ship spacing and station-keeping within the convoy formation, that had hitherto been illustrated in diagrams.

➢ An aerial photograph of Pearl Harbor on 30 October, 1941 which captures the difficulty of differentiating maps from photographs. Aside, however, from the angle of the shot, there is an absence of the graticule that shows that scale is integral to a map. Nevertheless, like a map, this photograph is designed to show certain points and relationships.

official survey was carried out in 1901–4 at a scale of 1:148,752, followed by another in 1932 at 1:59,000.

The process of mapping was expanded and given greater central direction after World War II. In 1946, the Colonial Office established the Directorate of Colonial (later Overseas) Survey and instructed it to map 900,000 square miles of Africa within 10 years, using aerial photography as well as ground survey.

A prime objective in the economic development of colonies in the 1920s and 1930s, and again after World War II, was the building of new communication routes and the related exploitation of minerals and cash crops. This led to considerable mapping. In the Sudan, for example, the British greatly extended the railway system – which they had initially built to help their conquest in the 1890s – and also developed the rivers, using mechanical dredgers to clear sudd (blockages of vegetation), then building port facilities. Another development, again involving mapping, was the expensive irrigation scheme, officially opened in 1926, which brought large-scale production of cotton to the Gezira plain near Khartoum.

This mapping also accorded with the environmentalism that was dominant in geographical thinking during this period. Affected by developments in the natural sciences – especially Social Darwinism – intellectuals, including geographers and historians, assumed a close relationship between humanity and the biophysical environment. This offered a way to analyse and seek to control change. Environmentalism played a crucial role in the organic theories of the country, nation, and state, and in the treatment of the culture of particular peoples and countries as defined by the integration and interaction of nature and society.

A belief in environmentalism encouraged a mapping of rivers and mountains. Prior to this way of thinking, these had generally served an illustrative rather than descriptive, let alone prescriptive, function, but now there was a stress on the thorough mapping of physical features.

In addition, advances in map production, and in the printing of colour, in particular, made it easier both to include more physical details such as colour-coded contour zones – for example brown for 1000–2000ft – and to juxtapose such details against those of states and societies. The use of colour increased the density and complexity of information that could be conveyed, and thus made the role of the map as an explanatory device easier and clearer.

The developing subject of geopolitics added another dimension to mapping. Germany's leading political scientist, Friedrich Ratzel (1844–1904), and his disciples presented international relations as a struggle for survival. The conflict for space was central to Ratzel's *Die Erde und das Leben* (*The Earth and Life*, 1901). He emphasized the role of environmental circumstances in affecting the process and progress of struggle between states. Ratzel's environmental determinism was to be criticized in the early 20th century by "possibilists", more concerned to promote the role that human action might play within the context of the possibilities presented by the environment. However, both Ratzel's and the possibilists' approaches required detailed maps and encouraged mapping as an important aspect of their development.

In addition, there was extensive mapping of areas that hitherto had been scarcely covered. This was particularly true of Saudi Arabia and of the polar regions. Travellers in the 19th century – for example, William Palgrave (1862–3), Carlo Guarmani (1864), Charles Doughty (1876–8), and Wilfrid Scawen Blunt (1879) – had made it possible to map parts of the interior; however, much, particularly in the south of the Arabian peninsula – the Rub' al Khali, or Empty Quarter – remained unexplored by Westerners. Bertram Thomas (1930–1), Harry St John Philby (1932), and Wilfred Thesiger (1946–8) all showed that individual explorers could still contribute much.

The explorers' efforts were soon to be superseded as oil companies sought to fix frontiers. The precision of oil concession areas was imposed on a desert society where the traditional movement of Bedouin and their flocks had instilled a less territorially fixed understanding of boundaries.

This territorialization was at issue in the negotiations between Saudi Arabia and Britain over the Saudi-Trucial Coast frontier in 1934–44 and again over the frontier between Saudi Arabia and Abu Dhabi in 1947–57.

The British urged the Sultanate of Muscat and Oman, a client state, to claim a western boundary with Saudi Arabia in the 1940s, and this, in turn, exacerbated Saudi–Muscat relations. In 1954, the dispute between Abu Dhabi and Saudi Arabia over the Buraimi oasis became more serious because of the issue of oil concessions. In 1954–7, the British arbitrated the borders of the Northern Trucial States and, in 1957–60, most of those between Oman and the Trucial States. It was with maps that all these disputes were fought out and, as competing claims were asserted, clarified, then decided, and finally settled.

In the polar regions, the role of explorers on the ground was supplemented by aerial exploration. This greatly helped the process of surveying and mapping. In 1926, Richard Byrd flew over the North Pole for the first time, and in 1929 he did the same for the South Pole. He also used aircraft in his exploration of Marie Byrd Land in 1928–30. Other regions that had hitherto been little mapped included parts of the Tropics, such as the interior of New Guinea and many of the islands in the western Pacific. Much mapping in this area was not carried out until World War II, when it became a battlefield.

Mapping from the skies

The Mercator projection was unhelpful in the depiction of air routes: great circle routes and distances were poorly presented in this projection, as distances in northern and southern latitudes were exaggerated. Air travel, air power, and assumptions about the need to encompass the aerial perspective, all encouraged

DAMAGE TO BUILDINGS KOSOVSKA MITROVICA, SERBIA

BUILDINGS INTACT

BUILDINGS DAMAGED

KOSOVSKA MITROVICA

PRISTINA

8 APRIL

DAMAGED BUILDINGS

⋏ Depicting the news. This combination of photographs and a location map was made during the Yugoslavian crisis in 1999. The photographs depict Kosovska Mitrovic before (above) and after (below) the destruction of homes by Serbian forces. The location map (inset) is integral to fixing the information.

"real space" mapping of land and sea, because this was the background against which moves in the air could be planned.

Aerial mapping was also useful for less dramatic reasons. Aerial surveying and photography were extensively used after World War II, as the expertise developed during wartime was employed to map large areas previously mapped only poorly. This was particularly valuable in inaccessible terrain. Aerial photography became central to the surveys carried out by the Directorate of Overseas Survey – for example, in Gambia and Kenya – not least because it could achieve more rapid results than those obtained from the ground.

The problems of aerial photography emerged in the post-war mapping of the Antarctic Peninsula and nearby areas carried out by the Falkland Islands Dependencies Survey in order to underline Britain's title to the area. The explorer Sir Vivian Fuchs (1908–99),

the eventual leader of the survey, noted of the 1948–9 coastline survey that there were many errors in existing maps: "The maps had been compiled by air photographs without the control of accurate fixed points on the ground or rigid flight control".

Mapping was linked to naming. In 1932, the British had established the Antarctic Place Names Committee in order to ensure that British maps at least reflected official views. Names of existing territories, towns, or islands, names in any foreign language, names of sledge dogs, "names in low taste", and "names with obscure origins" were eliminated. British maps omitted names found on Argentine and Chilean maps of the Antarctic Peninsula. Mapping and naming were seen as crucial to sovereignty claims, and thus of justifying the expense of surveys.

The costs and time taken by ground surveying engendered greater support in the 1950s for aerial photography, leading to the taking of 10,000 photographs in parallel traverses in the summer seasons of 1955–6 and 1956–7. Height could be measured by the use of overlapping photographs. The unpredictable weather, however, was a major problem, while ground-based observations were still also necessary for the most accurate interpretation of aerial photography.

In a wider sense, aerial surveying and photography had more specific benefits, for example, helping to transform archaeology. From the air, it was possible both to survey terrain that was otherwise difficult and to discover sites and information that were not visible on the ground. Aerial photography threw new light on a host of issues, including the routes of Roman roads, the settlement patterns of Roman Britain and Alsace, and urbanization in Aztec Mexico. Droughts were especially helpful, those in Britain in 1976, 1984, and 1988 leading to conditions that produced more information from aerial photography.

Wartime news

Across the century, wars greatly increased public interest in maps; newspaper readers and television viewers expected news coverage to be accompanied by them. Maps were used both to provide objective accounts and for propaganda. Frank Capra's film *Prelude to War*, produced by the Film Production Division of the US Army, used maps to underline the theme of challenge: the maps of Germany, Italy, and Japan were transformed into menacing symbols, while the world map depicted Axis attacks on the New World.

Large numbers of maps were printed in newspapers in order to locate areas of conflict. They provided a more valuable addition to text than photographs and were especially valuable for the distant areas that were not well covered in conventional atlases, for example, the Eastern Front and the islands of the Pacific. In addition, the colour photography that was to come later in the century was not yet an established part of newspaper publishing. Black-and-white maps were not, therefore, overshadowed.

Providing helpful newspaper maps, however, was not easy. The simple black-and-white maps generally included little, if any, guidance to terrain or to the difficulties of communications. Thus, for example, the impact of autumn rains and spring thaws on the roads on the Eastern Front were not apparent. In addition, the notion of a front line was singularly inappropriate in some areas, especially the Pacific, where a number of important Japanese bases, such as Rabaul and Truk, were leapfrogged or bypassed thanks to superior American air and sea power, features that could not be captured on the maps.

Aside from individual maps, there was also a rapid production of atlases to satisfy consumer interest in both world wars. These included the *Atlas of the European Conflict* (Chicago, 1914), the *Daily Telegraph Pocket Atlas of the War* (London, 1917), *Géographie de la Guerre* (Paris, 1917), *From the Western Front at a Glance* (London, 1917), *Petit Atlas de la Guerre et de la Paix* (Paris, 1918),

Bretano's Record Atlas (New York, 1918), *Atlas of the War* (Oxford, 1939), *The War in Maps* (London, 1940), and *The War in Maps: An Atlas of* New York Times *Maps* (New York, 1943). *The Esso War Map* (1942) emphasized the wartime value of petroleum products – "Transportation – Key to Victory" was the theme of the text – and also provided an illustrated section "Flattening the Globe" showing how the globe becomes a map. North America was placed central to the map, which made Germany and Japan appear as menaces from east and west. The map shows sea and air distances between strategic points such as San Francisco and Honolulu.

The combatants also used and produced large numbers of maps. They were crucial for the trench warfare of World War I, especially for artillery locating their target. This need had not been anticipated by military cartographers. The French, for example, had concentrated their military mapping on fortified positions, only to discover that most of the fighting took place nowhere near these and that they were not well prepared for the mobile warfare within France in 1914.

Instead, it became necessary to respond to the need for detailed trench maps, in order to be able to plan both effective defences and successful assaults on them. Effective infantry-artillery coordination was important to British success in attack on the Western Front in 1918. Accurate surveying and mapping reduced the need for the registration of targets by guns prior to attacks and allowed the British an element of surprise.

When the British Expeditionary Force (BEF) was sent to France in 1914, one officer and one clerk were responsible for mapping, and the maps were unreliable. By 1918, the survey organization of the BEF had risen to about 5000 men and had been responsible for more than 35 million map sheets. No fewer than 400,000 impressions were produced in just 10 days in August 1918. Due to the nature of trench warfare, maps were produced for the military at a far larger scale than those with which they had been equipped for mobile campaigning.

The factors of scale were even greater in World War II. The British Ordnance Survey produced about 300 million maps for the Allied war effort, and the American Army Map Service produced more than 500 million. A shortage of maps in military collections when the United States entered the war in 1941 necessitated extensive government borrowing of them – from the New York Public Library, for example – but this situation was swiftly remedied. Units in the field were not only provided with plentiful maps, but were also able to produce them in response to new opportunities and problems.

The need to coordinate air and land, air and sea, and land and sea operations ensured the increased complexity of many maps, especially to help in planning in the three dimensions. This was true of bombing and tactical ground support operations and, for example, of airborne attacks by parachutists and gliders. The development of the operational dimension of offensives,

➢ Coastal Command chart of the British Isles for September 1940 and a *Weekly Diagram of U-boat Warfare*, 1940. These charts plot the presence of Royal Navy ships, merchant convoys, aircraft and other anti-submarine patrols, as well as U-boat sightings, and sinkings in home waters. The Weekly Diagram clearly shows clusters of U-boat activity around the bottleneck off western Scotland, where the density of British shipping offered easy targets. Karl Dönitz, commander of the U-boat fleet, estimated that, if Germany could destroy 600,000 to 750,000 tons of British shipping per month for a year, Britain would have to surrender. However, in August 1940, he had 27 ocean-going U-boats for operations, and only 13 of these were on station. The British, nevertheless, were vulnerable. Much of the fleet was in home waters, prepared to resist invasion; there was a lack of anti-submarine aircraft and convoy escort vessels; and the Germans benefited from their conquest of France and the consequent opening of Atlantic ports, such as Lorient, to the U-boats. Combined with the German conquest of Norway earlier in the year, this made the British task of containing the U-boats far more difficult.

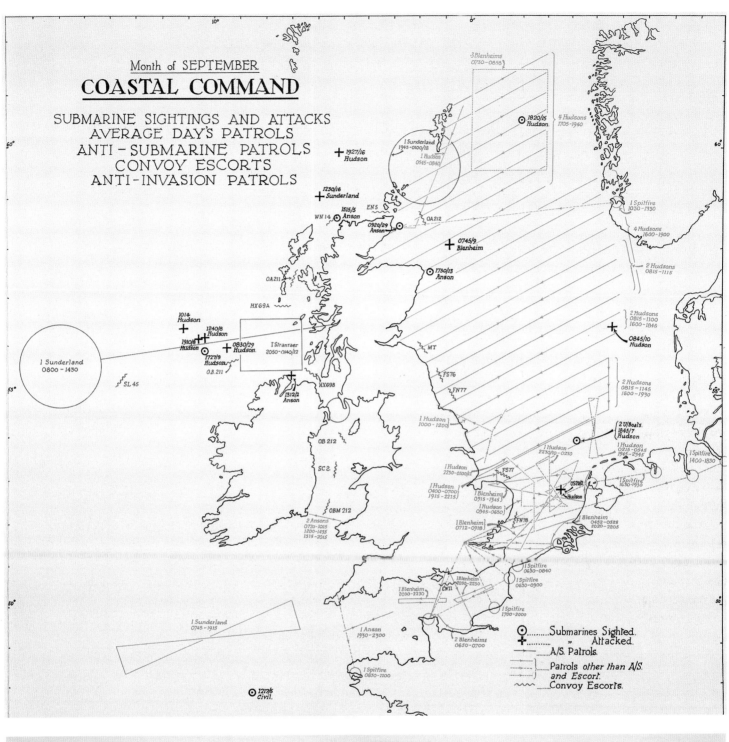

Month of SEPTEMBER

COASTAL COMMAND

SUBMARINE SIGHTINGS AND ATTACKS
AVERAGE DAY'S PATROLS
ANTI-SUBMARINE PATROLS
CONVOY ESCORTS
ANTI-INVASION PATROLS

⊙——Submarines Sighted.
✛—— „ Attacked.
✛——A/S. Patrols.
——Patrols *other than* A/S.
and Escort.
~~~~Convoy Escorts.

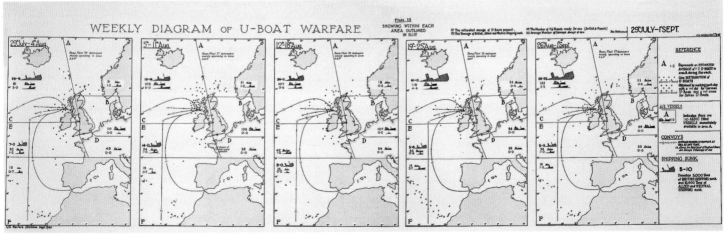

WEEKLY DIAGRAM OF U-BOAT WARFARE.   SHOWING WITHIN EACH AREA OUTLINED IN BLUE   29 JULY–1 SEPT.

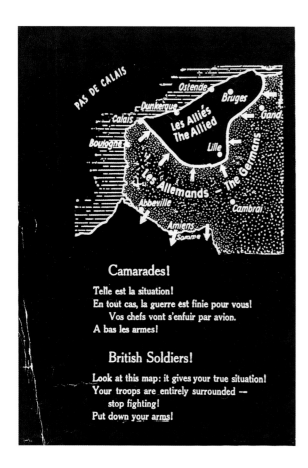

Camarades!

Telle est la situation!
En tout cas, la guerre est finie pour vous!
Vos chefs vont s'enfuir par avion.
A bas les armes!

British Soldiers!

Look at this map: it gives your true situation!
Your troops are entirely surrounded —
stop fighting!
Put down your arms!

Plotting political propaganda

Propaganda maps were also produced in the "cold wars" between competing ideologies. For example, the *Atlas of Empire* (1937) by the British Socialist James Horrabin, a work published by the left-wing house of Victor Gollancz, showed on its cover a picture of the globe encircled by a chain that included the symbols of the American dollar, the British pound, and the French franc.

The Nazis were far more blatant in their expectations of maps, although this was more the result of widespread compliance with Nazi thinking, than of a coherent propaganda offensive. The major theme was ethnographical — pressing hard the cause of the German people, many of them under foreign rule — and drew on the development of right-wing geopolitics in the 1920s. The quest for an Aryan geography produced some surprising proclamations. In *Die Entdeckung des Paradieses* (*The Discovery of Paradise*, Brunswick, 1924) the author, Franz von Wendrin, argued that the Garden of Eden had been in Germany, but that the Jews had claimed it for Asia.

The *Saar-Atlas* (Gotha, 1934) supported the German case for the reintegration of the Saarland. The first spread included a linguistic map that showed both the Saar and Alsace as clearly German. Bernhard Kumsteller's *Werden und Wachsen, Ein Geschichtsatlas auf Völkischer Grundlage* (Brunswick, 1938) presented Germany as vulnerable to France, Czechoslovakia, and Poland, and also focused on the supposed threat from communists and Jews.

In turn, Nazi agricultural and regional policies, and autobahns (motorways) were mapped in order to suggest that, just as Germany was the "bulwark against Asia", so the Nazis were the saviour of Germany. In 1938, in order to avoid harming relations with Mussolini's Fascist regime in Italy, Hitler ordered the withdrawal of a map of German culture showing the German ethnic areas in the South Tyrol which had been transferred from Austria to Italy after World War I. This type of authoritarian confusion was a central feature of Nazi rule; in 1941, for example, the Ministries of the Interior and of Propaganda had contrasting views on the colour to use for depicting Germany on maps.

Aside from maps in publications, the Nazis also encouraged maps in public displays. These emphasized areas where Germans lived under foreign rule — in 1933 a cartographic play on this theme was staged in Berlin — and maps were also used in German films. A map displayed at the 1938 Nazi Party convention showed the danger of Soviet attack on Germany by indicating the routes that could be used.

Propaganda could also be found in communist atlases. In the Soviet Union, maps were used alongside posters, murals, and cinema trains to present a visual account of the triumphs of the Communist Party. The role of central control was such that standardization in presentation and style was taken further than under the Nazis. The fall of communism was to be followed by

◄ German propaganda leaflet of 1940. Thrown from aircraft over Allied positions, this was designed to exploit the *blitzkrieg* breakthrough to the Channel; crudely printed, but effective. The use of arrows gave the impression of dynamism to the German advance. Attacking on 10 May, the Germans had reached Abbeville on the 20th. Calais surrendered on the 27th, and the Belgians capitulated on the 28th. On the 26th, the British had begun Operation Dynamo, the evacuation of the British Expeditionary Force (BEF) from Dunkirk.

especially by the Soviet army in 1943–5, required an ability to seize and retain the initiative and to outmanoeuvre opponents, and this heavily depended on staff work that was well informed about the distances and locations involved. Similarly, long-range bombing — for example, by the Americans of Japan — required particularly accurate maps because much of it was at, or close to, the limit of the bombers' flying range.

As a result of such needs, cartographic expertise was at a premium. For example, Walter Ristow, the Chief of the Map Division of the New York Public Library from 1946 to 1978, became head of the Geography and Map Section of the New York Office of Military Intelligence, while Armin Lobeck (1886–1958), Professor of Geology at Columbia University – who had published a major study of geomorphology in 1939 – produced maps and diagrams in preparation for Operation Torch, the successful American invasion of French North Africa in 1942.

Lobeck also produced a set of strategic maps for Europe. D-Day, the Allied invasion of Normandy in 1944, was preceded by precise study and mapping of climatic conditions, as these directly affected the troops' ability to land. In addition to predicting average weather conditions, there was also work on five-day forecasting. More generally, with the help of reconnaissance, models were prepared as aids to the planning of bombardment and attacks, as with the Soviet assault on Berlin in 1945. Governments also restricted the distribution of maps that might help enemies: in the United States, topographic maps and nautical charts.

much more freedom in mapmaking, especially, but not only, in Hungary and Poland.

More generally, as in the 19th century, nationalism in Europe led to the production of maps and atlases as an assertion of identity. In 1923, Pàl Teleki, a geographer who had been a Hungarian delegate to the post-World War I peace conference at Trianon (1920) that had deprived Hungary of much of its territory, published an ethnographical map of Hungary designed to support its territorial claims. In 1937, the prominent Ukrainian geographer, Volodymyr Kubijovyč, prepared and edited an *Atlas Ukrainy i sumerzhnykh kraiv* (*Atlas of the Ukraine and Adjoining Countries*) in Ukrainian and English. It was published in what was then Lvov in Poland – in other words, outside the Soviet-controlled Ukraine – and represented an assertion of Ukrainian identity against Soviet rule. In 1941, at a time when Kubijovyč was cooperating with the Germans, he prepared an atlas in German based on his 1937 work, although it was not published.

The Cold War also saw a range of ideological mapping. The sense of threat was expressed in map form, with both the United States and the Soviet Union presenting themselves as surrounded and threatened by the alliance systems, military plans, and subversive activities of their opponents. These themes could be seen clearly not only in government publications, but also in those of other organizations. The dominant role of the state helps to explain this close alignment in the case of the Soviet Union and its Communist allies, but in the United States there was also a close correspondence between governmental views and those propagated in the private sector, not least in the printed media.

News magazines offered an important illustration of the situation and served actively to propagate such governmental themes as the need for the containment of communism. Thus, in the 1 April 1946 issue of *Time*, RM Chapin produced a map entitled "Communist Contagion", which emphasized the nature of the threat and the strength of the Soviet Union. The latter was enhanced by a split-spherical presentation of Europe and Asia, making the Soviet Union more potent as a result of the break in the centre of the map. Communist expansion was emphasized by presenting the Soviet Union as a vivid red, the colour of danger, and by categorizing neighbouring states with regard to the danger of contagion, employing the language of disease: states were referred to as quarantined, infected, or exposed.

A very different world was displayed on the cover of *Time* on 15 May 1950, with the image very much that of an American counter to the Soviet Union and communism. The cover depicted a globe with facial features eagerly drinking from a bottle of Coca-Cola being offered from behind the Earth by an animated planet that was Coco-Cola. Again, the perspective was instructive. The image of the Earth was Atlanticist, with the nose on the face

➤ Skin, hair, and eye colour in central Europe: illustration from Hans FK Günther's *Rassenkunde des deutschen Volkes* (JF Lehmanns Verlag, München) 1935. This German map reflected Nazi concerns with racial characteristics. The geography of *Mitteleurope* was also interesting. It included Alsace and Lorraine, although these had been returned to France after World War I, as well as the territories lost to Poland, including the Polish Corridor. The blondish character of Sudetenland in Czechoslovakia would have underlined its German character to the map's German readers.

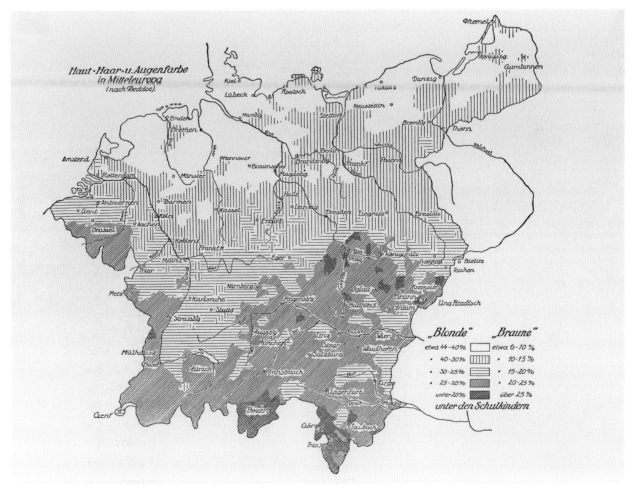

13·MÄRZ 1938
EIN VOLK EIN REICH EIN FÜHRER

⊰ A card which
commemorates the
Anschluss of 1938 by
which Austria was
annexed to Germany.
The map fused the
country, the leader,
and the Nazi Party,
and also presented
Czechoslovakia and
Poland as challenges
pressing on the German
space from the east. By
printing the names of
five Austrian cities, it
helped to educate
German readers
about their newly-
extended country.

appearing between Brazil and West Africa, and a bead of perspiration on the brow sliding down from Greenland. The Soviet Union was only partly seen, and, at that, on the edge of the map, while newly communist China and war-torn Korea were not seen on this perspective. The title and caption, "World and Friend. Love that piaster, that lira, that tickey, and that American way of life", referred to the seductive, worldwide model of American culture. It seemed fresh, vital, optimistic, and democratic, certainly compared to the war-scarred and exhausted societies of Europe.

Its cultures weakened or discredited by defeat, collaboration, or exhaustion, much of Western European society, especially that of West Germany, was reshaped in response to American influences and consumerism, which were associated with prosperity, youth, fashion, and glamour. American culture also replaced European models elsewhere, particularly in Canada and Latin America. Thus, the image on the front of *Time* captured the particular nature of America's cultural impact, offering a different vision of global politics and a different account of geopolitics to those provided by maps that emphasized military threats.

Independence from colonial rule was followed by the publication of national atlases such as *Atlas for the Republic of Cameroon* (London, 1971), *Atlas de la Haute-Volta* (Paris, 1975), *Atlas de Côte d'Ivoire* (Abidjan, 1975), *Atlas de Burundi* (Gradignan, 1979), and *Atlas for Botswana* (Gaborone, 1988). These works proclaimed national independence as a historical goal. The *Atlas de Madagascar* (Tananarive, 1969), prepared by the country's association of geographers and with a foreword by the president, emphasized unification and unity, the formation of a united people, a united state, and a "unité morale". The *National Atlas of Ethiopia*, produced by the Ethiopian Mapping Authority (Addis Ababa, 1988), offered a work in accordance with the aggressive Marxism of the regime, not least its opposition to Somalia. Similarly, the *Atlas de Cuba* (Havana, 1978), produced in 1979 to commemorate the 20th anniversary of the Cuban Revolution, accorded with communist ideology.

The production of these atlases tends to be ignored in works on cartographic history, but they were important to one of the most neglected aspects of mapping over the past half-century: the situation outside the West. That is where the majority of the world's population lives, but we know very little about how they see maps and how their senses of space has changed. Instead, the history of the map in the modern world is presented in terms of the spread of Western cartographic assumptions and products.

To turn to atlases such as those mentioned above is to see products that conform to the Western model; indeed, some have been published by Western firms. Government surveys in developing countries were derived from agencies established under colonial rule. The training, tools, and, indeed, maps of the colonial period have persisted. In addition, governments have sought to benefit from mapping provided by Western governments and agencies.

From this perspective, it is possible to present developing-world views of the globe in terms of Western cartography, albeit a Western cartography that is less well funded and is thus a pale shadow of the more intensive mapping conducted in more affluent countries.

Alongside this, it is necessary to consider the degree to which the spatial awareness of developing-world populations is not shaped in these terms. The extent to which societies such as Madagascar are suffused in cartographic images is far less than is the case for Britain or the United States. This is a matter of different educational practices, varying rates of book ownership, and contrasting access to television. Indeed, the role of television in providing daily exposure to maps, particularly in weather reports, cannot be exaggerated.

Exposure to television increased greatly in the second half of the 20th century. By 1986, there were 26 million television sets in Brazil, 10.5 million in India, and 6.6 million in Indonesia. Such figures are put in perspective by the 195 million then in the United States. Per head of population, television use was far higher in the developed world, and, in contrast, was particularly patchy in sub-Saharan Africa and Southeast Asia. However, the numbers of people involved were such that a rise in the per capita rate, especially in China and India, was very important.

Thanks, in particular, to satellite transmission, access to television continued to spread after 1986, especially in India, and this facilitated increased access to maps and images of the globe, for example, on networks such as CNN or the BBC's Asian services. Thus, those who had previously relied on radio stations, such as the BBC's World Service, for their news could now see, in the form of maps, exactly what they could formerly only hear.

For all the disparity in television ownership, literacy levels were rising worldwide, and this enabled access to another category of maps. Across most of the world, thanks to a marked increase in education, especially for women and the poor (both of whom had largely been marginalized in educational terms), literacy rose greatly – this was particularly impressive given the rapid rate of population growth.

By the end of the 20th century, most people in the developed world able to achieve literacy were literate; at the same time, the literacy rate in China had risen to about 80 per cent, and across most of the developing world the number of literate had also risen rapidly but was still lower than in developed countries. In 1995, approximately 900 million people worldwide were illiterate, with the majority of this number in India and with illiteracy rates in general being higher for women than for men.

The spatial sense of the illiterate and their awareness of maps await study. Because illiteracy in the modern world is far more clearly a product of social differentiation, the situation now is presumably different to that of societies – including those discussed in chapter two – in which all, or most, people were illiterate. Because of their dependence on text – for titles, captions, keys, and scales – modern maps, unlike those discussed in chapter two, are not readily accessible to the illiterate, and the use of such maps is geared to a literate culture attuned to visual imagery.

It would be interesting to see how far a history of maps can be offered that takes due note of the illiterate and of their mental mapping, which is quite distinct from our standard Western account of cartographic history. A failure to at least mention this issue would undermine any story of maps that focuses on improving technology.

Mapping the news

The impact of politics on mapping varied greatly. In South Africa during the apartheid regime, numerous substantial black settlements, particularly townships and squatter settlements, were ignored or minimized on maps. In part, this reflected the difficulties of mapping such settlements, especially squatter settlements, but the main reason was a deliberate bias towards the white population. Thus, small white-dominated towns, especially in rural areas, were given a misleading prominence in maps.

A good example of the inextricable link between maps and the news – a link that helps to keep maps in the public eye – can be seen in *The Economist* magazine of 21 December 2002, No. 8304, with maps serving both illustrative and interpretative purposes. Thus, an article on Russia's Baltic enclave of Kaliningrad was supported by a map showing its location and, thanks to a scale, its distance from the rest of Russia; inset is a map of Europe showing the location of the detailed map, offering all the necessary information with an economic use of space.

Similar maps (and insets) illustrate articles on the province of Aceh in Sumatra and the problems of road transport in Cameroon – maps for the latter complement the text with a visual account of events such as a collapsed bridge and sections of flooded roads. In contrast, the map showing existing and proposed communication links between the Spanish province of Aragon and southern France relies on the text to describe issues such as economic and political constraints, and the fact that, because Spanish trains run on a wider gauge, goods must be transhipped or bogies changed. Costs and transhipment can be mapped, but the nuances of the political context cannot.

In contrast, in the same issue are two interpretative maps designed to clarify the position and prospects of the American Republicans and the British Conservatives. The first shows heavily Republican counties in the 2000 election, defined as those where George Bush won 60 per cent or more of the vote, and major centres of population; the second shows the safer Conservative parliamentary seats, defined as those with at least a 10 percentage point margin of victory, and, again, major centres of population.

In fact, the choice of what to include on the map, and what to leave out, somewhat undermines title and text. The title of the

A Soviet cartoon criticizing American foreign policy, 1952. The Americans are talking about "peace, defence and disarmament" while preparing for war. Unlike NATO maps, this cartoon makes no reference to Soviet additional control. Soviet military facilities are ignored, but NATO bases are depicted by aircraft. The defeat of the Communists in the Greek Civil War leads the American general to place a base there. The powerful American presence in East Anglia, where B-29s were based, is also referred to.

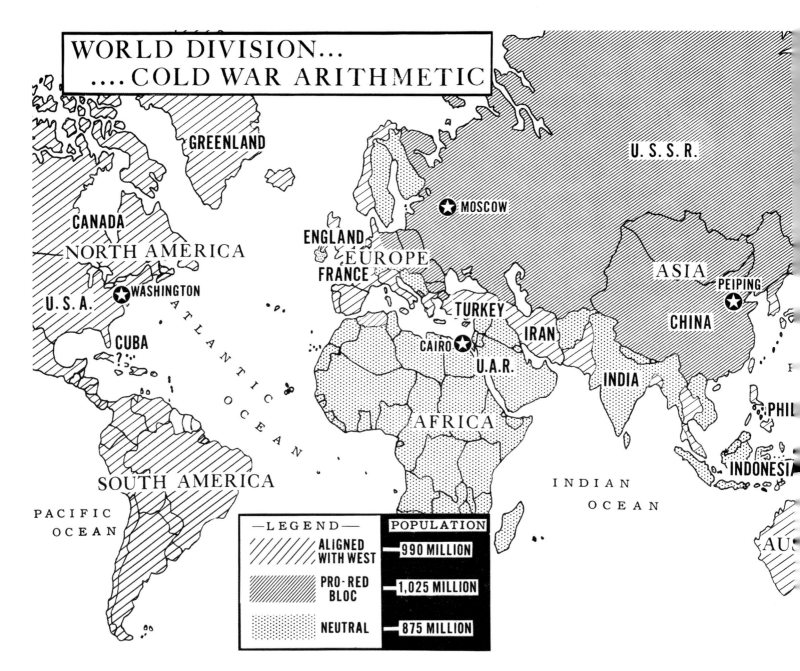

WORLD DIVISION...
....COLD WAR ARITHMETIC

GREENLAND

U.S.S.R.

★ MOSCOW

CANADA

NORTH AMERICA

ENGLAND

EUROPE

FRANCE

ASIA

PEIPING

★

★ WASHINGTON

U.S.A.

CHINA

TURKEY

IRAN

CUBA

?

CAIRO ★

U.A.R.

INDIA

ATLANTIC

OCEAN

PHIL

AFRICA

INDONESI

SOUTH AMERICA

INDIAN

OCEAN

PACIFIC

OCEAN

AU

—LEGEND—

POPULATION

ALIGNED WITH WEST

990 MILLION

PRO-RED BLOC

1,025 MILLION

NEUTRAL

875 MILLION

American map "Yee-hah!" is accompanied by a text stating that the Republicans "are now much closer to a national party (see map)". The title for the British map is "Ageing, rural and dwindling" and the text describes the Conservatives as "a regional party". Yet, the inclusion on the American map of major centres of population which are not heavily Republican lessens the impression created by the many counties shaded in. Moreover, the failure to offer population-based cartograms affects the value of both maps.

Aside from these maps, the influence of maps can be seen in articles discussing the "road map" as a possible solution to the Israel–Palestine crisis and a cartoon about the passing of the year in which the head of a UN Weapons Inspection Team gestures towards the globe. Thus, in this issue of a prominent news magazine, as in many others, images of the world and the language of maps and mapping play an intrinsic role in news coverage.

Lift off into the space age

The rocket age, which began when the first satellite, the Soviet *Sputnik*, was launched in 1957, enhanced the mappability of the world. Orbiting satellites offered the potential for the radio dispatch of images and also for material from recoverable cameras. The earliest pictures from space were provided from the American satellite *Explorer 6* by the former method in 1959.

Every day the Earth is photographed by weather satellites, and this has led to a great improvement in the understanding and mapping of global and regional climate, and, in particular, in the understanding of how they interact. The first weather satellite, *Tiros* (Television and Infra-Red Observation Satellite) *I*, was launched in 1960 to provide systematic images of the cloud cover.

Satellites were also important for photo reconnaissance, in order both to keep track of other powers and to improve the mapping of the world and thus enhance the precise aiming of

⋏ With the Cold War at its height, this American news map from 1960 explained, by reference to the arithmetic of population numbers, why the non-aligned world was regarded as so important. The question mark for Cuba indicates that it was still a member of the Rio Pact, but that, under Castro, the government was becoming increasingly anti-American. In July 1960, the month in which this map was

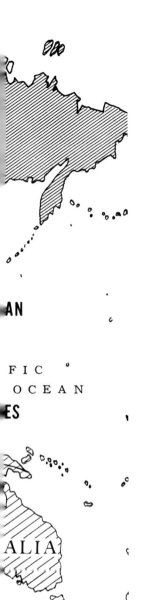

warheads. In 1960, the first pictures were received from *Discoverer 13*, the first in a line of successful American military photo-reconnaissance satellites. For their Soviet opponent, *Cosmos 4* followed in 1962.

Unlike the high-flying American U-2 spy plane, one of which had been shot down in 1960, satellites were too high to shoot down and therefore offered the possibility of frequent overflights and thus of increased observations. This was important to the arithmetic of deterrence during the Cold War between the United States and the Soviet Union, and the range of observation was increased with the American development of the space shuttle, which provided images from a low orbit.

In terms of their importance to mapping, satellites helped to improve the accuracy of the mapping of the polar regions, as well as to improve our understanding of the Earth's shape – especially its flattening at the Poles. Because the Earth is not a regular geometrical shape, in order to be precise about distances, it is necessary to measure them, rather than to extrapolate from observations, and satellites have made this possible.

Satellite photography played a role in the Second World Geodetic System, which was established in 1966. The development of satellite geodesy (the science of measuring the Earth) from 1987 superseded traditional methods of surveying, in the same way as electronic distance measuring had replaced triangulation in the 1960s.

In 1972, the Earth Resources Technology Satellite (renamed Landsat) was launched by the United States. Landsat relied not on the television cameras used by Tiros, but on a telescope and spinning mirror that scanned the Earth's surface to build up a digital image. NASA, the American National Aeronautics and Space Administration, produced pictures which served as maps by a technique known as remote sensing by Landsat imagery, in which images are generated from electromagnetic radiations outside the normal visual range. Using different wavelengths, it is possible to focus on different, specific aspects of the Earth's surface; infrared is especially valuable for vegetation surveys and for detecting water resources. Infrared images are generally presented in false colour: the infrared part of the spectrum normally being shown in red. There are, however, alternatives such as simulated natural colour.

Satellite location-finding provided a major new tool for mapmakers. The US Department of Defense developed a global positioning system (GPS) that depended on satellites. GPS was made available to civilians, although the accuracy of the signal was degraded by a process known as "selective availability" so that positions would be accurate to within 100m (328ft) only 95 per cent of the time.

Rockets took further the transformation of geopolitics by air power. Confrontation between the United States and the Soviet Union was demonstrated by maps that used a polar azimuthal projection. By being centred on the North Pole, this projection

shows shortest distances or trajectories as straight lines through the Pole as if a great circle passing through the ends of the trajectory also passes through the Pole. This was a suitable image for a world threatened by intercontinental missiles because surface geography was less important than shortest distance. Such maps served to demonstrate the threat to the United States posed by a Soviet Union that was closer over the North Pole than across the Atlantic. Thanks to the shift in mapping, St Petersburg and New York appeared closer than hitherto.

Satellite data also served as the basis of enhanced weaponry. "Smart" weaponry, such as guided bombs and missiles, makes use of the prior precise mapping of target and traverse in order to follow predetermined courses to targets actualized for the weapon as a grid reference. Cruise missiles use digital terrain models of the intended flight path. However, there are some discrepancies in the mapping that such systems rest on, and this can affect the pinpoint accuracy they seek. For example, there is a lack of consistency about the positioning of coastlines, in particular about the use of a median position between high and low water marks.

The sense of the world as a mapped target was captured in the James Bond film *Diamonds Are Forever* (1971), as the map shows Washington coming towards the range of Blofeld's space-mounted laser gun. Automated aiming and firing techniques have reduced the need for the human use of maps on the battlefield, but, in large part, these rest on accurate surveying and mapping.

Since its inception, there has been a rapid improvement in satellite observation of the Earth and this is true of a number of characteristics. For example, the resolution of satellite cameras has improved. In 1972, the first Landsat camera system had a resolution of 80m (262ft), while there were four separate channels in the multi-spectral scanner covering visible and infrared parts of the spectrum.

In contrast, Landsat 4, launched in 1982, had as its scanner a thematic mapper with seven spectral channels and a spatial resolution of 98ft (30m). The increase in the number of channels made it possible to go further into the infrared wavelengths, and thus reveal colours invisible to the naked eye. The use of false colour systems aided analysis of vegetation and land use.

With time, there was also an increased use of satellites and a greater range in their use. Indeed, satellite information has become a crucial adjunct in both planning and monitoring. In terms of monitoring, it has proved possible to check the implementation of regulations, thus it is now possible to gauge the failure of the European Union to control rampant fraud in agricultural subsidy programmes and also to chart the growing of crops that yield substances illegally manufactured into narcotic drugs.

Satellite information served to correct, as well as to supplement, information acquired by ground surveys, leading, for example, in the 1980s to a bleaker account of the rate of forest clearance in the Tropics.

produced, the Cubans began expropriating all American-owned property. The UAR was the United Arab Republic, which comprised Egypt and Syria. The strategic importance of Indonesia, where the United States supported the overthrow of the Sukarno regime and the defeat of the Communists in 1965–6, emerges clearly.

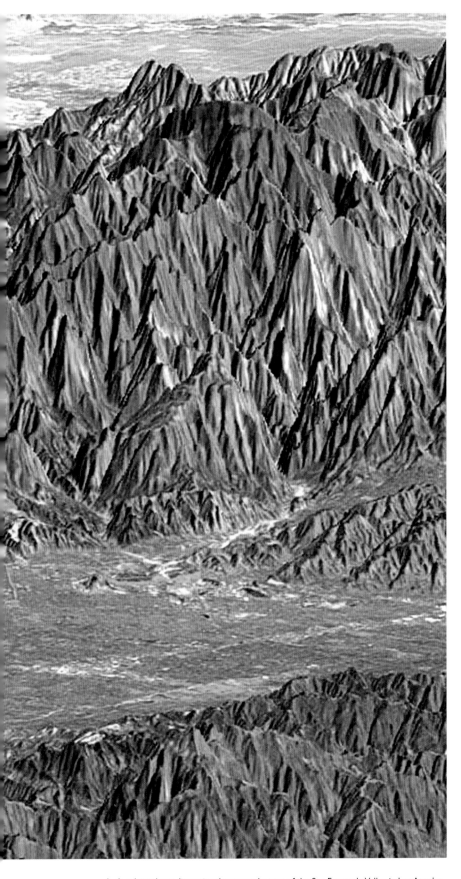

The governmental purposes served by satellites are increasingly non-military and have been complemented by a greater range of private enterprise goals. The profitable uses to which satellite observation systems can be put encouraged states other than France to launch satellites for such purposes. Until 1986, the United States alone had high-resolution remote-sensing systems, but that year the French launched the SPOT satellite the sensor of which has a resolution of 10m (32ft). France was followed by other powers, including India, Japan, and Canada, to which the United States responded by seeking greater commercial benefit from its satellite programme.

It also pressed ahead with military surveillance satellites. By 2000, these had a resolution better than 100mm (4in). The potential of this mapping became a major political issue in 2002, as the United States and the United Kingdom claimed that satellite information made it clear that Iraq was stockpiling weapons of mass destruction and evading the ground-search programme being carried out by United Nations inspectors. This highlighted the extent to which it was possible to overcome one of the major characteristics of totalitarian regimes – information management.

At the same time, the availability of satellite surveillance systems using digital sensors and transmitting, almost instantaneously, their pictures over encrypted radio links, highlighted the difference in capability and potential in mapping and information that has been true from the outset of cartography. The frustration displayed by Iraqi leaders in late 2002 was instructive in that it was more pointed than earlier responses to Western cartography, as the Iraqi leadership was more aware of its relative disadvantage than, for example, Chinese leaders in 1860 when British and French forces advanced on Beijing.

New projections

Projections of the Mercator type were the most influential in the 20th century, but there were others. Concern with maritime routes and familiarity with Mercator-type projections encouraged an essential conservatism in presentation, not least because one alternative, an equal-area projection developed by J Paul Goode in the 1920s, required cuts not only at the margins, but also in the oceans, and there was a cultural preference for flattening the globe into a two-dimensional shape without any obvious joins or cuts except at the margins.

The Van der Grinten projection, invented in 1898, continued the Mercator projection's practice of exaggerating the size of the temperate latitudes. Thus, Greenland, Alaska, Canada, and the Soviet Union appeared larger than they were in reality. This projection was used by the American National Geographic Society from 1922–88; as such, it was very influential. The society's maps were the staple of educational institutions, the basis of maps used by newspapers and television, and the acme of public cartography for a period when the United States was the most

⋏ A colour three-dimensional topography map of the San Fernando Valley in Los Angeles, California. The image was created by the Shuttle Radar Topography Mission (SRTM) on board the Space Shuttle Endeavour on 16 February 2000. A 1986 Landsat colour image of the area was overlaid on the elevation data. This densely populated area of California is prone to earthquakes and it is hoped that modelling the landforms in this way will enable new buildings to be built in areas at least risk of earthquake damage.

powerful nation in the world. In that projection, a large Soviet Union appeared menacing, a threat to the whole of Eurasia and a dominant presence that required containment. This was a cartographic image appropriate for the Cold War.

The geopolitical menace was abruptly reduced in the Robinson projection adopted by the National Geographic Society in 1988. This offered a flatter, squatter world and one that was more accurate in terms of area. Compared to the Van der Grinten projection, in the Robinson projection the Soviet Union moved from being 223 per cent larger than it really is to being only 18 per cent larger; Greenland went from 554 per cent larger to 60 per cent larger; Canada from 258 percent larger to 21 per cent larger; and the United States from 68 per cent larger to three per cent smaller.

An alternative, and influential, projection was devised by the German Marxist, Arno Peters, and presented in 1973. It was, however, far weaker than many other equal-area maps because it distorted shape far more seriously, greatly elongating the Tropics so that, for example, the length, but not the width, of Africa was greatly exaggerated. Coastal shapes were therefore considerably distorted, and the standard cartographic images of continents – the iconic language of map shapes so important to map readers – was changed. Distances on the Peters's projection could not be readily employed to plot data.

Peters portrayed the world of maps as a choice between his projection – which he presented as accurate and egalitarian – and the traditional Mercator world view. Arguing that the end of European colonialism and the advance of modern technology made a new cartography necessary and possible, Peters pressed for a clear, readily understood cartography that was not constrained by scientific cartography and European perceptions. The map was to be used for a redistribution of attention to regions that Peters felt had hitherto lacked adequate coverage.

This struck a chord with a receptive, international audience that cared little about cartography, but sought maps to support its call for a new world order. Peters's emphasis on the Tropics matched concern by and about the developing world and became fashionable. The Peters world map was praised in, and used for the cover of *North-South: A Programme for Survival* (1980): the "Brandt Report" of the International Commission on International Development Issues, although critics pointed out the weaknesses and, indeed, derivative character of the projection and the tendentious nature of many of Peters's claims.

Alongside explicit engagement with the issue of projections has come a more open willingness to face the different ways in which material can be mapped. It is helpful to read Malcolm McKinnon's instructive preface to the *New Zealand Historical Atlas* (Auckland, 1997). Referring to plate 52, "Space Transformed", he provides an account that is worth quoting in full because it provides a model for the self-reflective atlas, as well as making

explicit the process of selection that exists in all mapping, and also indicating the range of options available with which to map late 19th-century communications:

"The maps and graphics on this plate present information at the local, regional, colony-wide and global levels. This sequence is followed anticlockwise round the page. There is also a chronological sequence – 1850s/60s, 1870s/80s and 1890s – which is followed through both the local/regional maps (Lyttelton precedes the two upper South Island graphics) and also the 'quickest journey' and 'rail/telegraph/cable' maps.

The map perspectives are not just randomly chosen either. The style of the Lyttelton map – a logarithmic projection – is chosen to emphasize the centrality of the port to communications in the period before the extensive development of telegraph and rail. The upper South Island telegraph map makes a deliberately contrasting point to those of its two neighbours. Notice that it is now Christchurch that is prominent, not Lyttelton. And compare the character of the map with that of the 'Nelson problem' map to its right: relief is more important for understanding rail than telegraph. The Nelson graphic also makes its own point. We think of Nelson as being 'isolated'. But Nelson was well-connected by sea (in the foreground), and if it had been able to establish equivalent connections by land (in the background) it might have been Wellington that was 'isolated'. As it transpired, Nelson's political leverage was not able to 'move mountains'.

The 'quickest journey' maps draw attention to the compression of space by compressing the map. For their part the three colony maps are drawn identically, so that comparisons can be made between three dates. The southern perspective is designed to emphasise that development occurred first in the east and south of the South Island. Finally, the global map deliberately uses a Mercator projection. This was the traditional projection for showing time zones and the like because it allowed bearings to be mapped as straight lines. In sum, the choice and juxtapositioning of the images, in respect of both their design and their content, is always quite deliberate."

As with other non-historical maps, there is the question of what to depict, in this case, which aspects of the past and of change to show, and also the inherent danger that what is shown implies a causality that may be absent, exaggerated, controverted, or, indeed, more complex.

A good example is provided by the spread "Abolitionists and Runaways. The Failure of the Underground Railroad" in *Mapping America's Past: A Historical Atlas* by Mark Carnes, John Garraty, and Patrick Williams (New York, 1996). This includes a map "The myth

of the 'underground railway'" (p. 106) which depicts the "mythic representation of runaway exodus" (p. 106), a textual comment "The underground railroad was neither as organized nor as extensive as legend suggests ... it did not exist in any of the slave states", and a map showing the escape itineraries of eight prominent fugitives (p. 107).

In the introduction to the atlas, Carnes explains how the attempt to map the "railroad" convinced him and his colleagues that it was a misleading thesis and that it was inability to escape which was more significant (p. 5). As an instance of the maturity of this atlas, the introduction makes clear that the choice of topics, which reflects interest in social and cultural topics, has led to a downplaying of others.

One of the ambiguities of map production relates to the tension between what might be seen, in terms of the techniques of information display, as the clutter of too many place names, and the emphasis only on those names that fit in with the cartographer's ostensible story. This reveals the ambiguity between what the cartographer hopes to call attention to and what the end user of the map may need to learn. Without detailed – and hence more open-ended – atlases, the possibility of the reader seeing a hitherto overlooked spatial pattern, regularity, or relationship, and therefore of engaging in acts of consideration or discovery independent of the cartographer's intent, is diminished.

Into the oceans' abyss

Knowledge of the oceans – which cover most of the world's surface – was transformed in the 20th century. Before then, knowledge of the deep seas had been limited, although the laying

Mapping the Universe

The landing of Neil Armstrong and Buzz Aldrin on the Moon in July 1969 is one of the landmark events of the 20th century, indeed, of all time. Our fascination with the Moon remains undiminished, and thanks to modern satellite and telescope technology we can make detailed topographical maps of its surface. Other rocket and space-probe missions are now travelling further afield helping us to build up a more detailed map of the Solar System and the surfaces of the planets within it. The Hubble Space Telescope, launched in April 1990, is now showing us what parts of the universe looked liked billions of years ago.

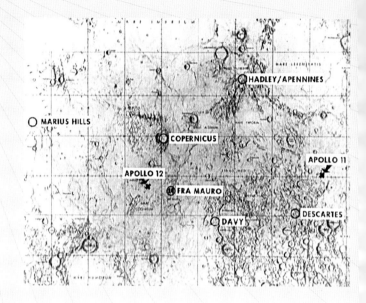

Rockets have allowed the exploration of outer space, and the resulting photography was fed directly into maps. The Soviet *Lunik-3* rocket sent back the first pictures of the far side of the Moon in 1959, providing information on the 41 per cent of the moon's surface that is permanently hidden from the Earth. The Soviet Union produced an atlas based on the rocket's photography, distinguishing between areas that were accurately represented and those that were not, and mapping ray patterns emerging from craters, "seas", and areas darker than the surrounding landscape, as well as naming certain features. Measurements on photographs had to be carefully related to orbital computations.

The mapping of the Moon by orbiting satellites was followed, in 1969, by the first manned moon-landing. Mapping had played an important role in the selection of a landing site for this momentous event.

This was followed by an attempt to use space probes to supplement earth-telescopes in mapping the planets and the stellar systems. The American *Voyager* mission, launched in 1977, provided images of Jupiter, Saturn, Uranus, and Neptune. The ability to send back radio signals that could travel at the speed of light – such as those that sent pictures of Neptune in 1989 – ensured that these images could be received and used, like earlier mapping, to supplement existing material.

The quest to understand the solar system, and what lies beyond it, is far from complete, but the ability to map and analyse it from both Earth and space led to a major leap forward in human knowledge, and the production of images of the universe, or cosmological maps, that were considerably more complex than those of earlier ages.

The *Voyager* mission, like those to the Moon and Mars, revealed no signs of life. The absence of any encounter with extraterrestrial life-forms ensured that there was no new challenge in cartography, as well as no fundamental questioning of the relative nature of human values. Thus, the depiction of hummankind in relation to cosmic themes and powers that had been an important aspect of early mapping was not revived. The predictive power of the imagination seen in films such as Stanley Kubrick's *2001: A Space Odyssey* (1968) proved deficient, as the massive increase in man's ability to scrutinize other planets did not lead to the transforming discoveries that had been anticipated.

⋀ Lunar map showing landing areas for Apollo manned lunar landing missions, 1970. This map shows the landing areas that had already been used and the locations of six candidate sites for the remainder of the *Apollo* flights. Those indicated are: Sea of Tranquility (*Apollo 11*), Ocean of Storms (*Apollo 12*), Fra Mauro (*Apollo 14*), Hadley/Apennines (*Apollo 15*). and Marius Hills, Descartes, Davy, and Copernicus. Maps of the Moon introduced the public to a whole new area of cartography and also posed problems for cartographers.

➤ Coloured topographic map of the Moon's western hemisphere. Colour provided a means to give far more information for maps of both the Earth and the Moon. Here, the Moon's right-hand side is Earth-facing, the left is on the Moon's far side. The mean radius of the planet is represented by the border between blue and green; dark blue and magenta are the lowest areas, yellow and red the highest. The image clearly shows the difference between the near side with its oceans and the mountainous far side. The Mare Orientale impact basin (blue circle) is just below the centre, with the deep SP – Aitken Basin bottom left. The data for this image was gathered in 1994 by the Clementine satellite.

of telegraph cables had brought some information about the ocean floor. Knowledge came in a number of ways: from satellites, aircraft, submersibles, surface ships using sonar, and from boring into the ocean floor. The ocean floor's effect on the water surface, and thus its contours, could be picked up on radar images taken from aircraft and satellites. Water temperatures, measured in the same way, provided warning of forthcoming storms.

Ship- and air-borne towed magnetometers and deep ocean borehole core sequences gathered widespread data about magnetic anomalies. Submersibles able to resist extreme pressure took explorers to the depths of the ocean. In 1950, the *Morskoi Atlas* brought together all the new information on the oceans for the first time. In 1960, Jacques Piccard (*b.* 1922), in the bathyscaph *Trieste*, explored the deepest part of the world's oceans, the Marianas Trench near the Philippines. From the 1970s, metals on the ocean floors were mapped. Unmanned submersibles with remote-controlled equipment furthered underwater exploration and mapping. Thanks to such information, mapping of the ocean floors became more ambitious.

By the end of the century, thanks to Seasat imagery produced from 1978, a full map of the ocean floors was possible. It revealed the processes of change, whereby new material forced its way up, for example, in the mid-Atlantic ridge, causing volcanoes, while elsewhere matter was pushed down to form trenches. Thus continental drift and the clash of tectonic plates could be mapped, and fault lines clarified. The mapping of plate boundaries accompanied their classification, and this helped to make sense of the location of volcanic and earthquake zones, as well as hot spots such as that beneath the Hawaiian chain.

Interest in the oceans encouraged one oceanographer, Athelstan Spilhaus (1911–98), to remap the world emphasizing its water surface. His mapping of the so-called "water planet" had a world ocean as the dominant feature. In 1942, Spilhaus produced a three-lobed map, centring respectively on the Atlantic, Pacific, and Indian oceans, with the map joined around Antarctica.

Although it did not centre on the oceans, the notion of a map joined around a pole (in this case, the North Pole) was also seen in the Dymaxion projection of Buckminster Fuller (1895–1983), published in *Life* magazine in 1943 and patented in 1946. This was in some respects the obverse of the Spilhaus projection because it stressed the connectedness of the continents and presented them as a world island surrounded on every side by water.

Mapping our damaged planet

Advances in modern mapping, especially the use of satellite imagery, made it possible to construct maps that addressed one of the central issues of the age: the state of the environment. In many senses, mapping had an ambivalent relationship with environmental damage. For a long time, one of the major purposes of maps had been to reveal resources for man to

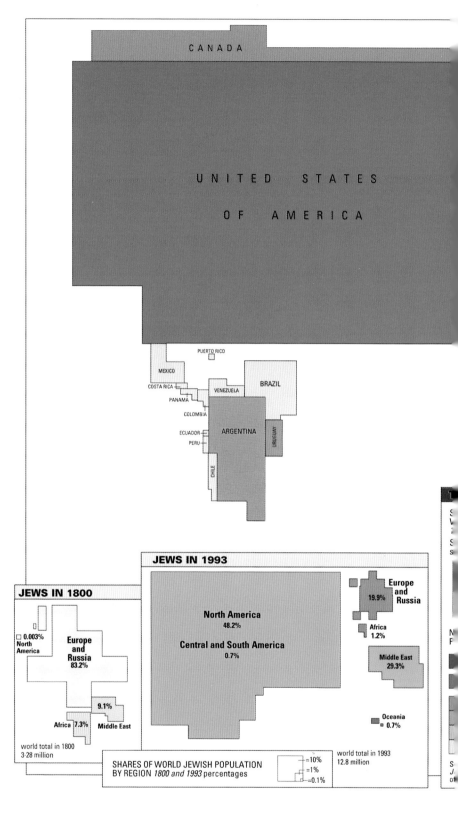

exploit. Thus, in the 19th century, maps were produced in order to assist gold rushes. In 1851, Charles Drayton Gibbes's *New Map of the Gold Region in California from His Own and Other Recent Surveys and Explorations* was published in New York.

Similarly, in the 20th century, maps showed drivers how to reach new destinations. Alongside the increase of car ownership and road use, map use grew greatly in the 1920s and 1930s in both North America and Europe. Demand for maps rose, and

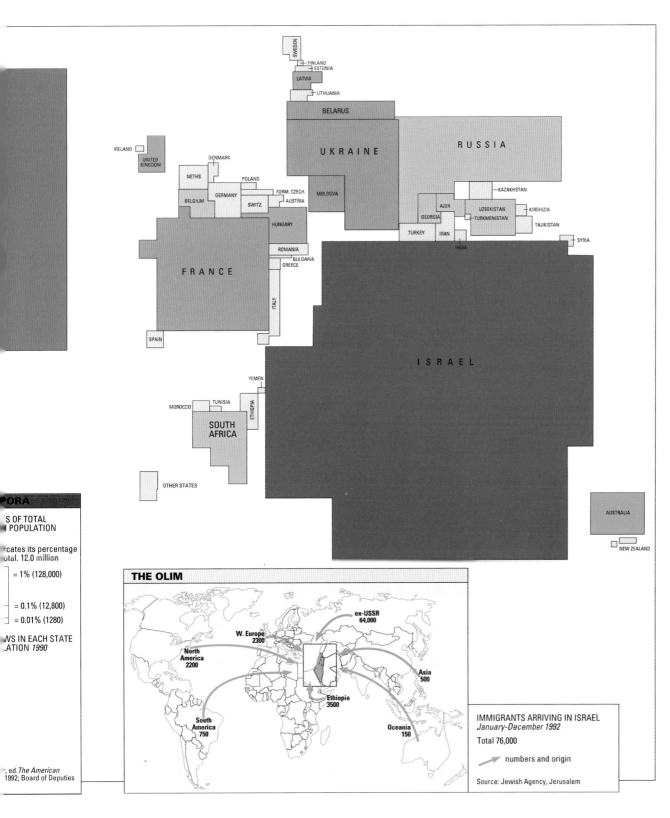

◁ "The Jewish Diaspora", taken from *The State of Religion Atlas* of 1993. This map uses the device of a block diagram to provide a visual impression of the distribution and importance of the Jewish diaspora, with the diagrammatic representation bearing no relation to the size of countries. Instead, an equal-population cartogram depicts the size of countries by their percentage of the world's population of Jews in 1990 and colour-codes them by the number of Jews per 1000 people. The prominence of the United States alongside Israel emerges clearly.

map companies responded, producing and distributing readily useable and relatively inexpensive road maps or maps in which roads were prominent. Countries were depicted for drivers, and for them alone. In contrast, from about 1850 until the 1920s, general American maps depicted railways but not roads.

By the second half of the 20th century, however, the human impact on the environment had become a major topic for mapping. Pollution and environmental degradation have not only been mapped in specialist works, but also become an issue in mainstream cartography. Indeed, this helped lead to a tempering of the relentless emphasis on progressivism – the assumption that "more equals better" – in the texts that had accompanied atlases. Maps had for so long concentrated on human activity within an intellectual context that saw such activity as beneficial, as improving the world. Thus, to map more towns and roads, or the expansion of the cultivated area, was to reveal the march of progress.

More recent mapping has focused on the negative impact on the environment of human activity, as with the mapping of the Gaia hypothesis – the proposition that the biosphere operates in an organic fashion using natural feedback mechanisms to sustain life. This interdependence was emphasized in *The Gaia Atlas of Planet Management* (1985), and the globe was presented as an environmental system affected by human activities, such as atmospheric pollution.

Similarly, in the aftermath of the 1976–7 Californian drought, the publicly funded and produced *California Water Atlas* (1978) emphasized the politics and problems of water supply systems. It showed how these were developed by man to address specific historical circumstances, and were not natural and immutable. The Atlas was offered as a public service, presenting the information collected by the government in order for the public to better understand the causes of drought.

Thus maps were to be used to educate the public – their very appearance indicated public concern. Satellite information was used to map closed canopy rain forests for *The Conservation Atlas of Tropical Forests: Africa* (New York, 1992), and also revealed, then mapped, the hole in the ozone layer over Antarctica. Changes in the layer were then dramatized in maps.

⋏ Aqua satellite map of water vapour in the atmosphere over the oceans. The amount of vapour, which forms clouds, is colour-coded from light blue (least) to dark blue (most). The small yellow areas correspond to areas of high precipitation. Snow and ice are yellow, deserts are dark green, other land

is black. Aqua, a joint mission between NASA and NASDA (the Japanese space agency), was launched on 4 May, 2002 as part of NASA's Earth Observing System (EOS) of satellites. This image was taken by Aqua's Advanced Microwave Scanning Radiometer for EOS (AMSR–E).

More generally, environmentalists use maps to highlight risk. And maps are also used to define and understand bio-regions in the search for ways in which mankind and nature can coexist without damaging the environment. The inclusion of environmental-issue maps in many modern atlases indicates a rising awareness of the usefulness of mapping such issues.

These maps also appear in other sources that testify to a growing concern for the environment. Thus, *Strategic Assessment 1999*, published by the Institute for National Strategic Studies of the America National Defense University, included maps which showed water shortages in 1999 and the probable situation in 2025, as well as a map depicting per capita international debt. Maps were also were used to plan irrigation schemes. By both highlighting environmental issues and helping us make the best use of the environment, maps proved their flexibility; in other words, maps can be seen as a medium, not the message.

They are also a changing medium. Satellites have seen to that. The maps produced for the *Land Utilisation Survey of Great Britain*, published in 1933–46, for example, relied not on satellites, but on schoolteachers and their pupils carrying out surveys in the field. The survey was designed to help plan land use in the event of war, and was employed after the war to aid land-use planning,

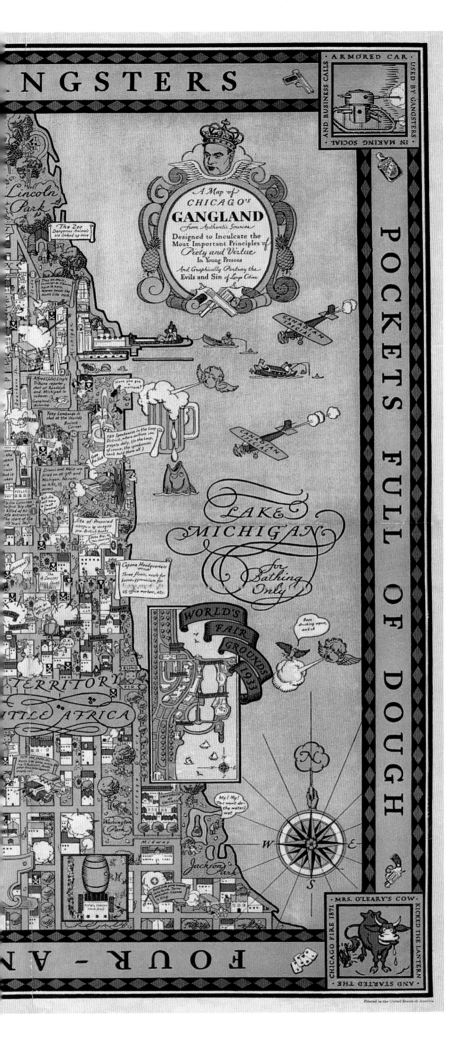

When the US Congress enacted the Volstead Act in 1919, making the manufacture and sale of alcoholic beverages illegal, the peddling of bootlegged beer and liquor became a $30,000,000-a-year business. Though their creators claimed to convey the message that crime does not pay, pulp publications such as this *Map of Chicago's Gangland* (1931) inevitably glorified the gangster lifestyle, turning many gang figures into celebrities.

especially in the regulation of urban development. Such mapping suffered from the fact that it could not easily be updated as satellite mapping could be. Thus it now seems very dated.

Mapping the urban sprawl

Much of the world's population lives in cities, but cities are difficult to map comprehensively. City maps are organized around streets, and dwellings emerge as the spaces between streets. Differences within the cities – for example, of wealth, or environmental or housing quality – are generally neglected. Different neighbourhoods, upwardly or downwardly mobile quarters, and areas largely inhabited by families or single people are ignored.

Maps of cities are very much a picture of what is going on at ground level. There is little, if any, suggestion of the vertical, and thus of the many people who live and work in skyscrapers or more modest multi-storeyed buildings, or, indeed, of the difficulties these buildings pose in terms of access (stairs, lifts etc). This neglect of the vertical dimension of urban life is the flip side of our obsession with mapping the city in terms of its roads.

Depending on the availability of information, it is possible to map other aspects of cities. For his *New York City in the 1980s: A Social, Economic and Political Atlas* (New York, 1993), John Mollenkopf used the 2200 census tracts of the city's 1980 census, each of which contained about 3300 people. Mapping household income, as well as income from dividends, interest, and rent, enabled him to show which areas benefited most from economic developments in the 1980s. Such mapping faces problems, for example, the availability of information, but it does allow us an insight into some of the more hidden workings of society.

The mapping of ethnic and religious groups can also be problematic. Maps that simply produce blocks of colour separated by clear boundaries are misleading, because definitions of race and ethnicity are fluid and contested. The impression of homogeneity in such maps plays down the complexity of minority groups.

Mapping techniques such as unit-dot maps or the use of interdigitated diagonal bands of different colours can be used to display heterogeneity. Unit-dot maps, where one dot represents a fixed quantity and demographic diversity is shown by having different coloured dots on the same map, are very confusing, but this very confusion is instructive: it is an accurate reflection of the reality of racial, ethnic, religious, or linguistic diversity.

Bruce Macdonald's *Vancouver: A Visual History* (1992) maps the use of highest ethnic concentrations by census tract. It mapped the single highest density of each ethnic group that made up more than five per cent of a census tract's population, in order to show the degree of concentration or assimilation of each group. New groups, visible minority groups, and groups retaining the culture of their home country – for example, the Chinese – are shown by the map to have a tendency to congregate.

Cities have been mapped in many different ways, in accordance with particular interests and opportunities, and this process was accentuated in the 20th century as more information became available. Most mapping has been serious, but there has also been a rise in humorous mapping, as entrepreneurs have seen the commercial possibilities of producing such maps as souvenirs and for other purposes.

The most famous series offer mental maps, as in a Manhattan or Chelsea view of the immediate city and of the wider world, but there are many other examples, including *A Map of Chicago's Gangland from Authentic Sources. Designed to Inculcate the Most Important Principles of Piety and Virtue in Young Persons and Graphically Portray the Evils and Sin of Large Cities* (1931) which divided the city into gangland territories, such as "Capone Territory". It also marked the location of gangland killings and mixed time and space with a text-number sequence: "numbers in red circles give the sequence of important events in Chicago's ten-year gangland war"; these included locations such as the site of the St Valentine's Day Massacre. Other places were accompanied by pertinent text, such as "Drainage Canal (A favourite disposal station)" and "County Morgue. The Gangster's Clearing House".

Other aspects of the city that can be mapped are the routes of parades and processions. Political, social, and ethnic distinctions were, and are, mirrored in the use of public space for collective action and demonstration. Disputes over where marches can proceed reflect perceptions of spatial identity. Cartographically, however, it is difficult to capture a moving spectacle on a static map, whereas electronic maps or plans can show multiple levels of information: the route of a parade, for example, juxtaposed alongside the city's ethnic mix; a plan of the city's sewerage system alongside its schools. This type of information has hitherto been difficult to manipulate in map form.

Although most of the world's population lives in cities, they are underplayed in most maps and atlases because of their emphasis on space: Montana occupies far more space than New York City. Any equal-area or real-space map, such as the one produced by Peters, thus exaggerates the role of thinly populated areas, for example Xinkiang in western China or the Australian interior.

However, new technology, especially the combination of computers and Geographical Information Systems, makes it possible to make dynaimc presentations of space. Thus, census information can serve as the basis for computer-generated population cartograms. Their equal-population areas, focusing on those with a high population, highlight developments in cities. At the same time, whatever the scale, real space is of importance, and the traditions and views of specific localities are not captured by demographically weighted maps.

Imaginary worlds

The spread of mapping has affected most areas of modern life. Overlapping, as it does, with graphic presentation, mapping has become central to issues such as industrial design and

⋏ Endpapers of the 1974 edition of AA Milne's *The House at Pooh Corner*, originally published in 1928. The map helps to fix the locations in Pooh's world. There is, of course, no scale, and the use of pictures is an appropriate visual aid for the book's likely audience. Heffalumps do not exist outside of Pooh's imagination,

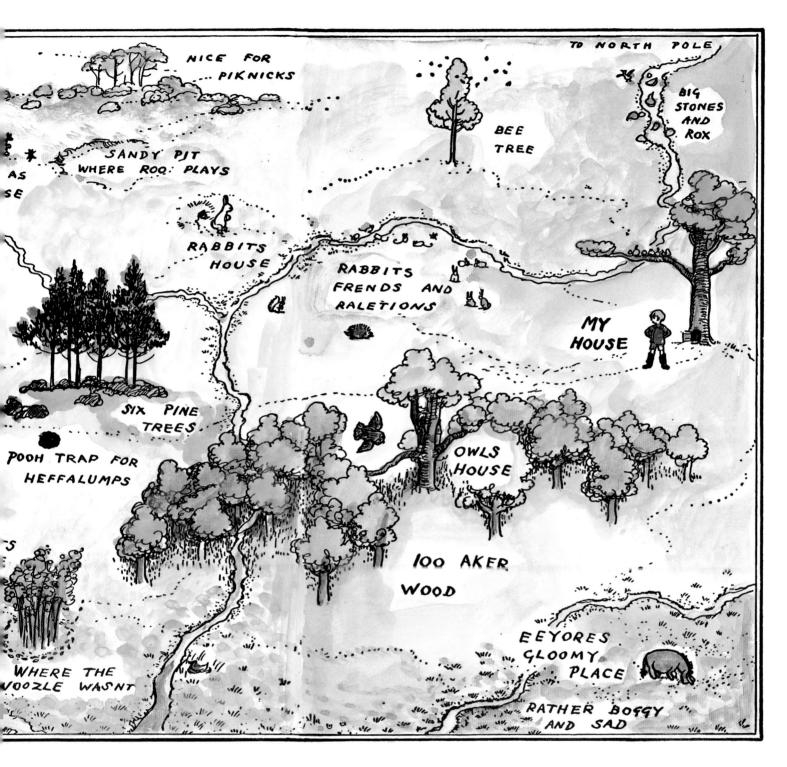

Within the map:

NICE FOR PIKNICKS

TO NORTH POLE

BEE TREE

BIG STONES AND ROX

SANDY PIT WHERE ROO PLAYS

AS SE

RABBITS HOUSE

RABBITS FRENDS AND RALETIONS

MY HOUSE

SIX PINE TREES

OWLS HOUSE

POOH TRAP FOR HEFFALUMPS

100 AKER WOOD

EEYORES GLOOMY PLACE

WHERE THE WOOZLE WASNT

RATHER BOGGY AND SAD

but he creates a trap for them, which Christopher Robin places on his map, thus rendering the Heffalumps a more concrete reality. The caption "To North Pole" reflects a child's sense of his own familiar surroundings and the unknown wider world.

organizational method, and to a range of technological and presentational systems, from flow diagram to microchip board.

Mapping has also played an important role in imaginary worlds. This reflects both the pervasive character of mapping and the extent to which such worlds have captured modern imaginations, as had older religious narratives, many of which also had a strong spatial sense.

Thus, JRR Tolkien's trilogy The Lord of the Rings (1954–5) was accompanied by a map of Middle-earth, drawn by the author, which was subsequently published separately, in large format and in colour. On the one hand, the map gives no real sense of the

spatial range of Middle-earth or of the relative potency of the forces of good and evil at work in th narrative. The ring at the centre of the conflict cannot be expressed or explained in a map. On the other hand, the map of Middle-earth is important to the readers' understanding of locations and of the mission that has to be accomplished. Similarly, the map of Wilderland in Tolkien's The Hobbit (1937) helps the reader to follow the narrative. The Atlas of Tolkien's Middle-earth (1981) by geographer Karen Wynn Fonstad is a comprehensive atlas of the lands, locations, and journeys undertaken in Tolkien's writings, drawn to scales and distances extrapolated and estimated from the text.

◄ In-car navigation systems, such as this Navman iCN 630 are now state of the art. This particular model has 12-channel multi-directional GPS receiver, and gives voice directions to the driver. These systems can have city maps installed in their memory, and can help motorists plan routes from door to door.

Epics of former eras, such as the *Odyssey* or *Beowulf*, lacked such maps, but nowadays we expect them. Indeed, in 1867, Alexander Keith Johnston's *School Atlas of Classical Geography* included a map of the geography of the *Odyssey*. We also now expect maps to help create less threatening fictional worlds, whether that of Arthur Ransome's *Swallows and Amazons*, the Reverend W Awdry's *Thomas the Tank Engine*, or AA Milne's *Winnie-the-Pooh*. All modern editions of these books now contain maps. It is less clear how far maps will continue to perform the same role of reference point in visual media. In part, this is because many stories are often depicted in a visual form anyway so a map may not make any further contribution.

Aside from the creation of completely imaginary worlds, such as Tolkien's Middle-earth, maps now help to add verisimilitude to fictional works. Thus, in a series "The Roman Mysteries", written for children, Caroline Lawrence includes maps that locate her characters. The map of the Bay of Naples in 79 AD in her *The Secrets of Vesuvius* (2001) marks Rectina's villa and Uncle Gaius's farm, alongside real places such as Neapolis, Cumae, Herculaneum, and Pompeii.

The map of Ostia in *The Thieves of Ostia* (2001) similarly locates, for example, the houses of Avita, Cordius, Flavia, and Jonathan. The maps help readers to solve the puzzles posed in such books, as do the building plans that are also included. The maps also answer the readers' need for a sense of place, which is now expected in a complete fictional account. The spaces, accuracy, and nuances of past fictional works, for example, the Sherlock Holmes stories, have been probed and, in some cases, mapped.

Other imaginary worlds, such as the Disney theme parks in California (1955), Florida (1971), Tokyo (1983), and Paris (1992), all depend on maps (in brochures and publicly displayed) in order to guide visitors around an unfamiliar landscape.

In addition to this use of conventionally understood maps, in order to further imaginary worlds, maps and mapping of spatial relationships through mediums such as dance, drama, and procession – what could be called "performance cartographies" – are now represented. This abandonment of the conventional definition in terms of "flat" maps, whether on stone, paper, bronze, copper, or, more recently, screen, is not without its problems. For example, in making everything a map – or at least making anything involving space a place – there is a risk of the subject losing analytical precision. The world of art, whether paintings or architecture, could readily be subsumed into this looseness, as could the entire language of space and distance. On the other hand, this extension in definition of captures the extent to which spatial relationships and representations vary greatly.

Where do we go from here?

The future of maps will be determined by the impact of technologies such as geographical information mapping systems which enable predictive mapping. Such systems make it easier to study patterns. Moreover, as more information is digitized, so its potential for mapping increases. Maps are regularly used in town and country planning at all levels, from individual plots to large-scale developments. The improvement in display systems makes it easy to link these maps with models and to scrutinize both from different angles.

Three-dimensional computerized maps will become fairly common or even widespread. Such maps could show variation by degree. A topography, for example, could be based on economic scales, such as prosperity or unemployment, or on religious density, as in signs of conformity or fervour. A third correlation, with an independent variable such as time, could be added.

There are still, however, major problems with such approaches. There are aesthetic considerations as well as practical differences between a printed map and a map viewed on a computer screen. Most screens lack the resolution, colour quality, and size of the printed page. Size is especially important. Screens are not generally big enough to see an entire double-page spread without moving the image on the screen; and this has implications in terms of density and range of information, as well as the scope of the area that can be effectively comprehended in a given map.

As with all mapping, data availability and accuracy will always be crucial. There are important issues, such as the intensity of religious belief or the strength of political conviction, that cannot be easily mapped, or at least mapped without major problems in interpretation. In other areas, much modern statistical information is based on sampling, but the sample is frequently too small to serve as a basis for reliable mapping. Issues of data availability also ensure that differing standards are frequently used to compile maps in different areas. This poses particular problems for creating composite maps or atlases.

Software packages allow changes between temporal and across spatial data points to be animated. Such non-traditional, historical atlases are currently being developed on the computer and delivered via CD-Rom or over the Internet. *The History Machine*, for example, is a GIS-based software package which enables students to manipulate, then display cartographically, county-level US census material from 1790 to 1990.

The great strength of such material is the possibility of discovery, through trial and error, or via hypothesis testing. The weakness of this brave, new cartographic world is the growing amount of data that has not been properly assessed for its potential usefulness. Thus, constraints on publishers of book-bound historical atlases are being compounded by other difficulties.

Major problems though they are, none undermines the importance and value of mapping, either for today or for the future. But we should recognize that mapmaking and maproading both involve and reflect choices: choices both about what is important and about how best to include, present, and understand that information.

Improvements in technology will not overcome this element of choice, so it is not helpful to think of mapping becoming "better". What it is becoming, though, is more common and more insistent. Maps increasingly store or process information for organizations and individuals. Shoppers can now find their way around shopping centres by maps, not memory.

Increasing personal mobility brings with it the need for more journey planning. As the human environment is increasingly moulded by the car, so we need to acquire the cartographic knowledge relevant to car usage. Whereas rail systems have a limited number of routes and access points, road transport is far more flexible in routes, access, and service. At the same time, maps only provide part of the information. For example, the side streets that become rat runs – quick shortcuts linking busier roads – are difficult to gauge from maps. Even one-way street systems are not readily comprehensible.

Instead, what was once an improbable fantasy, such as the homing device, radar, and moving map in James Bond's exotic Aston Martin DB-5 in the film *Goldfinger* (1964), are now the basis of the route-finding systems in many cars. Their use of global positioning systems (GPS) and computers, makes them, in fact, rather more sophisticated. The computer game for world domination played by Bond and the villain Largo in the film *Never Say Never Again* (1983), in which they fire missiles at maps of countries (each of which has a financial value), would now be considered standard fare. And the screen maps displayed in aeroplanes that record the plane's position in real time, at a variety of scales, are a quantum leap forwards from the in-flight magazine route-maps which were all that travellers once had. We live in a mapped world. That will not change.

Selected Further Reading

Andrews, J.H., *A Paper Landscape: The Ordnance Survey in Nineteenth-Century Ireland* (1975).

Andrews, M., *Landscape and Western Art* (1999).

Bagrow, L., *A History of Russian Cartography Up to 1800* (1975).

Barber, P. and Board, C., *Tales from the Map Room* (1993).

Bell, M., Butlin, R.A., and Heffernan, M., (eds.), *Geography and Imperialism* (1995).

Benes, P. (ed.), *New England Prospect: Maps, Place Names, and the Historical Landscape* (1980).

Black, Jeremy, (ed.), *DK Atlas of World History* (1999).

Black, Jeremy, *Maps and History* (1997).

Black, Jeremy, *Maps and Politics* (1997).

Bosse, D., *Civil War Newspaper Maps* (1993).

Browne, J.P., *Map Cover Art: A Pictorial History of Ordnance Survey Cover Illustrations* (1990).

Buisseret, David (ed.), *Envisioning the City. Six Studies in Urban Cartography* (1998).

Buisseret, David (ed.), *Monarchs, Ministers, and Maps* (1992).

Buisseret, D. (ed.), *From Sea Charts to Satellite Images: Interpreting North American History through Maps* (1990).

Bunge, W., *The Nuclear War Atlas* (1982).

Cortesão, Armando *History of Portuguese Cartography* (1969–71).

Cosgrove, D. and Daniels, S. (eds.), *The Iconography of Landscape* (1988).

Crone, Gerald, R., *Maps and Their Makers: An Introduction to the History of Cartography* (5th edn., 1978).

Cumming, W.P., and De Vorsey, L., *The Southeast in Early Maps* (3rd edn., 1998).

Cunningham, I.C. (ed.), *The Nation Surveyed. Timothy Pont's Map of Scotland* (2001).

Daiches, D. and Flower, J., *Literary Landscapes of the British Isles: A Narrative Atlas* (1979).

Delano-Smith, C. and Kain, R.J.P., *English Maps. A History* (1999).

Delano-Smith, C. and Ingram, E.M., *Maps in Bibles, 1500–1600* (1991).

Dilke, O.A.W., *Greek and Roman Maps* (1985).

Dodds, K., *Pink Ice. Britain and the South Atlantic Empire* (2002).

Edney, M.H., *Mapping an Empire: The Geographic Construction of British India 1765–1843* (1997).

Ermen, E.V., *The United States in Old Maps and Prints* (1990).

Fordham, H.G., *John Cary: Engraver, Map, Chart and Print-Seller and Globe-Maker 1754 to 1835* (1925).

Godlewska, A. and Smith, N. (eds.), *Geography and Empire* (1994).

Harley, J.B., *The New Nature of Maps. Essays in the History of Cartography* (2001).

Harley, J.B and Woodward, D., *The History of Cartography. Cartography in the Traditional Islamic and Southeast Asian Societies* (1994).

Harley, J.B., and Woodward, D., *The History of Cartography. Cartography in the Traditional Islamic and South Asian Societies* (1992).

Harley, J.B. and Woodward, D., *The History of Cartography. Cartography in Prehistoric, Ancient, and Medieval Europe and the Mediterranean* (1987).

Harvey, P.D.A., *The History of Topographical Maps: Symbols, Pictures and Surveys* (1980).

Harvey, P.D.A., *Maps in Tudor England* (1993).

Harvey, P.D.A. *Medieval Maps* (1991).

Hayes, D., *Historical Atlas of Canada* (2002).

Hindle, P., *Maps for Historians* (1998).

Hodgkiss, A.G., *Understanding Maps: A Systematic History of Their Use and Development* (1981).

Johnson, H.B., *Order upon the Land: The U.S. Rectangular Land Survey and the Upper Mississippi Country* (1976).

Kagan, Richard L., *Urban Images of the Hispanic World, 1493–1793* (2000).

Konvitz, J.W., *Cartography in France, 1660–1848: Science, Engineering, and Statecraft* (1987).

Lanman, J., *On the Origin of Portolan Charts* (1987).

Lewis, G.M., 'Cartography, History of', *International Encyclopedia of the Social and Behavioral Sciences* (2001).

Lewis, G.M. (ed.), *Cartographic Encounters: Perspectives on Native American Mapmaking and Map Use* (1998).

Macdonald, A., *Mapping The World: A History of the Directorate of Overseas Surveys, 1946–1985* (1996).

McElfresh, E.B., *Maps and Mapmakers of the Civil War* (1999).

Maling, P.B., *Historical Charts and Maps of New Zealand* (1996).

Monmonier, M., *How to Lie with Maps* (1991).

Monmonier, M., *Maps With The News: The Development of American Journalistic Cartography* (1989).

Monmonier, M. and Schnell M.S., *Map Appreciation* (1988).

Nebenzahl, K., *Maps from the Age of Discovery* (1990).

Nebenzahl, K., *Maps of the Holy Land* (1986).

Nicholson, T.R., *Wheels on the Road: Maps of Britain for the Cyclist and Motorist 1870–1940* (1983).

Norwich, O.I., *Maps of Africa* (1983).

Oliver, R., *Ordnance Survey Maps: A Concise Guide for Historians* (1993).

Penfold, P.A. (ed.), *Maps and Plans in the Public Record Office. II. America and West Indies* (1974).

Peters, A., *The New Cartography* (1983).

Reinhartz, D. and Colley, C.C. (eds.), *The Mapping of the American Southwest* (1987).

Rhind, D.W. and Taylor, D.R.F. (eds.), *Cartography Past, Present and Future* (1989).

Ristow, W., *American Maps and Mapmakers: Commercial Cartography in the Nineteenth Century* (1985).

Robinson, A.H., *Early Thematic Mapping in the History of Cartography* (1982).

Robinson, A.H., *The Look of Maps: An Examination of Cartographic Design* (1952).

Robinson, A.H. and Petchenik, B.B., *The Nature of Maps: Essays toward Understanding Maps and Mapping* (1976).

Ruggles, R.I., *A Country So Interesting: The Hudson's Bay Company and Two Centuries of Mapping, 1670-1870* (1991).

Sobel, D., *Longitude* (1995).

Thrower, N.J.W., *Maps and Man: an Examination of Cartography in Relation to Culture and Civilization* (1972).

Turnbull, D., *Maps are Territories, Science Is an Atlas* (1989).

Tyache, S. (ed.), *English Map-Making, 1590-1650* (1983).

Wallis, H. and Robinson, A.H., *Cartographical Innovations: An International Handbook of Mapping Terms to 1900* (1987).

Whitfield, Peter, *New Found Lands: Maps in the History of Exploration* (1998).

Whyte, I.D., *Landscape and History since 1500* (2002).

Wolter, J.A. and Grim, R.E., *Images of the World. The Atlas Through History* (1997).

Woodward, D. (ed.), *Art and Cartography* (1987).

Woodward, D. (ed.), *Five Centuries of Map Printing* (1975).

Woodward, D. and Lewis, G.M., *The History of Cartography. Cartography in the Traditional African, American, Arctic, Australian and Pacific Societies* (1998).

Zandvliet, Kees, *Mapping for Money. Maps, plans and topographic paintings and their role in Dutch overseas expansion during the 16th and 17th centuries* (1998).

There is much of value in the specialist journal literature. Journals of note include *American Cartographer, Cartographica,* and *Imago Mundi.*

Index

Page references in *italics* indicate illustration captions.

Picture credits

(In page order) 1 Bridgeman Art Library/Hamburger Kunsthalle; 2 The Art Archive/Uppsala University Library/Dagli Orti; 6-7 Corbis/Lindsay Hebberd; 8-9 Pitt Rivers Museum, University of Oxford, accession number 1966.19.1; 10-11 The Art Archive/Bodleian Library, Oxford; 12-13 Science Photo Library/CNRI; 14-15 The Art Archive/Biblioteca Nazionale Marciana, Venice/Harper Collins Publishers; 17 © British Library, London; 18-19 The Art Archive; 21 AKG-Images/ Biblioteca Nazionale Marciana, Venice; 22 Bridgeman Art Library/British Museum, London; 24-25 Bridgeman Art Library/British Library, London; 26-27 Bodleian Library, University of Oxford; 28-29 AKG-Images/Postmuseum, Berlin; 30 Bridgeman Art Library/Hereford Cathedral, Hereford; 32-33 Bodleian Library, University of Oxford; 34 Corbis/Museu Maritim, Barcelona/Ramon Manent; 35 Corbis/Museu Maritim, Barcelona/Ramon Manent; 36-37 Bridgeman Art Library/ Lauros-Giraudon/Bibliothèque Nationale de France, Paris; 38-39 The Art Archive/Maritiem Museum Prins Hendrik Rotterdam/Dagli Orti; 41 The Art Archive/Biblioteca Estense Modena/ Harper Collins Publishers; 42 The Art Archive/Bodleian Library, Oxford; 43 Corbis/Gianni Dagli Orti; 44 Corbis/Gianni Dagli Orti; 47 The Art Archive/Naval Museum Genoa; 48-49 Photos12.com/Bibliothèque Nationale de France, Paris; 50-51 Bridgeman Art Library/British Library, London; 52 The National Trust/Steve Davies, Camera Craft; 53 The National Trust/Chris Bowden; 54-55 Bridgeman Art Library/Raymond O'Shea Gallery, London; 56-57 Bridgeman Art Library/ Private Collection; 58-59 © British Library, London; ; 60-61 Uppsala University Library; 62-63 The Art Archive/John Webb; 64-65 Corbis; 66-67 The Art Archive/Maritiem Museum Prins Hendrik Rotterdam/Dagli Orti; 68-69 The Art Archive/Fondation Thiers, Paris/Dagli Orti; 71 Wellcome Library, London; 72-73 Photos12.com/National Maritime Museum, London; 75 The Art Archive/National Archives Mexico/Dagli Orti; 78-79 Bridgeman Art Library/Bibliothèque Nationale de France, Paris; 80-81 Corbis; 82-83 Royal Geographical Society, London; 84 The National Archives, London; 85 The National Archives, London; 86-87 © British Library, London; 88-89 Bildarchiv Preussischer Kulturbesitz; 91 Bridgeman Art Library/Archives du Ministère des Affaires Étrangères, Paris, France; 92-93 Bridgeman Art Library/Musée de la Révolution Française, Vizille, France; 94 The National Archives, London; 96-97 Reproduced by permission of the Trustees of the National Library of Scotland, Edinburgh; 98-99 Photos12.com/Hachedé; 100-101 © British Library; 102 Skinner, Auctioneers and Appraisers of Antiques and Fine Art, Boston, MA; 105 © British Library, London; 106-107 Corbis; 108-109 The Art Archive/Bodleian Library, Oxford (N.12288b after p88); 110 Corbis; 112-113 © National Maritime Museum, London; 114 Mary Evans Picture Library; 115 The National Archives, London; 116-117 Corbis; 118-119 The Library of the London School of Economics and Political Science; 120-121 Corbis; 122 Octopus Publishing Group Ltd; 123 © British Library, London; 124 The Art Archive/Bodleian Library, Oxford/John Johnson Collection, Empire and Cartoons; 125 top Collection Kharbine-Tapabor; 125 bottom The Art Archive/Bodleian Library, Oxford; 126-127 The National Archives, London; 129 Getty Images/Hulton Archive; 130 © The Natural History Museum, London; 132-133 Reproduced by permission of Marie Tharp; 134 London Transport Museum; 135 London Transport Museum; 136-137 The National Archives, London; 138 Getty Images/Hulton Archive; 139 TRH Pictures; 140-141 Corbis Sygma; 143 top The National Archives, London; 143 bottom The National Archives, London; 144 TRH Pictures; 145 AKG-Images; 146 AKG-Images; 148-149 Corbis; 150-151 Corbis/Bettmann; 152-153 Science Photo Library/NASA; 154-155 Corbis/Hulton-Deutsch Collection; 156 NASA; 157 Science Photo Library/NASA; 158-159 "The Jewish Diaspora" reproduced with permission from "The State of Religion Atlas" by Joanne O'Brien and Martin Palmer copyright © Myriad Editions Limited / ww.MyriadEditions.com; 160-161 Science Photo Library/NASA; 162-163 Chicago Historical Society; 164-165 Line illustration by E.H. Shephard copyright under the Berne Convention. Colouring copyright E. H. Shephard and Egmont Books Ltd. © 1973. Reproduced by permission of Curtis Brown Ltd. London; 166-167 Courtesy of GPS Warehouse